Developing Exce
in Autism Pract

CW01513345

This ground-breaking book gives an accessible overview and synthesis of current knowledge of relevance to the development of excellence in autism education. By situating understandings of autism within a 'bio-psycho-social-insider' framework, the book offers fresh insights and new ways of thinking that bring together global pedagogic practice, research, policy, and the insider perspective.

Guldberg critiques current notions of Evidence-Based Practice and suggests ways of bridging the research–practice gap. She explores the interrelationship between inclusive principles, distinctive group learning needs and the individual needs of the child or young person. Eight principles of good autism practice provide a helpful framework for how education settings and practitioners can adapt classroom environments and teaching so that autistic children and young people can thrive.

Written for anyone who wants to make a difference to the lives of autistic pupils, *Developing Excellence in Autism Practice* provides practitioners and students on education courses with tools for best practices, and shows how to draw on these to implement true positive change in the classroom.

Karen Guldberg is Professor of Autism Studies and Director of the Autism Centre for Education and Research (ACER) at the School of Education, University of Birmingham, UK.

Developing Excellence in Autism Practice

Making a Difference in Education

Karen Guldberg

 Routledge
Taylor & Francis Group

LONDON AND NEW YORK

First edition published 2020
by Routledge
2 Park Square, Milton Park, Abingdon, Oxon, OX14 4RN

and by Routledge
52 Vanderbilt Avenue, New York, NY 10017

Routledge is an imprint of the Taylor & Francis Group, an informa business

© 2020 Karen Guldberg

British Library Cataloguing-in-Publication Data
A catalogue record for this book is available from the British Library

Library of Congress Cataloging-in-Publication Data
A catalog record has been requested for this book

ISBN: 978-0-367-22671-8 (hbk)
ISBN: 978-0-367-22673-2 (pbk)
ISBN: 978-0-429-27628-6 (ebk)

Typeset in Melior
by Newgen Publishing UK

Contents

Acknowledgements vii

Preface ix

1 Introduction 1

Part I – Current evidence and knowledge from different domains in autism studies: implications for education 13

2 The bio-psycho-social-insider model 15

3 Contributions from biology and the medical domain 23

4 Contributions from psychology 47

5 Learning from autistic perspectives 62

6 Contributions from the social sciences 75

7 Evidence-informed practice 92

Part II – Inclusive practice and distinctive pedagogies for autistic pupils 111

8 Inclusion and inclusive pedagogy 113

9 Inclusive pedagogy for autistic children and young people 126

10 Eight principles of good autism practice in education 140

11 Professional development 169

12 The scholarly practitioner 182

References 193
Index 221

Acknowledgements

This book is a result of working for a number of years in the field of autism, and with some amazing people along the way. First and foremost, the autistic people I have known and worked with have transformed my thinking and practice as an educator. I want to extend my deepest gratitude to them all. My thanks also go to the parents and professionals I have worked with, my passionate and committed students and the fantastic group of regional tutors. Our large community of students, alumni, regional tutors and research partners has been an important learning space and keeps me in touch with the day-to-day issues faced by autistic people, their families and practitioners.

There are a number of individuals who have had a formative influence on me and whom I wish to thank too. They include fellow academics, autistic colleagues, practitioners and research partners. There are too many to mention, but I will highlight a few. I start with Dame Stephanie Shirley because I would not be working at the University of Birmingham if it were not for her. A number of autistic colleagues and friends have a unique and powerful ability to support others to develop deeper understandings of autism and have influenced me in a variety of ways. They include Damian Milton, Larry Arnold, Simone Stabilini, Wenn Lawson, Zaffy Simone, Sara Hendrickx and Dean Beadle.

Research partners and practitioners have kept me firmly embedded in the issues practitioners face. The Communication Autism Team (CAT) at Birmingham City Council works in innovative and exceptional ways. With Lesley Baker at their helm, they are a strong team who never avert their gaze from how they can best meet the needs of the autistic children and young people whom they support. My special thanks go to Lesley Baker and Pam Simpson for being inspirational role models.

As a result of working with the CAT team, the Autism Education Trust (AET) and other local authorities and schools through the AET partnership for the last ten years, I have experienced being part of a strong community of practice. By working towards the goal of improving autism education, the partnership has made a difference in the education of autistic children and young people. For that, I want to thank several past and current colleagues from the Autism Education Trust, including Steve Huggett, Bob Lowndes, Sarah-Jane Critchley and Sarah Broadhurst.

Closer to home, in academia, I have some inspirational people to thank for their support, encouragement and academic leadership over the years. They include Julie Allan, Graeme Douglas, David Gillborn, Mike McLinden, Sarah Parsons, Kaska Porayska-Pomsta, Ann Lewis, Gary Thomas and Wendy Keay-Bright. My team at the Autism Centre for Education and Research (ACER) has had a defining influence on my ideas over the years. We have worked together closely to break new ground and have remained focused on bringing research and practice together in a way that can lead to meaningful change. It has been a pleasure to work with Alexia Achtypi, Dan Corlett, Paul Edwards, Danielle Hinton, Glenys Jones, Rita Jordan, Lila Kossyvaki, Andrea MacLeod, Damian Milton, Despina Papoudi and Claire Robson. Ryan Bradley, Kerstin Wittemeyer and Simon Wallace deserve a special mention. We worked together on a couple of projects this year that have supported the development of this book.

Over the years, I have had the privilege of being on a transformative learning journey into social learning theory, with Etienne and Bev Wenger-Trayner and I look forward to continuing this. On a personal level, I want to thank my steadfast and patient partner Pete, my lovely boys Marcus, Aidan and Stefan, as well as Anna and Jamie for being so positive and encouraging. Finally, I want to extend my deep gratitude to three people who are sadly no longer with us. Barbara Hickling was my tutor on my Masters course in autism studies. My wonderful mother and father gave me such a good start in life and I think of them every day.

Preface

Even under extremely challenging circumstances, our attitudes about and perspectives on people with autism and their behaviour make a critical difference in their lives—and in ours.

(Prizant, 2015: 10)

This book is primarily intended for undergraduate and postgraduate students in autism education who want to make a difference to the lives of autistic children and young people and their families. It is written for educators who want to know more about how to improve educational practice and provision and who have a special interest in taking a lead in developing good autism practice in education. They might work in mainstream classrooms, schools for children with special educational needs or specialist provisions for autistic children and young people, with three-year-olds in an Early Years provision, or with a 20-year-old in a Post-16 provision.

The book is based on the premise that it is important to understand how autism might impact on an individual and that good theoretical frameworks can help in this process. The objective is to take the reader on a journey that provides them with thinking tools *and* that enhances their ability to meet the needs of autistic children and young people. This requires both theory and practical guidance. Theory is important because it can provide meaningful explanations concerning observations and it can help frame thinking. Equally, guidance about practice can provide the reader with issues to reflect on and implement when developing their practice. Although this is a practical book, it does not aim to be a recipe book for what works, nor is it a set of 'tools for teachers', as there are no quick fixes in the education of autistic children and young people.

Instead, it explores how to facilitate change in education. I have a firm conviction that education is the arena that can make the largest difference to the lives of autistic children and young people. The dual aims of this book are therefore to support educators to 'learn in order to make a difference' and to 'learn to make a difference' (Wenger-Trayner & Wenger-Trayner, in press). This has also been described as the difference between the *know-that* of knowledge and the *know-how* of knowledge. The former is the accumulated knowledge one develops over time in a field. In other words, what do we need to know in order to make a difference? The latter is the knowledge that emerges from engaging in the world, and from learning in and through practice. In other words, how can we make a difference? The structure of the book reflects these dual aims, so the book is divided into two parts.

Part I focuses on *learning in order to make a difference* and the *know-that* of knowledge by giving an overview of the knowledge, theoretical frameworks and evidence we can draw on to inform good autism practice in education, with the aim of thinking critically about the knowledge that is available. This means drawing on the knowledge that has emerged from the perspectives of autistic people themselves, from theories regarding psychological functioning, from biology and medicine, and from the social perspective. This bio-psycho-social-insider model is based on the notion that autism will affect a child or young person biologically. This will in turn influence how the person processes and experiences the world, whilst their development and experience will also be affected by how they are supported and educated.

Part I of the book engages with identifying what matters in the education of autistic children and young people by giving an overview of evidence from intervention research in autism, discussing gaps between research and practice and addressing how to bridge those gaps. In so doing, it draws on the knowledge emerging from research, policy and practice (see Figure 0.1).

Chapter 1 is an introduction to the book and gives an overview of the issues that will be covered. Chapter 2 discusses theoretical models that inform thinking in disability studies, and explains why the bio-psycho-social-insider perspective is useful in education. This perspective

Figure 0.1 The knowledge bases that inform good autism practice in education

provides a holistic understanding of autism and autistic people, and enables a focus on the interaction between the person and their context. Chapter 3 provides an overview of the biological and medical aspects of autism that are important for educators to know.

Chapter 4 examines what the discipline of psychology contributes to understandings of good autism practice in education. After this, Chapter 5 gives a justification for why the insider perspective is a crucial starting point for understanding autism and the individual learner. Chapter 6 focuses on the importance of examining the contexts in which people live and learn, and identifies key challenges and social issues that currently affect autistic children and young people and their families. Chapter 7 gives an overview of the research evidence emerging from intervention research and puts the case for a transformation in the way that research is conducted.

Part II of the book focuses on the *'learning to make a difference'* element by examining *how* to work towards genuine inclusive practice for autistic children and young people. The know-how knowledge of the educator is tacit and practical knowledge. It is understandings drawn from and assessed in the context of one's own experiences and the experiences of others. In autism education, practitioners can draw on the generalised knowledge from research but need to make sense of it in relation to the localised practices of the classroom. This part of the book therefore looks critically at how to develop productive pedagogy for autistic children and young people. It highlights the need to assess and meet the needs of the individual child or young person within a framework of inclusive principles *and* understanding of the distinctive learning needs of autistic children and young people. The aim is to give practitioners the thinking tools to review best practices and to draw on these to implement change in the classroom by enhancing their own capacities and those of others to implement positive change and become agents for change.

The aim is to support practitioners to think critically, to develop confidence in practitioner knowledge, and to enable change by working in partnership with others. This involves sharing good practice and engaging with others in a joint effort to make a difference. Eight principles of good autism practice provide a framework for how education settings and practitioners can adapt classroom environments and teaching so that autistic children and young people can thrive. There is a careful focus on the importance of, and strategies to support, agency, choice and empowerment for autistic pupils, promoting the active participation of the learner as the primary aim whilst always recognising that the context in which a child or young person learns needs to be taken into account.

Chapter 8 provides an overview of inclusive principles and outlines the need for an interrelationship between inclusive principles, understanding of the distinctive group needs of autistic pupils and meeting the needs of individuals. Chapter 9 presents a pedagogic framework for good autism practice in education. Chapter 10 flows from this and presents eight principles of good autism practice that are core to the pedagogic framework outlined in Chapter 9. Chapter 11 focuses on the kind of professional development that can lead to real change in education, and provides an example of a professional development programme that has effected collective change. Chapter 12 provides practitioners with ideas about how they can embark on individual change through their development as scholarly practitioners.

Each chapter has a similar structure in that it starts with an overview. At the beginning of every chapter, the key question or questions that this particular chapter will cover are posed. Space precludes giving comprehensive coverage of every topic the book covers, so references are provided at the end of each chapter to reading material that can enable the reader to explore some of these issues in more depth. At the end of each chapter, the reader is provided with a summary.

Finally, I am privileged to have been working closely with the Autism Education Trust (AET) for the last ten years, and this has involved co-producing tools and frameworks to support teaching. The AET website has many practical tools and frameworks that can support practitioners in their practice, and I urge readers to look at these (www. autismeducationtrust.org.uk). This book will not give examples of tools and templates as such tools have been developed elsewhere. As educators, we need to step back, reflect on our values and thinking, and work out how we can best enable change. This is the process the book aims to support.

Introduction

Key question

How can we arrive at a positive framework for developing good autism practice in education?

Introduction

When I began work as a teacher at a special school many years ago, I quickly realised that five out of the seven children in my class were on the autism spectrum. They were all very different from one another though. Dominic was older than the other children in the class. He was seven and non-verbal, but communicated well through sounds. He was agile, moving around the classroom and playground with ease. With piercing brown eyes and the most wonderful smile, he could also get very frustrated and angry with those around him, especially when he was trying to communicate and others failed to understand him. Dominic had an older sister with a learning difficulty and two younger siblings with profound and multiple learning difficulties. Dominic later went on to be educated in a private residential facility where he settled in well.

Kylie arrived in our unit at the age of three. She was also pre-verbal at the time. She was very scared and nervous about interacting with anyone. She had a phobia about going to the toilet and was still in nappies. Two years later, her phobia about the toilets had gone, and she was toilet-trained. She talked lots and was a fluent reader and writer. Her literacy skills were ahead of her age. She soaked up information and had a special interest in other countries. Her geographical knowledge put a lot of her teachers to shame. She transitioned from the special school to mainstream school. I recently learnt that she went on to study at university.

Dylan was five. He arrived like a whirlwind, swiping everything in the vicinity and spitting on everyone who came near him. He often scratched his face and laughed, especially when people raised their voices. When we first undertook observations to try to understand why Dylan behaved as he did, we recorded over one hundred instances of spitting or swiping every five minutes. His parents told us that they had not been able to go anywhere in public as a family for two years and Dylan had already been expelled from a nursery and another special school. He was nevertheless a very cheerful, happy and funny child. Ten years later, I met a teacher who had taught Dylan in secondary school. He told me he had bumped into Dylan with his mother at the supermarket. Dylan was then a polite young man who was helping his mother with the shopping.

John was very active and ran round on tiptoe most of the time. He constantly talked, was a very noisy child and asked a plethora of questions on a regular basis. He was an excellent reader and had a particular interest in dinosaurs. Staff found John's continuous questions difficult to deal with. Like Kylie, John joined a mainstream school a couple of years later. He settled in well in the primary school he joined, but struggled with mental health difficulties in secondary school.

Liam was altogether different. He had high levels of stress, a very anxious look on his face all the time, and found any kind of change very difficult to deal with. He was also non-verbal and had difficulties in communicating his needs, beyond taking adults by the hand to show them what he wanted. He clearly had sensory sensitivities and loud noises were particularly distressing to him. He would often bite when distressed. Staff became frightened of him, and would often handle him in the wrong way because they thought he was just a 'naughty child'. Liam was a frightened child though and biting was the only way he could deal with that fear. Careful observation helped us draw the conclusion that the only time he bit people was during transition time, especially if a staff member took him by the hand to guide him to a new activity. By implementing a visual system using pictures to show Liam when there was a transition to a new activity, he gradually managed to cope better with change.

Those experiences were my entry into the world of autism. I look back at those early days and remember with embarrassment how busy and noisy my classroom was, how little time I gave the pupils to process information, and how verbal I was most of the time. I realised quite quickly that neither my training as a teacher, nor my instincts, equipped me to be a good enough teacher for those children. I knew nothing about autism then, and although I worked hard to understand the children, and developed good relationships with them, I knew there were major gaps in my knowledge. As a result, I talked to other staff members about my difficulties, and one colleague suggested I contact the University of Birmingham, as she had undertaken an Advanced Certificate in Education by distance learning with a focus on autism there. I followed her advice, found out that the University of Birmingham ran a Masters in Education, and enrolled on this.

I never looked back. The course was just the start of a journey of beginning to understand autism, how it impacted on the children I taught, how to implement approaches and strategies, and how to evaluate my practice. It made me think critically about my practice and it helped me to apply theory and research to what I did as a teacher. It gave me the knowledge, understanding and skills to better understand the individual children I worked with and to adjust my support for them based on their needs. I became more astute in my observations, spent time undertaking thorough assessments, changed the way I ran group activities, reduced my language and gave the children more time to process information. I became inspired to observe, reflect and work closely as a team with the people with whom I worked.

It shaped my thinking about autism and my deep realisation that how we think really does change how we act and what we do, and that change is needed in education so that we can become better at meeting the needs of autistic children and young people. My experiences also convinced me that education is a context in which we can facilitate genuine change for autistic children and young people and their families. Most of all, I was fascinated by the way in which small adjustments in my teaching and my own ways of interacting could make such a big difference to the children and young people I taught. I put in place an augmentative visual system for Dominic based on symbols. He actively used those every day. They supported him to communicate with staff and his outbursts reduced. When he came back to visit me years later, he ran straight to the communication board in my classroom, using the symbol cards to greet me but also greeting me verbally as he was now a verbal young man.

I worked with Kylie to help her lose her fear of using the toilet. I set up a corner area with cushions, noise-cancelling headphones and a screen round it so that Liam could go there and have some space to himself when the sensory environment became too much. We changed the lighting in the classroom, and introduced more soft furnishings to make the acoustics better. I set up a workstation for John and used his special interests in dinosaurs to work on different areas of the curriculum. These small changes all made a difference in supporting those children to access learning. I came to realise that I could play a positive role in enabling those children to have a better quality of life, in enhancing their wellbeing and in enabling learning.

Through my work, it also gradually became clearer to me that enabling teachers to develop *their* own agency was equally important. After having worked with children with learning disabilities and autism in a special school, I moved on to working in a local authority outreach team. Our work consisted of supporting teachers in mainstream schools who were educating autistic children and young people. I remember visiting a school, and a teacher took me aside, saying 'I have this child in my class, and he finds it difficult to focus during literacy hour. What should I do?' I tried to indicate that the answer to this was something we would need to arrive at together by observing the child in the classroom so we could understand why he found literacy hour so difficult. The teacher was unhappy with this answer, as she wanted a simple answer with a clear strategy to deal with what she perceived as being the child's problems.

The most striking point about her line of questioning was that she felt I was the expert and that she did not know what to do. Many other teachers I visited also had the same expectations. They felt they needed an expert to give them answers about what to do. They lacked the confidence that they could address the needs of the autistic children and did not know how to come up with solutions. To me, this emphasised the importance of professional development for teachers, of finding ways of enabling educators to develop their knowledge, understanding and skills so that they could make a difference. I therefore hope that this book will support educators to become confident about their own practices, and to enhance their knowledge and thinking tools to develop their practice. This requires an acceptance that there really is no such thing as a ready-made answer, and that there are no experts. In fact, the people who are closest to being experts are autistic people themselves and their families.

In this process of enabling educators to develop their knowledge, understanding and skills, and to change their practice, I am deeply convinced that a philosophical shift is needed towards seeing autism as a different way of being rather than presenting it as a disorder or a deficit. This entails moving past the psychological language of deficits and disorder to using a language that recognises the diverse ways of being human. Rather than seeing autistic people as lacking in something, or having an illness, autism is then considered as one of the many different ways of being human, as Barry Prizant so eloquently puts it in his book *Uniquely Human* (Prizant, 2015).

Rather than focus on the difficulties and 'problems' presented by pupils with autism, the focus needs to be directed towards the strengths of people with autism. An approach that presents autism as a difference rather than a disability, and that focuses on strengths rather than weaknesses, leads to practical ways of working that engage with the abilities of the person. It does, of course, also entail the need to understand and address the challenges and difficulties a child or young person faces.

Importantly, such an orientation sees autism as a transactional condition that requires *mutual adaptation* on behalf of the person with autism *and* those who live or work with that person. Barry Prizant captured this well when he wrote:

Autism isn't an illness. It's a different way of being human. Children with autism aren't sick; they are progressing through developmental stages as we all do. To help them, we don't need to change or fix them. We need to work to understand them, and then change what we do.

(2015: 4)

Such a transactional model is based on a deeply humanist perspective. It sees disability as being part of diversity, with difficulties arising from an interaction between the individual and the environment. As a consequence, rather than viewing autism as an 'impairment', or the autistic person as a 'collection of deficits' that need to be corrected and in which the difficulties are located within the pupil, it focuses the lens on the interactions between people. It puts those who care for and work with individuals with autism in a position in which they need to think about what *they* can do to change their practice.

The consequences of this is that in developing inclusive pedagogy for autistic pupils, solutions need to be located in both curriculum adaptation, and in changes in those who are engaged in planning and teaching that curriculum (Peeters & Jordan, 1999). This means that educators need to be open to thinking about the world and people in different ways, and to becoming more aware of how their thinking might shape their actions. It involves having a commitment to understanding difference, to making adjustments to one's own style of interactions and modifying how the curriculum is delivered. It means reflecting on the dynamic relationship between the child or young person and those around them, understanding the way the person processes and experiences the world and finding ways to empower and give the autistic child or young person control over their learning.

Even for those autistic people with the highest support needs, environmental change and the provision of appropriate assistive tools can reduce their challenges. Importantly, to minimise disability for autistic people, both the physical *and* social environments require change, as attitudinal barriers to inclusion and acceptance are often significant. Good autism practice therefore needs to be about having an interactional and transactional perspective that attends both to individual needs and to changing society, schools and classrooms.

When Liam screamed, holding his hands over his ears and biting anyone who came near him, the key to addressing this situation was therefore to understand why he reacted in this way. For a long time, teachers and support workers had responded to his behaviour by physically taking him by the hand to whatever activity was happening next as they felt he needed to learn to conform. The result of this was that Liam became more and more distressed. When the staff team took a different approach and carefully observed what was happening whilst trying to understand why Liam was reacting like this, they soon worked out that he was reacting to both sudden noises and to changes in the classroom.

As a consequence, they started preparing Liam for changes in routine by showing him pictures of what would happen next to prepare him, and they did the best they could to minimise sudden noises by introducing a 'low-arousal' approach in the classroom. This included keeping voices low, not touching Liam, nor using restraint. This helped to support him when he was in a crisis situation. It led to staff starting to treat him as a person to be understood rather than as a problem to be solved (Prizant, 2015). By observing Liam, staff started understanding what his behaviour communicated and realised, to paraphrase Carol Gray, that they held more than half the solution (Gray, 1994).

Finding ways of understanding the perspective of the autistic child or young person is crucial in education. It means having a commitment to listening to what they say and to what their behaviour tells us. Damian Milton is an autistic scholar, parent of a child with autism and teacher. He has developed the theory of the 'double empathy problem'. Milton (2012b) has proposed that theory of mind or empathy problems should not be associated solely with the autistic person. Rather, such difficulties are reciprocal, so a 'double empathy' problem exists. Both the autistic person and the non-autistic person struggle to understand and relate to the experiences and perceptions of the other. Milton presents the 'double empathy problem' as a breakdown in communication and social interaction between people who process information in very different ways, and that both autistic people and non-autistic people have difficulties in understanding one another. It goes both ways and is not a one-way street.

If a teacher looks at a child and thinks, 'he is just naughty and needs to be taught to behave in an appropriate manner', then the teacher is likely to focus on wanting to make that child conform. Equally, if a teacher looks at a child who is spinning, rocking or flapping, and feels that the most important thing to do is to reduce those behaviours, then the teacher will want to find ways of reducing these behaviours. If, on the other hand, the teacher sees those behaviours, and thinks that there is a need to observe and understand what functions they have for the child, the teacher might reflect on the fact that they could potentially have a soothing and meaningful function for the child. The energies of the teacher might then become focused on finding ways of helping the child to communicate in a different way. This different way of thinking about the child then leads to a very different set of actions. This highlights the need to think carefully about the values, ethos and the language one chooses to use in education.

People will come across a number of different terms for autism. These include *autism*; *with autism*; *autism spectrum condition*; *autism spectrum disorder* or *on the autism spectrum*, for example. Milton argues that the language we use frames the way we think about ourselves and others. He challenges the notion of autism as a 'disorder' as this has negative connotations of presenting autistic people as faulty and in need of being 'fixed' (Milton, 2012a).

Milton and Bracher suggest that if we present the person with autism as a 'disordered other', we can reduce that individual's sense of self-worth and self-esteem' (Milton & Bracher, 2013). As a result, they highlight the importance of talking about autism as a *different way of being* rather than a *disordered* way of being. They are not alone in arguing this. The disability rights lobby argues strongly for engendering positive acceptance of autism so that the focus is on participation and inclusion rather than looking for 'cures' and 'treatments' (Sinclair, 1993; Hacking, 2009).

There has also been debate about whether to use 'person first' ('an autistic person' rather than 'a person with autism') language or not. Many autistic people argue that autism is a core part of their identity, and therefore see themselves as autistic rather than 'with autism' (Sinclair, 1993; Milton, 2014a). Michelle Dawson (Dawson & Mottron, 2011) describes herself as autistic, for example, whilst Cunilla Gerland (2000) described autism as a living thing inside her. However, not all autistic individuals view their autism in the same way. In fact, the 'person first' language was first suggested by people with developmental disabilities who felt that they were being 'written off' and wanted to be seen as people first. Many young people do not see autism as central to their identity, and would therefore prefer the term 'with autism'.

Kenny et al. (2015) gathered the views of UK community members in the field of autism and found that a large percentage of autistic adults and their families preferred the term 'autistic', whilst the majority of professionals endorsed the term 'on the autism spectrum'. The debate about terminology is clearly complex and there is an argument for respecting the different justifications. In this book, the terms 'with autism' and 'autistic' are therefore used interchangeably to indicate acceptance of different perspectives. The terms 'autistic individuals, pupils, children and young people' or 'individuals, pupils, children or young people on the autism spectrum' are used interchangeably to include all those who have a diagnosis of autism or any other autism spectrum condition. The term 'disorder' is not used though, other than when quoting the work of people who have used this term.

One of the issues that have been identified as problematic in recent years in the field of autism studies is that professionals, researchers, parent organisations and autistic people exist and interact in different communities where they have developed their own language and culture, and are often at odds with one another. Much of the knowledge emerging from these communities exists in 'silos' with few shared practices (Arnold, 2010). I hope that this book will make a contribution to reducing the barriers separating these communities and to bridge different worldviews and practices. This involves working towards synergies between research and practice, between medical and social models, and between the perspective of autistic people and others. All these knowledge bases are important in the development of good autism practice in education as different domains of knowledge can sharpen understandings of autism and autistic people in a way that can enable the development of good autism practice in education.

The language we use shows that we all interpret individuals on the autism spectrum according to our own values and theories. This in turn affects how we act. It is therefore important to become aware of our own 'theories' or 'worldviews'. Autism is complex, with multiple factors involved in its emergence. There are many different knowledge bases and disciplines to draw upon when embarking on the journey of trying to understand autism, including psychology, psychiatry, education, philosophy, neuroscience and health. There is a need to pay attention to what these different disciplines contribute, and this is particularly so in education.

Crucial to our understanding are the perspectives of autistic people themselves, their parents and caregivers. It is particularly important to engage with the perspectives of autistic people through their narratives whilst acknowledging that each has a different, and important, lens for examining and understanding autism. Each has a different voice and by listening to those different voices, we can become better at seeing autism as a multi-dimensional tapestry of differences and abilities.

The key questions this book addresses

Arriving at a clear framework for good autism practice in education starts with asking some key questions about what actually matters in education. Each chapter of this book therefore poses key questions. These include but are not limited to the following:

Does the terminology we use matter when we talk about autism?

Can both medical and social models of disability inform educational practice?

How can a bio-psycho-social model that draws on the insider perspective support educators to develop a holistic understanding of autism and the autistic person?

What are the key contributions to knowledge that have emerged from biology, psychology, sociology and insider perspectives?

What can we learn from research and how can research influence practice?

Do autistic pupils need distinctive and different teaching approaches?

What are the principles for good autism practice in education?

How can practitioners decide on which approaches or strategies to use with an individual?

Why is it important to listen to the voice of autistic children and young people?

How can continuous professional development become transformative?

How can practitioners draw on research and theory, and what does it mean to be a scholarly and reflective practitioner?

Summary

This book takes a broad view of education and sees education as the process of facilitating learning. Education is also about values and beliefs, and these are important in informing how educators make decisions about the approaches and strategies they might want to use. As such, the overriding premise of this book is that education starts with understanding our learners. Understanding autism and how autism might impact on an individual is crucial. Knowledge is needed, and this knowledge needs to draw on different disciplines. As there is a clear biological basis to autism, which in turn affects how the person thinks and acts, it is necessary to have some understanding of what the autism field knows about both biology and psychology. The social structures of the family, the classroom, the school and community can become barriers or enablers to learning, so the context in which education happens also needs to be addressed.

All children and young people with autism are different from one another and they live and learn in different contexts. Research can offer us some understandings of what works in the research context, and might also be able to give practitioners some general pointers regarding the challenges and barriers autistic children and young people face, as well as ideas about how to overcome these. There is a need to make our classrooms more accommodating to our learners on the autism spectrum. This starts with identifying what matters in education, and it requires a commitment to changing ourselves and adapting the teaching and learning environments in which we teach. My hope is that this book will make a contribution to this process by providing clear guidelines that can inform good autism practice in education.

The book does this by bringing together the conceptual and the empirical, research and practice, and a number of stakeholder voices, including drawing heavily on the publications of autistic scholars to ensure that their perspective is central to the proposed pedagogies. It is based on the premise that in order to develop excellence in autism education, there is a need to consider theory, research *and* practice. It is intended to be a tool for thinking by inviting the reader to critique, interpret and understand our ever-changing field of autism education.

Recommended reading

Boucher, J. (2009) *The autistic spectrum: Characteristics, causes and practical issues.* London: Sage.

Prizant, B., with Fields-Meyer, T. (2015) *Uniquely human: A different way of seeing autism.* New York: The Associated Press.

PART I

Current evidence and knowledge from different domains in autism studies
Implications for education

2

The bio-psycho-social-insider model

Key question

How can a bio-psycho-social model that draws on the 'insider perspective' and subjective experiences support educators to develop a holistic understanding of autism?

Introduction

The most comprehensive and possibly most frequently used one-sentence definition of autism states that it is a 'neurodevelopmental condition that affects how people perceive, communicate and interact with the world'. In fact, this statement is so widely used that it is difficult to trace who first explained autism using these words. The word 'neurodevelopmental' in this definition highlights that autism is grounded in biology. In other words, autism affects a person biologically. It has a genetic foundation, is biological in origin and this leads to neurobiological differences. It is behavioural in manifestation though, so diagnostic criteria are based on observed behaviours and those criteria highlight differences in the separate domains of social communication and restricted and repetitive patterns of behaviour, interests and activities, including differences in sensory processing (American Psychiatric Association, 2013; World Health Organization, 2018).

The above definition also highlights that autism affects how people perceive and communicate. This shows that the biological difference can have an effect on the psychological functioning of the individual. Psychology is about how a person is feeling, thinking, perceiving, attending, listening and making sense of the world. Autism can therefore have an effect on thinking processes, levels of anxiety, self-esteem and wellbeing.

The final strand of the above definition highlights that having autism influences how the autistic person interacts with the world. In other words, the development and experiences of an autistic person will be affected by how the person is supported and educated. In summary, autism affects a person biologically. This will in turn influence how the person experiences and processes the world, whilst their development and experience will also be affected by how they are educated and supported. Individual differences interrelate with social factors to create challenges. A bio-psycho-social model can therefore provide us with a comprehensive way of understanding autism.

Models of disability

The bio-psycho-social-insider model in autism studies emphasises the need to understand the interrelationship between the biological, psychological and social whilst ensuring that individual and subjective experiences are also taken into account when developing understandings of autism and of autistic people (see Figure 2.1). How does this model differ from other theoretical models of disability in general and autism in particular?

The medical model encourages us to think of autism as a disease, pathology or abnormality with a focus on the impairments of autistic people. In fact, the word 'pathology' is crucial to the diagnostic and statistical classifications and it has been defined as 'the study of the causes and effects of diseases or injuries' (Royal College of Pathology website, 2019). The two main classification systems are the *Diagnostic and Statistical Manual* (*DSM*) and the *International Classification of Diseases* (*ICD*). The classifications of autism through the diagnostic and statistical manuals focus on deficits and impairments, on curing and fixing, and on changing the individual through interventions that improve performance. There is also an underlying assumption of the need to eliminate and reduce symptoms or behaviours.

Historically, special education was grounded in scientific, medical and psychological disciplines. Reid and Valle (2004) argue that this has primarily been about understanding disability within the medical framework and as located within the individual. Disability in US special education, for example, is defined in the Individuals with Disabilities Education Act (IDEA) as a pathological condition that exists within individuals (Department of Education, 2004). The legislation makes it clear that the task of the special needs educator is to offer the child intensive intervention in an attempt to remedy or, at least, lessen the child's learning 'disorder'.

Although IDEA (2004) states clearly that students receiving special education services are to be educated alongside their non-disabled peers to the fullest extent possible, the deficit approach has often been interpreted as being opposed to inclusive education. Many scholars have argued that the medical model ignores the social barriers to participation and inclusion (Oliver, 1996). In fact, the two models are often presented in opposition to one another, in that the medical model sees barriers as being faced by people as a result of their impairment, whereas the social model focuses on the social barriers to participation. In the social model, rather than seeing someone's difficulties as being 'innate' in that person, disability is seen as a social construct. Concepts of disability are seen as culturally relative and the product of specific cultural conditions (Corker & Shakespeare, 2002). The focus changes from 'fixing' the person to giving consideration to removing barriers and adapting the environment. In this way of seeing the world, the difficulties of autistic people are grounded in a discriminatory world.

Within the context of these debates, the disability rights lobby has argued for engendering positive acceptance of autism. Rather than looking for cures and treatments, the focus should be on the rights of disabled individuals, and on access, participation and inclusion. In this perspective, the person is not disabled by their impairment, but by the failure of their environment to accommodate their needs. In other words, disability results not from autism itself but instead from living in a society which is not accommodating towards autistic people. The lens is then directed to environmental limitations, the creation of a caring society and getting rid of stigma. The concern is with systemic barriers, negative attitudes and exclusion. In education, this means focusing on the institutional failures of an education system that is not flexible enough to include all children.

People are increasingly beginning to question whether the medical and social models should continue to stand in such stark contrast to one another though. Vermeulen (personal communication, 8 November 2018) has argued that linear models such as the medical or the social model can create a sense of cause and effect and blame, and that they are not much use in moving our understanding forward. Similarly, Shakespeare and Watson (2001) suggest that the social model creates a binary division between impairment and social disability. The notion of whether autism is a neurological difference to be celebrated or whether it is a disabling condition has been said to 'paralyze public discourses in ways that might ultimately be of little benefit to autistic people' (Moloney, 2010: 3). Shakespeare and Watson (2001) acknowledge that much discomfort with the medical model is based on an opposition to being defined solely on the basis of impairment, and that there is a need to challenge both the reduction to a medical condition, *as well as* stigma and negative cultural meanings around autism.

Shakespeare and Watson (2001) argue for the need to jettison the social model of disability as it stands in the UK today, and that we need to honestly appraise how different 'impairments' can have different social and individual implications. Furthermore, they highlight that:

> there is a complex dialectic of biological, psychological, cultural and socio-political factors, which cannot be extricated, except with imprecision.
>
> (Shakespeare & Watson, 2001: 24)

Disability is then seen as the 'result of an interaction between characteristics of the environment and the person' (Hollenweger, 2014: 11). It is perfectly logical then that one can reject the negative focus on impairment, disorder and deficit outlook of the medical model, whilst still take on board that biology, diagnostic and health perspectives can offer something positive. Such an interactive model takes into account the strengths and difficulties of a child or young person as well as the supports and barriers in the environment (Wedell, 1993).

The bio-psycho-social model

The bio-psycho-social model assumes that individual differences interact with social factors to create challenges (Grinker, 1964). Roy Grinker, a neurologist and psychiatrist, initially developed the bio-psycho-social model in the 1950s. It was later adapted to general medicine and health by Engel and Romano in the 1970s (Engel, 1977). Engel was a specialist in gastrointestinal conditions and his work focused on the fact that a holistic perspective grounded in general systems theory was necessary to address health.

The main tenet of his argument was that one must consider the psychological, behavioural and social dimensions that contribute to illness, and how the medical, psychological and social interact in a person's life (see Figure 2.1). Environmental factors interact with biological and psychological factors and the environment can significantly mediate difficulties for autistic people. This is therefore about addressing human health and education in a holistic and humanist way. In short, it takes into consideration the complex nature of individuals. The model also takes account of the fact that there are real challenges for people whose bodies and brains are different (Youdell & Lindley, 2019).

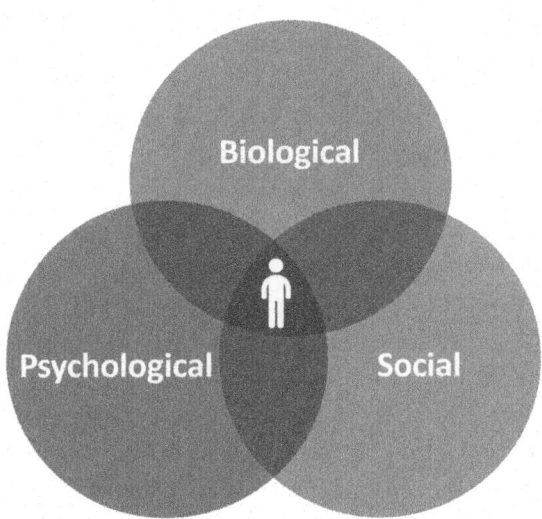

Figure 2.1 The bio-psycho-social insider model

bio-psycho-social-insider model draws out the 'kaleidoscopic xity' of autism (Orsini & Davidson, 2013: 12). It highlights that cannot be reduced to simple assumptions. There are no ready-solutions. Rather, it demands sensitivity and understanding of the complexity of autism and of autistic people. In autism studies, this suggests we need to consider the medical, neurological and psychiatric (biology); the emotional, cognitive and developmental (psychological), and the influence of family, culture, interpersonal, school, and physical environments (social factors) alongside how these aspects interact in complex ways.

In essence, such an approach moves away from a wholehearted objection to the medical model. It rejects the deficit-focused view of the medical model, but it does not reject what biology or neuroscience tells us about how the functioning of the brain or the human body might impact on a person's life. Medical and health considerations need to be taken into account, whilst understanding how the context impacts on the individual.

Let's take the case of Liam, who was introduced in Chapter 1. Liam responded with high levels of anxiety to transitions and his anxiety was often expressed by biting his caregivers or educators. He was particularly vulnerable to transitions. This included transition from one activity to another, between home and school, or from the class-room to the playground, for example. He reacted with behaviours that challenged the people around him during transition times. These behaviours were a result of an interaction between biological, psycho-logical and environmental factors. At the biological level, his neurology meant that he was extremely sensitive to sounds, so he would often react by becoming distressed and biting if there was a sudden increase in noise levels in the classroom, or if there were sudden noises.

His behaviour was also influenced by a number of other health factors. Liam had difficulty sleeping, and was often tired in school. He also had a very restricted diet, and was prone to getting colds and other illnesses. The main socio-environmental factors he would respond to were sound levels and the 'busyness' of the classroom. These were therefore triggering factors. Psychological features included that he could not attend to anything for more than a few minutes, and he had difficulty expressing his needs. His particular vulnerability lay in the fact that he could not communicate his frustrations verbally. He also had high levels of anxiety, as evidenced by the sounds he made and his facial expressions. In Liam's case it was important to understand these various factors for him to be able to learn, and to support him to learn.

This does not mean that it is always clear what the key biological, psychological and social or environmental factors are that impact on the individual, nor how these might interrelate. Rather, by taking an approach that aims to understand these factors, educators are more likely to identify the key issues that might impact on that person's readiness to learn. Such an approach is also more likely to enable a practitioner to develop appropriate interventions.

Summary

The issue of whether behavioural, social or biological influences are prioritised depends very much on what we are trying to understand. If someone wants to understand causation, they are more likely to pay particular attention to the biological. This might then lead to the bio-psycho-social model being seen as the complex interplay of biological and pre-natal environmental factors, or integrating biomarkers with mental health. Or, one might focus on addressing the relationship between biology and the physical and chemical processes that take place in the cell on a theoretical level.

In this book, the bio-psycho-social model is approached from the standpoint of what it is from these knowledge bases that are useful for teachers to know. It is about practical understandings and worldviews rather than testable scientific hypotheses, and it is about drawing on the knowledge bases in a way that can improve the understanding and practice of teachers. For an educator, the psychological and social disciplines are often more important when addressing educational needs. An understanding of genetics and the brain might be of less importance. Understanding the implications of the broader health needs of the person is nevertheless crucial.

The next three chapters give an overview of knowledge that has emerged from the different disciplines, with a focus on their importance for educational practice. In terms of the structure of the chapters, Chapter 3 gives an overview of knowledge from biology (medical, neurological, psychiatric) before providing an outline of the psychological (emotional, cognitive, developmental) dimension of knowledge in Chapter 4, followed by examining what can be learnt from the perspectives of autistic people in Chapter 5. Finally, Chapter 6 gives an overview of current social factors (family, culture, interpersonal, school, and physical environment) that contribute to understanding autism.

These chapters by no means represent an order of importance. Rather, the concern is with the knowledge, understanding and insights these different disciplines and knowledge bases can contribute to our overall understanding of autism.

Recommended reading

Roth, I. (2010) *The autism spectrum in the 21st century: Exploring psychology, biology and practice.* London: Jessica Kingsley.

Youdell, D. & Lindley, M. (2019) *Biosocial education: The social and biological entanglements of learning.* London: Routledge.

Contributions from biology and the medical domain

3

Key questions

What knowledge is relevant from biology and health in the development of good autism practice in education?

Can diagnostic criteria give pointers to educational needs?

Why is it important for education staff to be aware of the broader health needs of an autistic person?

Introduction

This chapter gives an overview of biological research, diagnostic classification and processes, co-morbidities in autism and broader health issues faced by many autistic people. It highlights some of the practical implications of these. Autism is a rapidly changing field, and knowledge about genetics, the brain and broader health needs are progressing all the time. Not very long ago, autism was seen as resulting from faulty upbringing. In the 1950s and 1960s, Bettelheim (1967) put forward the 'refrigerator mother theory'. His work claimed that children became autistic due to cold and unloving mothers who did not attend to their needs. This was an influential theory at the time and it led to some shocking practices of blaming parents, which resulted in many children being taken away from their parents.

As stated at the beginning of the last chapter, we now know that autism is a lifelong neurodevelopmental condition that affects how people perceive, communicate and interact with the world. For the majority of individuals on the spectrum, there is a genetic basis for their differences. In other words, genes can have an influence on someone having this neurodevelopmental condition. Current research indicates that it is likely that autism occurs as a result of the action of multiple genes. Heritability of autism is therefore very high, so if a family has a child with autism, they are more likely to have another autistic child.

Autism is also associated with changes in the structure and the function of the brain. Brain-imaging studies have come up with large differences in findings, both in terms of the size of brain regions and the connections between them. There is not enough evidence at present to draw firm conclusions as to whether differences in the grey or white matter of the brain are truly primary, but overall there is consensus that the cerebral cortex is probably organised in an unusual way in autism (Ecker, 2017). The cerebral cortex is the most developed part of the brain and is responsible for higher-order thinking, such as perceiving, producing and understanding language.

A strong association has been found between autism and patterns of electroencephalogram (EEG) signals. This could indicate differences in the organisation of large circuits that underlie the production of brain waves. Johnson (2017) sees autism as a variant of human brain development, with a developmental path that differs from the typical. This autism developmental pathway, Johnson argues, reflects differences related to altered signal processing at the synapses in the brain. That said, and despite the clear biological base to autism, there are as yet no reliable and valid biological markers (Gillberg, 2019). This means that there is no blood test that can identify autism, and neither can brain-imaging studies.

Diagnostic criteria

Whilst the results from research on biological causation, genetic and brain-imaging studies might not be of direct relevance to the practice of education practitioners, they can affect how autistic people relate to the world. These neurodevelopmental differences affect areas of development, and diagnostic criteria identify those areas of development that need to be present for a person to be autistic. Although the diagnostic classification system characterises autism as a list of deficits that are contrasted with corresponding abilities in typical development, it is possible to value the knowledge that biology, medicine and health research contributes to the autism field. The positive aspects of the diagnostic classification systems are that they provide a guiding framework for helping people understand the developmental domains that can be a challenge to autistic people.

The international classification systems for setting autism apart as a separate 'disorder', and the standards upon which a diagnostic decision is made, are the *Diagnostic and Statistical Manual* (*DSM*) and the *International Classification of Diseases* (*ICD*). In these, the core developmental differences in autism include social communication difficulties and restricted and repetitive patterns of behaviour, interests or activities. Sensory hypersensitivities have now been included in the stereotyped and repetitive behavioural domain.

The key change to the diagnostic classification systems in recent years is that the separate domains of social and communication difficulties in *DSM-4* and *ICD-10* have been collapsed into one domain of social communication and social interaction in *DSM-5* and *ICD-11* as there was recognition that one cannot really separate social interaction and communication because these developmental domains are so closely interrelated. Furthermore, previous diagnostic classifications included a number of conditions whereas the current classification specifies only one category for autism, namely 'autism spectrum disorder' (American Psychiatric Association, 2013; World Health Organization, 2018). Asperger syndrome, for example, no longer features as a separate syndrome in *DSM-5* as those involved in updating the manual felt that there was not enough to distinguish 'high-functioning autism' from Asperger syndrome.

Before outlining the developmental differences in more detail, it is necessary to make the point that individuals with autism will vary in terms of intellectual ability, personality, profile of strengths and needs, and the presence of other conditions, such as learning disability or epilepsy, for example, as well as their life experiences, just as all people do. Autistic campaigner Steven Shore emphasised this diversity a long while ago, when he highlighted that when you have met one person with autism, you have met one person with autism (Shore, 2003).

The same autistic person may have different needs at different times and in different contexts. Moloney (2010) considers this difficulty in the context of Asperger syndrome and suggests that:

> the received notion of a person being fixed at one point in an immutable autistic spectrum needs to be replaced by the image of a sliding scale or meter, which gives differing 'read outs' according to the given context, which will also include the person 'doing the reading.'

> (Moloney, 2010: 138)

The key point to take from this is that we need to understand the person and their development as dynamic. Nevertheless, diagnosis of autism is made if a person has significant difficulties in particular areas of development, and these will be outlined next.

Social communication difficulties

The psychiatrist Leo Kanner first introduced autism as a separate condition in 1943. He worked with a group of children whom he saw as having shared patterns of behaviour that set them apart from other children. Taken together, these features indicated a syndrome that had a characteristic set of symptoms. Asperger, a year later, published his paper 'autistic psychopathy' (Asperger, 1944). Both Kanner (1943) and Asperger (1944) included social and communication difficulties in their early clinical descriptions.

Kanner (1943) identified language delay in the children he saw, and also highlighted that some did not develop speech at all. He found that the children had difficulties relating to others from the beginning of life. Asperger pinpointed the lack of social quality in speech and the focus on their own preoccupations (Asperger, 1944). Both noted lack of eye contact, stereotypical movement, marked resistance to change and isolated special interests as being common to the children they studied. Lorna Wing (1996) later described autism as a 'triad of impairments' and grouped features of autism into three categories of social interaction, communication and imagination. The notion of a broader 'autism spectrum' was also coined by Lorna Wing in 1996 when she published her book entitled *The Autistic Spectrum*, and this term became widely used.

Diagnostic criteria are based on the notion that autistic children develop differently to 'typically developing' children in their early social communication. Autistic people have been shown to have difficulties in most areas of language and communication. The different components of communication include expressive communication such as spoken and written language and receptive communication such as understanding what others are saying. Many autistic people have additional language problems. These result from the effects of autism, but there can also be an additional language difficulty, or other cognitive difficulties. Where there are learning difficulties, for example, there may be difficulties in acquiring speech. There can also be an interaction of all three of those factors on the development of language and communication (Potter & Whittaker, 2001).

The communication and language development of autistic children and young people tends to take a different path to that of children and young people who do not have autism. In fact, autism is the only condition in which communication is separate from language in its development (Jordan, 1999). In all other conditions, speech and language arise out of communication, but in autism the development of speech can take a different route (Jordan, 2005). The fundamental difficulty is with communication, rather than language per se (Noens & van Berckelaer-Onnes, 2004).

To explain this point, it is necessary to define the difference between communication and language. Communication is a joint enterprise through which people share meanings with one another. Communication has many non-verbal elements to it, so it includes pointing, for example. When we point to something, it tends to be about sharing the meaning of a particular action. If I point at a bird flying in the sky, I am communicating to the other person that there is something up there to look at and that they should look at the bird flying in the sky. If I point to a glass of water whilst having a coughing fit, I am using pointing to mark what I want and to ask the other person to give me the glass of water. It is this shared aspect of communication that children and young people with autism have difficulties with, so if a child does not develop pointing, this is often a cause for concern.

In the first year of life, babies and toddlers tend to develop different ways of communicating. This can include requesting objects through pointing, sharing social meanings with others by waving goodbye, or commenting on objects by pointing them out. These pre-verbal abilities tend to be in place in typically developing children long before the development of language, but they are often delayed or do not develop naturally in children and young people with autism, leading to autistic children having difficulties in imitating others, sharing attention with others and playing social games such as peek-a-boo.

Language is a more formalised system that helps us share ideas and thoughts with others in more sophisticated ways. Structural aspects of language are not always a problem for pupils with autism, so a person can develop good language skills. They might have an extensive vocabulary, good grammar and syntax and the ability to use complex sentence constructions. The person can nevertheless have significant difficulties in communication. They might not understand the give and take of conversation, for example, and can, despite good language skills, have difficulty in the turn-taking of conversation, and in understanding conversation as something that is shared with others.

Roz Blackburn, an adult with autism, has often said that her greatest disability is her ability. She sees her abilities as masking her disabilities. This leads people to assume she can do much more than she can. She is an impressively eloquent and articulate speaker who can hold the attention of hundreds of people in an audience, but she finds it difficult to answer questions. Her talent in using the structure and form of language masks her difficulty dealing with the to and fro of conversation.

Those with good structural language skills can also have difficulties with articulation and semantics, especially those aspects of meaning that shift according to context. This makes it difficult for the person to understand how others use intonation to mark whether they are changing topic or whether they are emphasising a particular point. Difficulties with the rhythm and pattern of language are also marked, with speech often sounding flat. The difficulties extend to all aspects, including gestures, indicative pointing, eye-signalling, facial expression and body posture. These abilities are essential for using language productively as language is used to share meanings, to relate to others, to identify topics and to take turns.

Children and young people with autism will therefore need to be taught what communication is for and will need support in developing their communication, regardless of apparent language skill. A group of three young autistic men in a school I visited had developed excellent vocabulary, great sentence construction and very good command of language. All three nevertheless had significant difficulties understanding the non-verbal aspects of communication, such as picking up on body language and facial expressions, and they had a very literal understanding of language. Their greatest challenge related to how to engage in conversation. When working with the three young men who had good language skills but who struggled with holding conversations, teachers decided to focus on explicitly teaching them how to start, maintain and end conversations as well as how to judge a listener's reaction. They needed to be explicitly taught these aspects of communication that many other children acquire naturally.

Needing to be taught what other children and young people might acquire naturally is also the case in relation to the social. Jordan et al. (2019) state that only in autism is the typical preference for noticing and responding to social information absent (or at least delayed) so that development that depends on social facilitation and support is significantly affected. Difficulties in joint attention, imitation, social and emotional identification and sensitivity to social signals, for example, affect not just relationships with others but also how individuals come to understand themselves and the world around them.

Social differences that have been identified in early childhood include not enjoying physical contact with parents and failing to respond to their own name along with difficulty in understanding other people's feelings and facial expressions. The child or young person might struggle with forming friendships and can have unusual responses to social approaches. In the teenage years, researchers point to a different set of challenges. Autistic children and young people are often bullied and are isolated socially. These challenges continue into adulthood with lower rates of friendship, romantic relationships and social independence.

A different way of processing the world

The term 'restricted and repetitive behaviour' is used in the diagnostic and statistical manuals. Many people object to the way in which this terminology pathologises behaviour, and autistic people have pointed out that these behaviours can give pleasure and comfort. Questions have been asked about whether these descriptions reflect an adherence to social expectations rather than necessarily being pathological.

The diagnostic and statistical manuals highlight that restrictive and repetitive behaviours are considered to be unusual in appearance, and seen as inappropriate to the context. They often follow rigid patterns. In the current version of the *Diagnostic and Statistical Manual* (American Psychiatric Association, 2013), the subset of behaviours linked to the domain of 'rigidity of thought and behaviour' includes, for example:

1. Stereotyped or repetitive speech, motor movements, or use of objects (such as simple motor stereotypies, echolalia, repetitive use of objects, or idiosyncratic phrases).
2. Excessive adherence to routines, ritualised patterns of verbal or non-verbal behaviour, or excessive resistance to change (such as motoric rituals, insistence on same route or food, repetitive questioning or extreme distress at small changes).
3. Highly restricted, fixated interests that are abnormal in intensity or focus (such as strong attachment to or preoccupation with unusual objects, excessively circumscribed or perseverative interests).
4. Hyper-or hypo-reactivity to sensory input or unusual interest in sensory aspects of environment (such as apparent indifference to pain/heat/cold, adverse response to specific sounds or textures, excessive smelling or touching of objects, fascination with lights or spinning objects).

Research is unclear as to how restricted and repetitive behaviours change over time and what predicts these developmental patterns but there is some evidence that behaviours classed as repetitive and sensorimotor remain high, whereas insistence on sameness starts low and increases with age (Richler et al., 2010).

Implications for education are that change and transitions can be difficult for autistic children and young people, whether this relates to transitions from home to school, between different activities during the school day, or between different physical environments in the school, such as between the classroom and playground. Martin was a young child with whom I worked, who would find it very difficult if his mother had to take a different route to school in the morning. She dreaded it when roadworks meant that she had to change the way they drove to school, as Martin would become extremely distressed at the change.

When thinking about the issue of rigidity of thought and behaviour, there are a couple of key points to make here about the terminology and the notion of 'rigidity of thought and behaviour'. Whilst the diagnostic criteria can provide a framework for understanding particular behaviour patterns, they do not *explain* the behaviour. There is a need to understand what specific behaviours represent and signify. Prizant (2015) makes the point that a preoccupation with changing someone's behaviour is not the right way to go about it. Rather, the point needs to be to understand the behaviour. Prizant (2015) indicates that autistic people have difficulty with emotional regulation and constantly need to deal with regulating their emotions. He describes this as being dysregulated. This can impact on behaviour; therefore, many of the observed behaviours are about coping with dysregulation.

Furthermore, people often become preoccupied with the behaviour element of this because it is the behaviour that is observed. We cannot easily observe how someone is thinking or even feeling inside. Yet, behaviour is often a consequence of thought processes. The rigidity of thinking element is at least as important as understanding the behaviour. Many autistic people can find it very difficult to deal with thought patterns. My brother, Johnny, who has a diagnosis of Asperger syndrome, tells me about some of the issues with which he contends. He says that when he becomes anxious, in particular, he cannot think straight and it becomes impossible to learn. The other thing that happens is that certain thought processes take hold of him and he finds it difficult to control them. He says he knows these are not rational and they do not help him, but he finds it difficult to stop them.

He gave me an example of becoming totally preoccupied about finding a particular pen in his house. The pen did not have any emotional value to him. There was no reason to have to find it because he had lots of other pens. But his mind became completely preoccupied with finding this pen. He looked for it for six hours and turned the house upside down in the process. Other thought processes have also led to rigid thinking on bigger issues and topics for him, and these have often lasted for a while. When he was in his late teens, for example, he became very preoccupied with farmers and the subsidies they were getting in Norway, from where we come. He would argue and have monologues about how angry he was about this.

He has now started to find ways of dealing with preoccupations that might not be serving him well. When he feels that he gets locked-in to certain thought processes that lead him to going over the same issues over and over again in his head, he now tries to deal with these thoughts by asking himself one key question. This is 'what effects are these thoughts going to have?' When he makes himself think about this, he realises that the effect of the thinking is to make him feel worse. It is still difficult to stop the thoughts from going out of control, but he is working hard to put himself in control and to manage the difficult thought patterns.

Lawson (2010), drawing on Murray's (1992) earlier theories, has argued that one thing autistic people have in common is the ability to focus intensely on one interest. The term 'monotropism' was coined to indicate that autism can be attributed to a spread of attention. Monotropic attention is focused attention allowing a tighter, smaller set of interests at any one time whereas polytropic tendency is described as 'having many interests less highly aroused' (Murray et al., 2005: 140).

The other side of having 'rigidity of thought and behaviour' is then that this often means that autistic people have special interests that they can become very immersed in. Sometimes these are described as obsessions, but this is a very negative way of viewing something that can also be positive. The notion of 'highly restricted interests' used in the diagnostic and statistical manuals can also be seen as special interests and can, as we will see in later chapters, be a real source of strength for autistic people.

Rather than use the word obsession or rigidity of thought and behaviour, Prizant (2015) suggests using the term 'enthusiasms'. He highlights that enthusiasms can help the person manage their sensory processing or emotions. By joining in with a person's enthusiasms, one can help build relationships and trust. Enthusiasms can lead to people with autism becoming incredibly knowledgeable on the subjects in which they are interested.

Although my brother's negative thought cycles regarding farmers became difficult for him because these thoughts always made him angry, his interest in this topic also made him incredibly knowledgeable about the Norwegian government's policies on farming. Likewise, a young man in a residential provision had an enthusiasm for Birmingham's buses. He used to travel on them regularly. His memory was incredible because he knew every single bus route in Birmingham. He also knew all the drivers, their birthdays and the birthdays of all their family members. His special interest made him happy and content. Had people around him viewed this as an unproductive obsession, they might have tried to stop him developing his interests.

In short, rigidity of thought and behaviour can be difficult to deal with for both the autistic person and other people around them, but it can also lead to special interests and enthusiasms that make the person happy and that contribute to their wellbeing. It can also lead to the person excelling in particular topics and skills.

Sensory processing

Sensory sensitivity is now included under the 'restricted and repetitive behaviours' domain in the diagnostic manuals, and this includes three categories of sensory responses. Sensory sensitivities include differences in responses to the taste, feel, sound, sight or smell of things or people. The first is hypersensitivity. This is an overreaction to or avoidance of a sensory stimulus. The second is hyposensitivity. This is an under-reaction to a sensory stimulus. Under- or over-responsiveness can lead to behaviours that either generate or avoid sensory stimuli.

The third is sensory seeking. This means there can be a strong interest in a particular sensory stimulus. Beyond the traditional senses, autism researchers have also identified differences in systems that integrate sensory inputs. This is also known as proprioception and balance or vestibular issues. It includes awareness of one's body in space. Sensory integration difficulties also mean that there can be disruption in the process of organising sensory information from all the senses. This can influence fine and gross motor development, balance, co-ordination, self-help and visual perception.

Research has found that more than 90% of autistic people are likely to have a sensory sensitivity (Leekam et al., 2007). Many autistic people have described sensory sensitivity as being a central aspect of their lives and strongly related to feelings of stress and anxiety (Grandin & Scariano, 1986; Williams, 1996a; Sainsbury, 2000). Noise levels in classrooms can be very high and can impact on learning. Autistic children and young people can find it difficult to distinguish speech sounds from background noise, much in the same way as a hearing-impaired child or young person might. This can cause distraction and discomfort.

This brings to mind a pupil in a primary school classroom. His teacher found that he was suddenly unable to concentrate and participate in the English lesson whereas he had previously enjoyed this lesson. For the first 10 minutes everything was fine. He was clearly a very bright young boy, and was engaged in the lesson, asking lots of questions. Suddenly, though, he disengaged. The teacher could pinpoint the moment at which that happened. At first she thought it might be that he simply lost his concentration, but then she observed that he kept looking anxiously out the window. Initially, she could not work out why he did this, so after the lesson was over, she asked him why he had been looking out the window. He told her that the noise of the digger was so loud that he could not concentrate on anything else.

It turned out that there was building work happening quite a distance from the school. The teacher had not been able to hear the digger, but Daniel's hearing was so sensitive that he was unable to concentrate once the digger started. For other children who have sensitive hearing, it might be more obvious that sounds can be distressing because they might hold their hands over their ears when noise levels rise. In fact, Damian Milton will do that when he predicts that an audience is going to start clapping as he is very sensitive to noise. He has asked that we do 'silent clapping' (e.g. clapping by waving our arms) after he has given a talk because the noise of clapping is distressing.

Touch sensitivity can make it very difficult in classrooms for autistic children and young people, such as having to sit close to others on the carpet or in assembly. Exploring materials in art and design or food technology can be hampered by sensory sensitivities. Visual sensitivities can also have substantial impact. Wenn Lawson is an autistic adult and professional. When he visited me many years ago, the lights were on in my office. Wenn had to ask me immediately to switch off the lights because the lighting caused him significant discomfort and pain. Many autistic children in schools use noise-cancelling headphones because they are sensitive to noise. These issues highlight that it is crucial for educators to understand the specific sensory needs of the children or young people they work with, and to understand the areas of development that are affected in autism. It is often the case that sensory needs must be met before the child or young person can learn.

Having outlined diagnostic criteria, and the developmental areas that are affected in people on the autism spectrum, there is a need to reflect on to what extent diagnosis can be helpful. Diagnosis signposts people to the developmental areas that autistic people have difficulties with. It can also help family and friends understand the autistic person better. Many autistic people have described getting a diagnosis as being the best thing that happened to them because it enabled them to understand their own needs better, whilst being a starting point for others to understand their needs.

Diagnosis is often a gateway to services, in that a diagnosis might be needed in order for a child or young person to get additional resources and support in education, including being able to access the right provision. On the other hand, many people have concerns about labelling children and young people, and parents can be resistant to diagnosis. There can be different reasons for this, ranging from finding it hard to accept that their child has difficulties, to concerns about their child being stigmatised.

Talks given by autistic adults have articulated the value of receiving a diagnosis, whilst rejecting the way that the diagnostic process focused purely on the 'deficits'. Dean Beadle, an autistic speaker and journalist, in particular, is very eloquent and clear about the impact of the deficit approach when he talks about his own diagnosis. Dean is a public speaker who shares his experiences of having autism. He describes the diagnostic process and the way in which he was told everything that was wrong with him when he received his diagnosis. He comments that this was not 'a good way of selling autism to me' and wondered why there was not a focus in everything he *could* do rather than this focus on everything he could not do. He takes a positive view of his own autism and prefers to focus on his abilities and talents. As a result, he is a confident and highly articulate young man.

The diagnostic process

Autism can be detected through screening, and then followed through with diagnostic assessment if screening throws up 'red flags'. Screening is usually about facilitating earlier diagnosis and access to early intervention. Tools that have been developed to facilitate screening have included the M-CHAT, which stands for 'Modified Checklist of Autism in Toddlers' (Baron-Cohen et al., 1992). This is a questionnaire for the parents of children who are 18 months old.

It will not give a diagnosis but can indicate whether a child might be autistic. This is just one example of a screening tool and although this is widely used, there are many others. The key point to make here is that very few countries have adopted universal screening for autism in young children. This is partly because it is difficult to ensure that the screening instruments are specific and effective enough. There can be many factors impacting on a child's development. Screening is also a very expensive process and is not a substitute for diagnosis.

Diagnosis is a clinical judgement based on a developmental history of the behavioural symptoms of the person and other possible reasons for the behaviour. In most countries, medical professionals undertake diagnosis. This usually involves several different processes. Regardless of the age at which an individual is referred for diagnosis, an essential part of the diagnostic process is to take a developmental history of the person. Secondly, an experienced clinician or team of assessors will undertake an interactive assessment with the individual to determine differences in social communication and repetitive and stereotyped behaviours or speech.

The gold standard professional guidance in the field is for diagnostic assessment to be made in multidisciplinary clinics with professionals from different backgrounds being part of the clinical decision-making. In the UK, for example, the National Institute of Health and Care Excellence (NICE, 2011) and Scottish Intercollegiate Guidelines Network (SIGN, 2016) have set the criteria for a robust diagnostic process as being multidisciplinary assessment, direct observation of the individual across settings and the use of standardised assessment tools such as the Autism Diagnostic Observation Schedule and the Autism Diagnostic Instrument-Revised. Although there are a number of assessment tools available to clinicians and these enable diagnostic information to be gathered in a uniform manner, there is no agreement regarding the use of specific tools.

It is possible to diagnose autism at two years old, but this quite often does not occur. Research in the UK has shown that between 2004 and 2014, the age of diagnosis did not decrease and was relatively stable at an average of 55 months of age (Brett et al., 2016). In the United States, the median age of diagnosis is 52 months (Baio et al. 2018). Crane et al.

(2016) found that the time interval for UK families between initial expression of parental concern to a health professional and diagnosis was on average 3.6 years. Factors that influence the age of diagnosis include whether the child has more 'autistic symptoms', severe language delay or regression. Ethnic minority children appear to be at particularly high risk for diagnostic delay.

There is increasing evidence that unusual behaviours observed outside the home, either in pre-school or kindergarten, can be useful pointers to a possible diagnosis of autism. If education professionals suspect that a child might be autistic, they should discuss this with other professionals and sensitively consider how they might then raise their concerns with parents. If parents want to pursue diagnosis, they might need advice about referrals to the appropriate health professionals.

Broader health issues in autism

Understanding the possible biological and health implications of autism is also crucial for education practitioners as all aspects of health affect how a person develops and learns. The World Health Organization defines health as a state of complete physical, psychological and social wellbeing, not simply the absence of disease or infirmity. Health needs incorporate the wider determinants of health such as deprivation, diet, education and employment. Good health and wellbeing is central to effective learning and preparation for independent living.

This highlights the importance of looking at the wider influences on health, so the next sections give an overview of what is described in the medical profession as co-morbidities, as well as the potential impact of sleep disturbances, diet, intellectual disability and mental health difficulties on autistic children and young people. All of the discussed medical co-morbidities and consecutive processes can impact behaviour, socialisation, communication, cognitive function and the sensory processing of individuals with autism.

Co-morbidities

Autism can co-occur with almost any other 'disorder' outlined in the diagnostic and statistical manuals. Studies have found that children with autism had a much higher rate of a number of medical conditions, including eczema, allergies, ear and respiratory infections, gastrointestinal problems, headaches, migraines and seizures (Matson & Goldin, 2013). In a study of 300,000 children, children with autism were 60% more likely to have Irritable Bowel Syndrome (IBS) than children who did not have autism and they were four times more likely to have gastrointestinal complaints (Edelson, 2019). Autistic children are also more likely to have sleep problems and to have food, respiratory and skin allergies (Edelson, 2019).

Gillberg and Fernell (2014) coined the term 'autism plus' for cases where someone has autism as well as a significant co-morbidity. Gillberg (2019) has also highlighted that co-morbidities are the rule rather than the exception. Given that autism often co-occurs with other difficulties, researchers have suggested that people with a diagnosis of autism should automatically be investigated for these. Commonly available screeners for psychiatric disorders also appear to be effective in individuals on the autism spectrum. The conclusion of a number of studies is that an extensive medical assessment is appropriate in all cases and that treatment of co-morbidities can lead to a substantial improvement in quality of life both for the child and parents.

A recent study found that at least half of autistic people have at least four co-morbidities and more than 95% have at least one condition in addition to autism (Soke et al., 2018). In a survey of autistic children aged 10–14 in the UK, 70% met criteria for a psychiatric condition using the Child and Adolescent Psychiatric Assessment (CAPA) and 40% met criteria for at least two psychiatric conditions (Simonoff et al., 2008). The most common conditions that were identified in this study were anxiety, Attention Deficit Hyperactivity Disorder (ADHD) and Oppositional Defiant Disorder (ODD). Psychiatric co-occurring difficulties also include anxiety, depression, schizophrenia, Obsessive Compulsive Disorder (OCD) and Tourette's syndrome.

Almost half of the children with autism meet the symptoms of ADHD, but until the most recent version of *DSM* (*DSM-5*), it was not possible to diagnose both. A diagnosis of ADHD itself points to the need for specific intervention and adaptation. For children and young people with both autism and ADHD, the ADHD is often more associated with inattention than impulsivity (Gillberg, 2019). As a result, children and young people with a dual diagnosis of both autism and ADHD require clear explicit instructions and visual strategies. Girls with autism who have co-occurring ADHD usually also have high rates of reading and/or writing difficulties (Gillberg, 2019).

Epilepsy is also common in autism. The prevalence of epilepsy in autistic individuals with Intellectual Disability (ID) is estimated to be 21.5% and 8% in individuals without ID (Tuchman et al., 2013). Epilepsy has a later onset than seen in the non-autistic epilepsy populations, with the mean age being 13.3yrs. Diagnosis and treatment is medical, but education staff need to be aware of the symptoms of the many different types of epilepsy given that it often has late onset in autism and the disorientating effects of seizures may have a role in behaviours that challenge. Depression is increasingly common in able and older autistic individuals. About half of all 30-year-olds with childhood diagnosis of Asperger syndrome have recurrent depressive episodes. Anxiety is also common and 40% of youth with a diagnosis have been found to have substantial anxiety symptoms (Mikita et al., 2016).

Sleep

Physical issues that can have a significant effect on autistic children and young people and their parents include sleep disturbances. Autistic people tend to have less sleep than non-autistic individuals, including those with other developmental disabilities. Given that measures of EEG (electroencephalography) and rapid eye movement have been found to be different in autistic people, this could suggest a possible biological cause for some of the sleep difficulties. One biological marker that has been found to be different in autism is melatonin levels. Melatonin is the hormone released to control the sleep/ wake cycle and is sensitive to changing light conditions. Although the causes of sleep disturbance are still unclear, a recent paper based on expert opinion in the field suggested that sleep problems are the consequence of cognitive hyper-arousal, such as becoming fixated on certain topics and/or heightened physiological arousal. This can include body temperature and increased heart rate (Souders et al., 2017). The frequency of night awakenings had the greatest impact on behaviours that challenge (Engelhardt et al., 2013).

Diet

Many autistic people have a tendency to eat a limited selection of food, and even to be restricted to eating a single food. This can in part be due to sensory differences related to the taste, texture and temperature of food. Restricted diets have led to predictions that there might be poorer intake of nutrients but the findings in this area have been inconsistent. Some have found no difference from controls and others have reported poorer intake of certain vitamins or dairy products. Children who are on an exclusion diet, such as when gluten and/or casein is purposely removed from their diet, are more likely to have a different nutritional profile than autistic children not on an exclusion diet. This is in part negative, in part positive, showing the importance of getting nutritional advice before starting a specialist diet. Overall, there is no suggestion that any variation in nutritional intake has a negative impact on energy or physical growth in autism.

A limited diet, such as eating less fruit and vegetables, could be a contributory factor to why autistic people have a higher incidence of gastrointestinal (GI) problems (McElhanon et al., 2014). GI problems are reported to be more frequent in autism compared to non-autism control groups. These problems have been correlated with higher rates of behaviours that challenge and poor sleep. Children with anxiety and sensory sensitivity have also been found to have higher rates of GI problems. As a result of GI problems, and speculation around food intolerances, some parents believe that removing gluten and casein from their child's diet will improve symptoms.

In a large parental survey of 18 European countries, it was found that a quarter of respondents had used a dietary or supplement intervention within the last six months (Salomone et al., 2015) and from a UK survey, 83% of parents had tried a dietary intervention at some point (Winburn et al., 2014). A significant proportion of parents have reported that the change in diet has had a beneficial effect on their child's behaviour but independent research evidence has been harder to find. Given the strength of the evidence, the associated costs of being on an exclusion diet and the additional family pressure of trying to stick to the diet, recommendations are to advise parents to seriously consider whether using this diet is the best use of their resources.

One consequence of having a restricted diet and a less active life-style has been increased rates of obesity in autistic young children and adults. Beyond reduced engagement with physical activity and increased interest in passive activities such as watching TV, rates of obesity in autism have been correlated with sleep problems, mental health difficulties, socioeconomic status of parents and medication use. There is now strong evidence to suggest that there are significant health, mental health and behavioural benefits from autistic people participating in autism-specific exercise programmes.

Intellectual disability and autism

The World Health Organization classifies Intellectual Disability (ID) as being caused by various factors. For example, it can be genetic in origin or it can be acquired through brain injury. It is usually evident early in development and is characterised by intellectual functioning that is at least two standard deviations below the average level of intelligence. Prevalence of ID in the general population has been estimated in a meta-analysis study to be 10.37/1000 (Maulik et al., 2011). As the prevalence of autism has increased over time, and we have become more sensitive to the breadth of the spectrum, there has been a shift to recognising that the majority of individuals on the autism spectrum now do not have an intellectual disability (Lecavalier et al., 2011).

Mental health issues

The last five years have seen an increasing awareness of mental health difficulties in children and young people generally, including those with autism. Current research indicates that from a young age through to later adult life, autistic individuals are more likely to have a mental health condition and experience poor mental health than the general population. Although it is fundamentally important to recognise that mental health difficulties often arise from an interrelationship of biological, psychological and social factors, some of the key issues that have emerged from research are covered in this chapter given that mental health difficulties are often considered to be psychiatric in origin and tend to be defined as a medical condition.

Data indicates that up to 46% of children on the autism spectrum aged between three and 16 years have at least one co-morbid mental health condition. Within the group aged 10 to 14 years, the rate was up to 70% (Simonoff et al., 2008). Furthermore, the prevalence of co-occurring mental health conditions is higher for those children on the autism spectrum who also have an intellectual disability. Anxiety and depression are the most common mental health issues experienced. However, it is difficult to determine the true rates of depression and anxiety in autistic people as many features of autism such as social withdrawal and sleep problems overlap with symptoms of depression and anxiety, so it can be difficult to diagnose.

Symptoms have been found to increase during the adolescent period and extend into adult life. Accounts of autistic adults indicate that many feel very anxious for much of the time. In addition, they often have low self-esteem as they receive more critical comments from others and are often at a loss to know why others might consider something they have done to be inappropriate or insensitive. Having high anxiety and low mood underlies many mental health conditions. Reducing anxiety and giving more positive reinforcement to autistic children and young people is therefore likely to reduce the mental health problems now and in the future.

The reasons for the mental health issues seen in autistic children and young people are complex and can include both genetic and environmental factors, such as social exclusion, bullying, and the experience of criticism and stigma. Whilst every person on the autism spectrum experiences life in their own individual way, to a greater or lesser degree the experience of dealing with neurotypical physical, sensory and social environments means that autistic children and young people and their families can be more susceptible to stressors that may trigger mental health problems. Differences in communication can also make it more difficult for them to seek and obtain help, which can perpetuate mental health issues.

It is perhaps unsurprising that a combination of issues can lead to 'behaviours that challenge'. The term 'behaviours that challenge' (Tanwar et al., 2017) is now used rather than the term 'challenging behaviour' because this takes the focus away from seeing the behaviour as arising from something innate in the person, to considering the reason to why the individual is displaying that behaviour. It also encourages those who care for or work with an autistic person to consider what the behaviour might be communicating, as well as what might be triggering behaviour. In fact, autistic adults can display a higher rate of 'behaviours that challenge' than non- autistic adults, whether intellectually disabled or not (Matson et al., 2011). A large survey of parents with autistic children identified emotional and behavioural difficulties that included anger, sleep, dietary issues, overactivity and anxiety (Maskey et al., 2013). Triggers can include the sensory environment, physical disorders and discomfort, the social environment, changes to routines, communication issues or co-occurring mental health or psychiatric problems (Pilling et al., 2012). The emphasis needs to be on understanding what the behaviour may mean and the role that practitioners, society and the environment play in interpreting, eliciting and intervening with these behaviours.

Inter-professionalism

Legislation and advances in medical science have meant that many more children with complex medical needs are now attending both mainstream and school settings. Local authorities and schools in England have a statutory duty (Education Act, 1996: Section 16) to provide education for children with all health needs, including those children who cannot attend school due to their health needs. Schools must legally have a link person for medical needs whilst schools and local authorities have a legal obligation to make reasonable adjustments and ensure equality of opportunity by, for example, providing equipment needed for accessibility or making adjustments to the environment and curriculum. Schools should also have policies for children and young people with ongoing health issues.

There is therefore a strong emphasis on the need for education staff and health and social care professionals to collaborate to ensure they have an accurate picture of the child or young person's needs across settings. This highlights the importance of conducting multidisciplinary assessment as an essential part of determining a child or young person's needs.

Although it is difficult to achieve, policy and expert guidelines highlight the need to work towards interprofessional work. Inter-professionalism captures working practices across service boundaries (Ravet, 2015). It is about developing links across services and contexts. Ravet (2015) states that:

> The aim of interprofessional working is ultimately to facilitate more efficient and effective provision, to enhance inclusion and to ensure improved social, health and educational outcomes for children, young people and adults.
>
> (Ravet, 2015: 91)

Education practitioners can play an important role in supporting autistic people and their families to identify health issues and to liaise with health practitioners to receive help to address them. In fact, liaison between education and health professionals can make a big difference to how effectively autistic children and young people and their families are supported. Medical co-morbidities can be more difficult to recognise in autistic people than in the general population. Nearly a third of people with high-functioning autism reported that they did not receive appropriate medical care for physical health problems (Nicolaidis et al., 2011). Health concerns were often dismissed or not treated adequately. Successfully addressing health issues often leads to significant improvement in overall functioning.

The health and wellbeing of autistic children and young people can clearly benefit from partnership work across services. This includes between teachers and home link staff, health professionals, educational psychologists, as well as through individual support and pastoral care. Such links need to encourage the active support of parents, and should draw on specialist expertise when needed.

Knowledge of health needs also has implications for the interventions and approaches that are chosen. The Scottish Intercollegiate Guidelines Network recommends that:

> agencies and services develop a menu of interventions, including advice, therapeutic interventions and counseling for children, young people and adults with an ASD, that are appropriate and flexible to the individual need.
>
> (Scottish Strategy for Autism (2011: 78), Recommendation 10)

The strengths and positive aspects of autism

This chapter has painted a fairly grim picture of the number of different health concerns and co-morbidities autistic people can face. By explaining diagnostic criteria, it has also highlighted how constructions of autism are presented through the medical model, and that the impairment and deficit-focused lens needs to be challenged.

Fortunately, there are a number of researchers that have recognised the need to focus more on the strengths and abilities of autistic people and to change the way that research is conducted so that it is possible to draw conclusions about those strengths. One way to address these issues is to design research that enables a focus on the fact that many autistic people show no impairment, or even show above-average performance in many areas of development (Wallace et al., 2008). It is important to question the measures that are used too. IQ tests are one example as traditional measures of IQ tend not to be adapted to the strengths of autistic people and can therefore underestimate autistic people's intelligence (Dawson et al., 2007; Nader et al., 2016).

Furthermore, in some studies, researchers have reported superior performance by autistic individuals on a number of cognitive tasks. Subsets of autistic people have performed well on standardised vocabulary tests, for example (Jarrold et al., 1997). Superior cognitive skill in autism has been found in the ability to form and manipulate mental images (Soulieres et al., 2011) and may explain some of the abilities in completing puzzles (Stevenson & Gernsbacher, 2013). Autistic people can also exceed the performance of non-autistic individuals within education and the workplace (Lorenz & Heinitz, 2014) as they often have better skills of concentration, understanding of rules and patterns, and memory.

Some autistic individuals have what is described as 'savant' skills. This refers to having an exceptional skill in a specific area such as calculations. It is often assumed that many savant abilities are related to being able to focus on details and having superior attention skills for their topic of interest (Heaton & Wallace, 2004; Mottron et al., 2006).

Summary

Autism is a natural variation of the human condition and all humans should be valued. The functions of diagnostic criteria are to improve diagnosis, prognosis and treatment, so the diagnostic process involves clinical judgement by skilled practitioners. In this process, there is a need to reject the focus on trying to change or cure the person with autism and move to the more appropriate goal of supporting the person to be the best they can be without changing who they are.

Understanding the medical classifications of autism and the developmental areas that affect autistic people provide signposts to what autistic people have in common and to their needs. Diagnosis can also offer a gateway to services. The health, behavioural and psychiatric conditions that co-occur with autism should be priorities in terms of planning services for autistic people and for staff training programmes.

Managing these conditions are priorities for autistic people and their families, and can lead to significant improvements in quality of life, as well as increasing social participation. Co-morbidities should not be assessed and managed in isolation but consideration should be given to how these different conditions interact. Improved sleep may make weight problems easier to manage and interventions for anxiety may lead to a reduction in gastrointestinal problems. This highlights the need for educators to understand the health needs of an autistic child, and to be able to consider these when addressing need and delivering interventions.

Recommended reading

Casanova, E.L. & Casanova, M.F. (2018) *Defining autism: A guide to brain, biology and behavior.* London: Jessica Kingsley Publishers.

Grandin, T. (2014) *The autistic brain: Exploring the strengths of a different kind of mind.* London: Rider.

4 Contributions from psychology

Key question

What is the contribution of psychology to knowledge about how children and young people with autism learn?

Introduction

There are a range of different orientations in psychology, from neuroscience, to cognitive, developmental and behavioural theories and research. The psychological perspective brings together observed behaviours and attempts to infer what these mean for features of cognition. Psychology is a discipline that has created hypotheses as a way of explaining observed behaviour, and many theories have been put forward in the domain of autism studies. This chapter provides an overview of the key theories that have emerged from psychology and the relevance of these to education practitioners and educational practice. Given the plethora of publications in this area, the chapter does not go into detail about those theories but gives an overview of them in order to provide some guidelines for their relevance to education.

Fletcher-Watson and Happé (2019) argue that cognitive theories span the gulf between biology and behaviour by creating hypotheses about the mind: 'Cognitive theories are the explanatory models that attempt to link biological heterogeneity with behavioural heterogeneity via cognitive simplicity (if only!)' (Fletcher-Watson & Happé, 2019: 68).

Cognitive models are arrived at by examining observations derived from biological and behavioural data, which in turn provide the input and output to theories around cognition. Uta Frith, a pioneer in research on autism, for example, encouraged psychologists to work in a theoretical framework that distinguished between observed behaviour and the underlying cognitive and neurobiological processes that mediate that behaviour.

The aim of much psychological research has been to formulate testable hypotheses that can lead to predictable outcomes should that hypothesis be correct. Psychologists will argue that theories should be falsifiable in order to have explanatory power. This evidence can come from experiments, observational studies and a variety of other methods.

Uta Frith (2012) argued that many of the theories that have emerged in the last decades in autism are 'core deficit models'. She used this way of describing them because the assumption behind these theories was that there was *one* underlying problem that accounted for the wide range of difficulties observed in autism. One such influential cognitive theory has suggested that the key problem lies in understanding the thoughts, feelings and beliefs of others (Baron-Cohen, 2000).

Theory of Mind relates to the ability to attribute independent mental states to oneself and others in order to explain behaviour. This ability helps a person to make sense of and predict another person's behaviour, or put oneself 'in someone else's shoes' as one might say colloquially. Baron-Cohen et al. (1985) postulated that this ability was impaired in autistic people. He and his colleagues conducted a study that led them to conclude that 80% of children were 'unable to impute beliefs in others and are thus at a grave disadvantage when having to predict the behaviour of other people' (Baron-Cohen et al., 1985: 43).

Another well-known theory put forward to explain the difficulties of autistic people is Executive Functioning. The executive dysfunction hypothesis proposes that the symptoms of autism are a result of problems in the executive control of action (Hughes & Russell, 1993). This is about maintaining an appropriate problem-solving set to attain a goal. It includes functions such as planning, working memory, impulse control, inhibition and mental flexibility, as well as the initiation and monitoring of actions.

Central Coherence, on the other hand, relates to the ability to draw together 'bits' of information to make sense of situations or events, according to the context. In other words, to 'see the big picture'. Uta Frith's work (1989) found that autistic people showed a detail-focused cognitive and perceptive style. This could cause difficulties with generalising, sequencing, prioritising, organising, shifting focus, understanding new concepts and the general idea of what is being said.

Although cognitive theories have tried to identify a single cognitive difference in autism, it has become clear that none of these provide a satisfactory account for the full range of behaviours in autism or for understanding all autistic people. Criticisms of theory of mind, for example, have included that the tests used to measure whether someone had a theory of mind 'deficit' might have more to do with how autistic people process language, or with memory, rather than with theory of mind. The ability to pass the test also increased with age. It is also the case that 20% of the children who undertook the test passed it, so this has led many people to question the hypothesis of theory of mind. Furthermore, a number of research studies have found different results regarding hypotheses related to psychological functioning.

The theories have also been criticised for their lack of universality, specificity and explanatory power in describing autism. To be universal, a theory needs to identify something that affects all people on the autism spectrum and the identified feature should be specific to autism. Jordan, for example, makes the point that:

> There is as yet no one commanding theory that can offer an explanation for all the characteristic symptoms, that applies to all with autistic spectrum conditions, and is exclusive to that group. Most have something to offer our understanding of the condition, even if they are not entirely satisfactory as full explanations.
>
> (Jordan, 1999: 111)

Dr. Claire Evans-Williams points to the fact that all autistic people are complex beings biologically, socially and psychologically, so it is not advantageous to presume the essence of 'autisticness' can be captured and reduced to a single unitary theory (Evans-Williams, 2019). Rather, it is likely that a number of different influences work alongside one another and lead to the difficulties autistic people have. The theories are not necessarily mutually exclusive. In fact, they can be complementary, as they can address different aspects of development and can affect individuals differentially.

These theories can nevertheless provide insights into how people with autism learn even though they might not provide hypotheses that turn out to be appropriate for all people on the autism spectrum. The theories have contributed to understanding more about the role of information processing in learning and the need to strip down and chunk up information for many autistic people when their way of learning requires us to do that. Theory of mind can remind practitioners to make information more explicit. The notion of central coherence and a details-focused autistic style can help educators think about how autistic people's ways of learning might differ.

Roth (2010) highlights that Theory of Mind, Executive Functioning and Central Coherence have contributed to understandings about the difficulties autistic children and young people might have in daily life. These can include, but are not necessarily limited to:

▓ Writing: planning a piece of writing and not seeing the point of telling the reader something they might know already.

▓ Task planning: how long a task will take and what resources might be needed.

▓ Managing daily life: getting ready for school, navigating round school and getting to classrooms on time.

▓ Change and transitions: anxieties about changes in routine.

▓ Life skills: understanding relationships and sexuality.

▓ Unstructured periods: unusual behaviours and not knowing how to enter into playground games.

▓ Understanding instructions: needing simple instructions, having literal understandings, and finding it difficult to understand sarcasm, irony and jokes.

Although these are not the only theories that have been advanced to explain the difficulties of autistic people at the psychological level, these theories do demonstrate that psychological research in autism has tended to work at the cognitive level of explanation and rely on behaviours to make inferences from. The concept of cognition usually covers attention span and reasoning. It covers the parts of the brain that are considered to be responsible for complex mental processes, such as the process of knowing, perceiving and conscious intellectual activity.

Cognitive theorists have tended to take a perspective focusing on acquisition of knowledge and have tended to shift attention to academic behaviours and cognition. This has included seeing psychological functioning as something innate rather than culturally acquired and as a product of the culture and language of the society from which they emerge. It has been argued that they locate the difficulties within the mind of the individual autistic person (Milton, 2012b) and that by presenting autism as purely behavioural or cognitive, the disabling effects of society are not taken into account. This brings us on to inter-subjectivity theories.

Inter-subjectivity theories

Inter-subjectivity theories take a transactional approach to autism (Prizant et al., 2006) in that the difficulties of the autistic person are not seen in isolation or as existing within the child, but emerge in the interaction between the child and others. In his paper 'On the origins of self and the case of autism' (1990), Peter Hobson (1990) focused on autistic children to attempt to understand how people develop a concept of self. He stated that:

> I have argued that autistic children's awareness of themselves and other persons as subjects of experience, and ultimately their capacity to think of themselves as thinkers, is limited by disruption in their affectively patterned interpersonal relations.
>
> (Hobson, 1990: 177–178)

Some theories on autism therefore take the perspective that the mind cannot be reduced to the biological mechanics of the brain. The ability to think is tied with social interaction, not merely tied with brain development. There is a social interplay and social relationships have a profound impact on the development of thought and on the person. Many theorists in this tradition have put forward the notion that the intentionality of autistic minds is oriented differently, and is less directed at emotional connectivity with others. In other words, there are differences in what motivates individuals with autism. Right from the beginning, there is a lack of preference towards social stimuli and understanding of social situations.

People who do not have autism, on the other hand, develop intuitive understandings early on about other people's feelings. Hobson argues that empathy is the intuitive capacity to feel for and with other people. Early emotional engagement then forms the basis for both social and cognitive development. This emotional engagement, in Hobson's writing, involves experiencing what the other person might be feeling. Hobson built on Trevarthen's work (1979), which showed that infants and their mothers were pre-programmed to respond to each other's behaviour in a way that meant that their interactions were closely attuned and synchronised. Hobson believed that relating emotionally to others originated in these early interactions.

For those without autism, it is often other people that motivate them whereas in autism, social motivation is seldom effective (Jordan et al., 2019). Jordan (2005) has argued that this has implications in that autistic children and young people require education for those aspects of development that others just acquire intuitively. They need explicit teaching of how to attend to and learn from others. In summary, social orienting hypotheses predict that early signs of autism come from a lack of preferential attention to social content in the world. The core difficulty then becomes the difference in ability to perceive and respond to the affective expressions of others. This, in turn, leads to atypical social experiences in infancy and childhood, which in turn impacts on social understanding.

Autistic theorists have also engaged with a transactional approach. Both Milton (2012a) and Sinclair (1993) have highlighted that social understandings are constructed in the context of people interacting with one another. Interaction should therefore always be viewed by taking into account *all* the people involved in that interaction. Empathy, for example, then becomes a 'two-way street' (Sinclair, 1993). Damian Milton wrote a paper titled 'On the ontological status of autism: "the double empathy problem"'. In this paper, he argued that many discourses in autism studies ignore the importance of 'relationality and interaction in the formation of a contested and constantly reconstructed social reality, produced through the agency of its "actors"' (Milton, 2012a: 883).

As highlighted in Chapter 1, he coined the term 'the double empathy problem' to highlight the difficulties that autistic and non-autistic people have in understanding each other's worlds. This theory is gaining a lot of interest.

Recently, researchers have used the transactional approach to conduct research on how autistic people communicate with one another. Brett Heasman and Alex Gillespie (2019), for example, have looked into how autistic people interact with one another and create shared understanding. They make the point that it is strange that research has tended to focus on individual abilities given that communication is a two-way process, and that communication requires individual skills as well as an environment that supports interaction. They see communication as a socially situated activity, and that culture includes rules and norms that guide people in creating shared understanding. They therefore studied the communication of autistic people in an environment involving only autistic people where there were no 'neurotypical' norms. They found that when autistic people were communicating with other autistic people, they developed shared understandings through making generous assumptions about common ground and they had a low demand for social co-ordination.

Developmental psychology and psychosocial interventions

Developmental psychology considers how people change over the course of their lives. The focus is on broader developmental areas in reference to what is often described as 'typical' development. This approach takes a broad perspective on growth to include how thinking, feeling and behaviour can change over the course of someone's life. It is concerned with cognitive and intellectual changes as well as emotional and motivational development. It refers to the process of acquiring skills in stages, from simpler to more complex. In a child's development, one would expect a child to babble and make sounds before saying words, and be able to say words before saying phrases, for example.

Researchers have evaluated atypical sensory and perceptual functioning, differences in imitation, language, empathy, emotional expression and understanding, and social communication of autistic people through studies. This work has often focused on interpreting disruptions in the 'typical' developmental process, such as the fact that many autistic children will have language delay and have limited non-verbal communication in terms of their use and understanding of gesture, facial expression and body language, for example (Ozonoff et al., 2003).

Most children develop meaningful non-verbal communication, such as joint attention, turn-taking and understanding of gestures, before they develop language. Joint attention is essentially the shared focus of two individuals on an object or another person. In human communication, this is usually achieved when one person alerts another to an object by eye-gazing, pointing, or other verbal or non-verbal indications. Pointing is an important indicator of the development of joint attention and usually develops at the age of around nine months. Joint attention is disrupted in autism, so if a child does not point, this can be an area of concern.

There have therefore been many studies examining joint attention, communication and play skills in autistic children, and how these can have an effect on the development of language (Kasari et al., 2006). Research focusing on teaching early communicative behaviours such as joint attention shows that a focus on joint attention offers real potential for the later development of social and communication skills (Kasari et al., 2006; Parsons et al., 2011). There have also been many studies looking at the communication and language skills that help the individual to function in day-to-day life, as well as social understanding and joint attention, peer interaction and play (Ozonoff et al., 2003). Many of the interventions that have been developed have focused on shaping and increasing social skills (Howlin et al., 2004). Research has focused less on promoting self-regulation and autonomy (Ward, 2005) despite the fact that autistic people argue that this is crucial in their lives (Jarzabek, 2014).

Psychosocial interventions

In the context of meeting the needs of autistic individuals, there are many strategies, approaches, therapies and psycho-educational programmes. These often draw on research on psychological processes (Howlin et al., 2009). Many therapeutic interventions focus on techniques for improving communication, and on encouraging greater flexibility in thinking and behaviour, for example. Some focus on broad educational and therapeutic frameworks.

The definitions, criteria and classifications of these interventions have been categorised in different ways in the literature (Howlin et al., 2009). Comprehensive Treatment Models (CTMs) focus on many areas of development and on improving functioning across multiple domains. They represent a prescribed set of focused interventions or practices designed to achieve broad learning. They tend to be intensive and address a range of outcomes. Odom et al. (2010) identified 30 CTMs in the United States. Examples include Early Intensive Behaviour Intervention (EIBI), or Social Communication, Emotional Regulation Transactional Support (SCERTS) (Prizant et al., 2006).

Research on interventions in autism studies has tended to concentrate on focused interventions rather than CTMs. Focused interventions tend to occur within a short time frame and address a specific outcome. They cover fewer areas of functioning and behaviour such as specific targeted skills in areas of functioning. This includes play skills, areas of cognition or behaviour, as well as peer training and social skills packages. Examples of focused interventions are task analysis, reinforcement and time delay, for example. Task analysis is about breaking down complex tasks into discrete chunks. This is often used to teach self-help skills, toileting, or how to make a sandwich, for example. To teach a child to wash their hands, the teacher might break this down into step-by-step instructions by providing visuals for each step of washing hands, from turning the tap on, putting the hands under the flowing water, picking up the soap and rubbing it on the hands, and then rinsing this off again under the running water before switching the tap off again.

Reinforcement is about teaching replacement behaviours for an interfering behaviour to increase 'appropriate' behaviour and communication skills. Sometimes a token economy can be used for this. Time delay is about reducing and fading prompts during instruction. Focused interventions also include communication interventions, such as the Picture Exchange Communication System (PECS) (Bondy & Frost, 1998), and those that target early interactions between parents and children, such as Early Bird (Shields, 2001) and Pre-Linguistic Milieu Therapy (Yoder & Stone, 2006), among others.

Behavioural psychology

Applied Behaviour Analysis (ABA) encompasses a range of behavioural approaches in autism. Early Intensive Behaviour Intervention (EIBI) is largely based on ABA principles and is one of the most commonly used treatments for autistic children according to surveys of parents and service providers (Stahmer, 2007).

In simple terms, behaviourism is a science that aims to bring about meaningful change in a person's *actions and behaviour*, and that behaviour can be modified through reinforcement. Behaviourist approaches define desirable behaviour before working on that through prompts and small tasks in a structured format. In ABA, behaviour is examined as a three-step process. These three steps are antecedents (a cue), the behaviour and the consequence. So, if a person is thirsty (antecedent), they might drink some water (cue) and the consequence is that they have quelled their thirst. Through this process, the person learns that drinking water has positive consequences.

In ABA, this principle is applied to an intervention to produce positive consequences for behaviour. The focus is on encouraging and reinforcing positive behaviours whilst discouraging negative ones, to establish new and more productive behaviours and to ensure that the child is not rewarded for negative behaviours. The thinking is that rewards and consequences can make behaviour more or less likely to happen again.

A number of methods will be used to award positive behaviours, including discrete trial training. This is a teaching strategy that breaks down skills into small and discrete components and the teacher then systematically 'trains' these skills. Reinforcements and rewards are used to encourage the positive behaviour. An example of how this might work would be that the child is learning to sort yellow cubes in a tray. The child is given a combination of red and yellow cubes. If the child selects the yellow cube, the child receives an award, such as praise. If the child does not choose a cube or he chooses a red cube, the child does not get the praise.

ABA is the most comprehensively studied treatment model in research (Reichow, 2012). This is partly due to a study by Lovaas (1987), which subsequently stirred much debate. Experimental studies in which different programmes for early intervention have been compared have produced mixed results about ABA since then (NAC, 2009). Some studies have concluded that EIBI is an effective intervention, and that the average effects of EIBI appear to be strong, with increases in IQ and to a lesser degree in adaptive behaviour (Reichow, 2012). Magiati et al. (2012), for example, reviewed EIBI approaches, and found evidence that these are generally more effective in supporting the development of cognitive and language skills, and to some extent adaptive behaviours, than eclectic approaches.

Other studies have reported limited or no clinically significant benefits to EIBI approaches compared with other forms of provision such as specialist nursery provision (Reed et al., 2007; Remington et al, 2007). Interventions that used EIBI techniques have been shown to be successful in teaching specific skills for some children, such as joint attention and play-related skills (Howlin et al., 2009).

One of the criticisms of behavioural approaches has been that there has not been much evidence to show that children can transfer the skills they have learnt through behavioural interventions to other contexts outside those in which the skills were acquired. This indicates that children are not really learning to generalise through this approach (Jordan et al., 2019). It has also been criticised for producing dependent learning styles, and for taking away agency from the child. ABA approaches also emanate from a deficit-based medical model that is based on a normative focus on 'correcting deficits' (Milton, 2014b).

Psychosocial interventions and practical approaches

Behaviourist approaches are often contrasted with humanist, intersubjectivity or transactional approaches. Prizant takes a deeply humanist approach, which is also transactional in orientation. Barry Prizant (2015), in his book *Uniquely Human*, describes the main challenge in autism as being that of dysregulation. Dysregulation refers to a difficulty in regulating emotions whilst emotional regulation refers to the ability to use skills and strategies to modify one's emotional state. Prizant argues that emotional regulation is core in autism, as the neurological issues mean that autistic people are far more vulnerable to dysregulation than others. Autistic people will therefore have fewer innate coping strategies. Sensory processing difficulties can make vulnerable and they may be unaware of how .eir reactions when they are dysregulated.

.ocus on specific behaviours and argues that it is ɔcus more on the *causes for* behaviour. He argues .aviours autistic people display are not deficits, but ɡ strategies. They are a way of the person trying to ʋes. He uses the example of flapping arms. When an young person flaps their arms, this behaviour can mean veɪ ɔ things for different people, and can also have different meanings . the same person in different circumstances or at different times. The behaviour can be an indication of the person being excited, it could be that the person is in pain or it can be a calming behaviour for the person. It could also be a response to shutting out anxiety. Prizant (2015) makes the point that there is a need to stop viewing these as behaviours and start addressing them as coping strategies for dealing with dysregulation. There is therefore a real need to understand the true motivations of underlying behaviour and what the purpose of the behaviour is to the individual.

In a similar approach, Mackenzie (2019) puts forward the case for a social cognitive approach that focuses on the interaction among the learner, the teacher and the task, so that learning is seen as a shared effort with the child (Mackenzie, 2019). She argues that relationships have largely been overlooked in the field of autism interventions, and she talks about the importance of agency and on ensuring that the child or young person plays an active role in their learning. On a day-to-day level, this highlights the need to give children and young people opportunities to make choices, express their feelings, to think on their own and demonstrate knowledge.

The adult's role is then to develop their skills of active listening, acknowledging the child or young person's perspective, and being attentive to the child's emotional and intellectual states. The adults should also relate to the child with a sense of warmth, affection and acceptance. The adult should avoid orders and directives, and be respectful of the child or young person's views and expressions of concern, doubt or disagreement. The educator ensures that the child or young person understands the meaning and purpose of the task, and is given opportunities to think on their own and demonstrate knowledge. So, rather than focus on teaching particular behaviours and skills, the aim is to promote decision-making and choice, letting the child or young person make mistakes, and encouraging independent work.

This approach focuses on the relationship between the psychologist and the client or the teacher and the student, and this is seen as more important than the therapy or particular intervention. Rather than make a child or young person comply and follow a plan, the purpose is to foster social communication and find ways to support emotional regulation. That involves giving give the child or young person control over their life by giving choices within a predictable structure.

Core components of effective interventions

Another area of psychology is intervention research. Intervention research will be covered in more detail in Chapter 6, but there are a few points to make here. There is good evidence now that some non-intensive interventions, particularly those that focus on communication and joint social interaction, can have a significant and positive impact on children's general functioning (Morgan et al., 2018). Research has highlighted the potential value of interventions that focus on broader areas of development such as communication and social understanding rather than on specific skills (Tager-Flusberg et al., 2011). Research has also enabled the identification of the components of effective interventions for children with autism and key features of effectiveness. These features can and should inform pedagogic practice.

There has been significant effort to produce guidelines to support policy and practice, and to develop basic principles of good autism practice that can inform education and therapy. The National Autism Center (2009) in the United States, for example, conducted a systematic review of the evidence, and identified 11 'treatments' for which there is evidence of effective practice (NAC, 2009). Meanwhile the National Professional Development Center found 27 practices that met their criteria of strong evidence (Wong et al., 2014).

Another systematic literature review (Bond et al., 2016) found that interventions that were designed to increase joint attention and comprehensive early intervention programmes were rated as having most evidence for pre-school children. For school children, peer-mediated interventions supporting the development of social skills were the strongest (Bond et al., 2016). Guidelines from the National Institute of

Clinical Excellence (NICE) in the UK point to the importance of making adjustments to the social and physical environment, to support families, and to focus on the development of life skills (NICE, 2011 & 2013).

The NICE guidelines pinpoint that interventions need to be developmentally appropriate, that there should be a focus on increasing the understanding of caregivers, teachers and peers, and on anticipating and preventing behaviours that challenge. They also emphasise the importance of enabling environments, augmented communication, person and family-centred work, as well as collaborations and multidisciplinary work, such as professionals from different backgrounds working towards shared targets (NICE, 2013). There is evidence that an organised environment with visual cues can enable access to the learning environment. Taking account of sensory processing difficulties and the social demands of working with other children and young people has also been emphasised as important (NAC, 2009).

The Medical Research Council (MRC, 2001) guidelines stress the importance of entry into intervention programmes as early as possible. They highlight the need for the active engagement of autistic pupils in intensive instruction and for repeated and planned teaching opportunities with sufficient attention daily. These guidelines point to the need for systematically planned and developmentally appropriate activities that should target identified objectives, include a family component, and conduct ongoing assessment of progress. This should be complemented by specialised instructions in settings that permit ongoing interactions with typically developing children (MRC, 2001).

Summary

Psychological theories can go some way towards helping us make sense of seemingly diverse behaviours in a unified way and can help us connect lived experiences and biological data in a way which can have implications for good autism practice in the classroom. Psychology has undoubtedly made an important contribution to understandings of autism, and to knowledge about the psychological functioning of individuals. Work around central coherence, for example, has emphasised the need to pay attention to a different way of learning and to the way the person actually perceives and processes information and the environment.

The ability to learn and act effectively does not simply depend on the attributes of any one individual. Scholars have highlighted that when it comes to learning, we should not split the mind and the body, the individual and the social, or structure and agency (Hodkinson et al., 2008). Learning evolves in the mental, emotional, practical and physical, and these are all interrelated. In fact, it is the relationship between the above different factors that influence learning (Hodkinson et al., 2008).

At the level of thinking, perceiving, as well as the developmental, emotional and inter-subjective, psychology and psychological research has helped us gain insights into how children and young people develop and how relationships can affect the person. Psychology can also direct the gaze to what the underlying problem might be when someone behaves in a certain way. Psychological theories and research also give a clear rationale for many structured approaches that can be used in education, and research on interventions has highlighted some of the core components of good practice in both therapy and education.

Recommended reading

Bowler, D. (2007) *Autism spectrum disorders: Psychological theory and research*. London: John Wiley.

Fletcher-Watson, S. & Happé, F. (2019) *Autism: A new introduction to psychological theory and current debate*. London: Routledge.

Lawson, W. (2010) *The passionate mind: How people with autism learn*. London: Jessica Kingsley.

5 Learning from autistic perspectives

Key question

What can the insider perspective offer us that other knowledge bases are unable to offer?

Introduction

As we saw in Chapter 2, the diagnostic and statistical manuals are based on behavioural criteria for understanding autism. Donna Williams, autistic adult and advocate, challenged this perspective many years ago when she said:

> right from the start, from the time someone came up with the word 'autism', the condition has been judged from the outside, by its appearances, and not from the inside according to how it is experienced.
>
> (Williams, 1996b: 14)

Since the time of Donna Williams' quote, there has been increasing recognition of the need to ensure that all voices should be heard in the discourse of autism, and autistic authors have emphasised this point (Sinclair, 2010). Autistic people have stated that they have been frozen out of the processes of knowledge production and many have become distrustful of researchers and their aims (Milton & Bracher, 2013). Milton argues that due to a lack of interactional expertise with autistic communities (Milton & Bracher, 2013), a negative spiral has ensued. Milton highlighted the extent to which the autistic voice has been silenced:

> In the history of autism studies, expertise has been claimed by many differing academic schools of thought, practitioners, parents, quacks and so on. Yet, the one voice that has been traditionally silenced within the field is that of autistic people themselves.
>
> (Milton, 2014a: 7)

In recent years, this has gradually started changing. The autistic rights movement has gained strength and more people are taking note of the messages that are emerging from this movement. Most importantly, their voices are starting to be heard. There have been many powerful autobiographies, blogs, novels and movies written by and about the lived experience of autistic people.

The philosopher Ian Hacking (2009) has highlighted that autistic self-narratives have a critical role in conveying the subjective autistic experience. Through these self-narratives, we can gain greater understandings of certain 'behaviours'. Autistic authors have opened our eyes to the notion that we need to understand the *meaning* of behaviours, and the function a behaviour might have for an individual, rather than seeing them as behaviours that need to be eliminated. Hacking (2009) highlighted that hand flapping was perceived by many as a meaningless behaviour until autistic authors described the feelings of release and satisfaction incurred by the activity. Luke Jackson (2002), in talking about the difficulties he has with eye contact, states that:

> Sometimes it is hard to concentrate on listening and looking at the same time. People are hard enough to understand as their words are so often cryptic, but when their faces are moving around, their eyebrows rising and falling and their eyes getting wider then squinting, I cannot fathom all that out in one go, so to be honest I don't even try.
>
> (Jackson, 2002: 71)

Hacking argues that autobiographical writings are giving us a new and deeper perspective on autism, one that provides us with a new language and that sees autism as a culture rather than as a problem:

Autism narrative is a new genre: not expert reports by clinicians or reflections by theorists, but the stories about people with autism, told by the people themselves, or their families, or by novelists, or by writers of stories for children, they are enabling the development of describing experience for which there is little pre-existing language.

(Hacking, 2009: 1467)

Hacking (2009) also highlights that given that these stories are forging a language through which to talk about autism, this is helping to bring into being an entire new mode of discourse, and way of talking about autism (2009: 501). It provides a strong perspective on autism as a many-dimensional tapestry of abilities and limitations. He suggests that there is a truth about autistic inner life that these narratives are gradually revealing, that there is little ready-made language to describe this, and that the autobiographies, the blogs, the novels and the movies are creating it.

Many authors highlight how having autism affects every aspect of their experience and is central to how they understand the world. Jim Sinclair, autistic campaigner and advocate, said:

Autism isn't something a person has, or a 'shell' that a person is trapped inside. It is pervasive, it colors every experience, every sensation, perception, thought, emotion, and encounter, every aspect of existence.

(Jim Sinclair, 1993, www.autreat.com/dont_mourn.html)

Several accounts written by adults with autism (e.g. Grandin & Scariano, 1986; Sinclair, 1993; Williams, 1996b) offer a 'view from the inside' in describing their life as autistics. Dealing with ongoing anxiety is a major thread that runs through many of these narratives, as are difficulties with the curriculum, becoming bored, and facing significant sensory processing issues.

Autistic narrators talk about being perceived as being different, bullied or marginalised, and that they are not viewed as 'normal' members of society. They find it hard to make sense of others and want to be appreciated for themselves rather than fitted into a box. In Claire Sainsbury's (2000) *Martian in the Playground*, she eloquently describes her sense of alienation from others throughout her school years by drawing both on her own experiences and those of others to provide a strong account of what life can be like in the school and in the playground (Sainsbury, 2000). In *Freaks, Geeks and Asperger Syndrome*, Luke Jackson (2002) provides fascinating insights into life as a teenager on the autism spectrum.

Temple Grandin's (1995) *Thinking in Pictures: My Life with Autism* has had a major impact on enhancing people's understanding of the importance of visual thinking when she described her own visual thinking style, and that words were her second language. Grandin opened her book with:

> I think in pictures. Words are like a second language to me. I translate both spoken and written words into full-color movies, complete with sounds, which run like a VCR in my head. When someone speaks to me, his words are instantly translated into pictures.
>
> (Grandin, 1995: 1)

Due to her own sensory perceptual issues, she used these experiences to inform her work in animal sciences and is currently a Professor at Colorado State University. In *Emergence: Labeled Autistic*, she communicated her innermost fears and gave crucial insights into her own mental processes. In fact, Oliver Sacks, the neurologist, described her work as a 'bridge between our world and hers. It allows us to glimpse into a quite other sort of mind' (foreword to *Thinking in Pictures*, 1995).

Despite the strength of these narratives and their importance in creating a new genre that can shift understandings of autism, some people have responded with the warning that individual accounts offer us descriptions of one person's autism and therefore can only provide insights into that person's autism rather than everybody's (Jones et al., 2013). Naoki Higashida's *The Reason I Jump* is a book written by a 13-year-old boy from Japan who is non-verbal. Temple Grandin, in a review of this book, comments both on the similarities and differences between her own thinking style and Naoki's in that both have problems remembering long sequences, fear of certain noises and the tendency to see details of objects before seeing the whole. This suggests that although the insights from the writing of autistic people are based on individual experience, these narratives can highlight common experiences faced by many people on the autism spectrum.

The narratives are powerful ways of giving non-autistic people new insights into what life must be like for an autistic person and to step into the shoes of the author or narrator. They offer new and deeper ways of thinking about autism by revealing a truth about inner life in a way that can help bring people closer to understanding autism. As a result, this can lead to a more in-depth understanding of the issues faced by autistic people. It can enable the reader to take on board the reality of living with autism day in and day out, and from experiencing it first hand. Christopher Goodchild's narrative, for example, tells a powerful story of how he experienced the world as totally overwhelming:

> My earliest memories were of a world that felt totally overwhelming. Lights, sounds, movements and smells flooded into my senses, leaving me feeling distressed and anxious. For me it made perfect sense to remove myself from all social interaction. This way I felt safe from a world that was strange and alien to me, and the more I ventured out into the world the more I wanted to retreat from it.
>
> (Goodchild, 2009: 21–22)

Outsider views can give stereotyped perspectives of autism, such as the notion that all autistic people are good at maths, are like the character in the 1988 film *Rain Man* or that they all have low ability and 'live in a world of their own'. In fact, publications, stories and narratives from autistic people often state that it is not autism itself that causes difficulties, but the expectations, interactions and responses they get from other people. In particular, the expectation to act, respond and learn in the same way as 'typically developing' pupils. Christine Breakey (2006) notes:

> If we listen to what autistic people tell us about autism, then one of the first things that we learn is that even though they may describe a war, or a battle with autism, autism in itself is not a problem. Their relationship with us and the environment is.
>
> (Breakey, 2006: 124)

Autistic people also challenge the notion that the focus should be on encouraging autistic people to be 'normal'. They are producing discourses that are critical of the status quo as they question the deficit-focused model of diagnostic criteria for autistic conditions and argue

for putting the voices of autistic people to the fore. They of
resistance to narratives that see autism as a tragedy. In so
encourage the examination of assumptions about normal
ment and difference that underlie the medical model of aut

> People do seem to have trouble realising that we can lear.. ఎ ∪ʋiii-
> pensatory skill, but not how to be 'normal' (even if we wanted to
> be totally normal). They can't realise that our brains and thought
> processes are different and that we can't change that any more
> than the blind can learn to see with their eyes. Or that what is
> adaptive for normal may be maladaptive for us (and vice versa),
> and that, in most cases, our ways can be better for us (and can
> allow us to function quite well in certain situations and at certain
> tasks). I think a cure for 'normalcy' would be a much better goal
> than a cure for autism; normalcy is much more prevalent!
>
> Jared (1993 from a debate on the internet,
> quoted by Jordan et al., 1999: 16)

As Lawson notes in *Concepts of Normality*:

> Disability presents itself in a variety of ways, and for most of us
> living with disability, who we are is normal. For many people on
> the autism spectrum, which is certainly very disabling in a world
> that does not accept, value or accommodate "difference", being
> handicapped is an everyday reality. This text argues for the right
> to exist as oneself, with or without disability; this should be part
> of "the norm."
>
> (Lawson, 2008: 15)

The neurodiversity movement

Many autistic adults embrace an identity as autistic and reject
'neurotypical' behavioural norms by aligning themselves with the view-
point that autism is a natural identity with strengths and weaknesses that
contribute valuably to human diversity (Silberman, 2016). The concept
of neurodiversity has been attributed to Judy Singer, an autistic social
scientist in 1998. It is based on the notion that there is variability in the
brain structure and function of all human beings and that the resulting
cognitive processes account for the differences between all individuals.

This paradigm sees autism as a form of diversity rather than pathology, with many advocating that strengths and differences associated with autism are central to a person's identity (Ne'eman, 2010). It recognises that all neurological ways of being human should be respected just as any other way of being. The movement coined the term 'neurotypical' to describe the kind of brain most people have, and to distinguish this type of brain from the brain that autistic people have.

The neurodiversity *paradigm* is based on the notion that just as people are ethnically, culturally and sexually diverse, they are also neurologically diverse. It challenges the assumption that autism is a disease or an illness that needs to be eradicated. It also confronts the notion that there is such a thing as a healthy brain or a right style of functioning. The idea is that if we change people's awareness of seeing autism as difference rather than as a disease, then it is more likely that people with autism will be treated more humanely and with more understanding.

It can lead to people becoming more accommodating of different needs and behaviours and to creating more accommodations in schools and workplaces. The key contribution of the neurodiversity paradigm is therefore that it does not pathologise or focus solely on what the person struggles with. Instead it offers a more balanced view by focusing on strengths and what the person can do well. It also recognises that biological variation is intrinsic to people's identity, sense of self and personhood. It is grounded in a compassionate social view of disability and inspired by civil rights causes.

The neurodiversity *movement* is a social movement that promotes the neurodiversity paradigm. This movement sprang out of the autistic rights movement of the 1990s. It is a movement that campaigns for equal treatment and it has emerged from a social reality in which autistic people are not treated equally. It rejects the need to normalise autistic people and cure autism, and argues instead for expanding the definitions of what is considered 'normal' and acceptable rather than pathologising autistic people. Rather than attempt to cure, it is argued, the focus should be on supporting people to thrive.

Advocates therefore campaign for acceptance and respect for autistic people as valuable members of society, and highlight the need to fight for appropriate support and services to meet the needs of autistic people. This is often focused on improving subjective quality of life and wellbeing whilst respecting and preserving autistic ways of being, and seeing autistic individuals as having a complex combination of strengths and challenges. The goals of the movement include ending the use of harmful therapies and changing practices so provisions can become more 'autism friendly'.

This movement has been important in creating a sense of identity for autistic people and a feeling of belonging. Martijn Dekker, in his discussion about competing and opposing narratives in the autism field, talks about the development of the Autism Network International, which was established in 1992. He says 'for all our cultural, political and neurological diversity, we found plenty in common, not only in the shared experience of trauma and marginalization, but, for many of us, also in a certain fundamental autistic way of being' (Dekker, 2019: 26).

This movement has gained strength in recent years and the influence of it can be seen in a number of positive developments. The firm 'Specialisterne', for example, aims to only recruit autistic people as autistic programmers and software developers. The influence of this movement can also be seen in the introduction of autism-friendly screenings at cinemas and the introduction of quiet hours in supermarkets.

The strength of the movement is evident in its ability to influence laws. In the United States, a law was passed by Congress and it was initially named the 'Combat Autism Act'. Neurodiversity campaigners organised a campaign against this and the name of the act was changed to the Autism CARES Act (Autism Collaboration, Accountability, Resources, Education and Support). The US government has also created a body called the IACC (Interagency Autism Co-ordinating Committee), which now advises federal government on autism policy. Meanwhile, the Labour Party in the UK has launched an autism neurodiversity manifesto. Importantly, the neurodiversity movement has empowered many people with autism and enabled people like Greta Thunberg to describe having autism as a superpower.

Criticism of the neurodiversity movement

Like any movement, people will have a number of different perspectives and do not speak with one voice. Critics of the neurodiversity movement tend to focus on the notion that many autistic rights advocates are on the 'high-functioning' end of the autistic spectrum, and claim that they ignore the very real challenges that many autistic people and their families face. They argue that most activists are people who have language, and are unlikely to have learning difficulties. They counter the neurodiversity paradigm by highlighting that there are autistic people and families who face major challenges and who struggle in any environment. They might have significant physical challenges alongside their autism, as well as developmental delay.

Critics of the neurodiversity movement point out that many autistic people are too affected by their condition to speak up for themselves. In California, for example, the National Council on Severe Autism has been set up. They state that their aim is to pursue awareness of and solutions for the individuals and the families of those who have severe autism. They exclusively advocate for individuals with autism who need high levels of support. This group is very wary of the neurodiversity movement as it claims that the movement marginalises those with more severe needs.

In recent years, there have been quite extreme positions taken on either side. Some people in the neurodiversity movement have been accused of fanaticism and a cult-like outlook. People with strong convictions are seen as browbeating people with different views, and as closing down debate in the process. Social media is rife with examples of accusations being levelled at both sides of the debate. Those criticising the neurodiversity movement have been accused of eugenics, being ableist, and have been likened to Nazis.

On the other side, the neurodiversity movement has been accused of denying that severe autism exists, and that by not allowing parents to speak for autistic people, they exclude severely autistic people. They are accused of dividing the autism community as it creates a sense of 'us and them'. They are seen by some people as fostering deep mistrust of the medical and scientific community. Neurodiversity champions have been accused of monopolising public discourse, silencing dissenting voices and closing down debate when people disagree with them.

The most contentious debate is concentrated on the notion of whether autism should be cured. Some neurodiversity advocates have argued against the notion that money and energy should be spent on finding a cure, or that there should be a world without autistic people. As a result, autistic advocates have been charged with the accusation that they do not think autistic people need support or intervention in any form. In fact, the debate is often presented as a counter position between whether autism should be celebrated or treated. This is a misguided criticism as most people belonging to the neurodiversity movement acknowledge that autistic people and their families might choose different interventions to support them lead a better life. Most are not saying they do not want to ameliorate challenges faced by autistic people. Rather, the focus is on increased acceptance, accommodations and support. Research and interventions that improve life are welcomed.

Neurodiversity advocates have also been accused of arguing that autistic people do not have disabilities. Despite accusations to the contrary, leaders of the neurodiversity movement do see autism as a disability and they often describe the disabilities they have. They also maintain that those difficulties are contextual and that living in a society designed for non-autistic people exacerbates their challenges.

This in-fighting can distract different communities from opportunities to learn from one another, and to create new knowledge and understandings based on this learning. In an attempt to reconcile the perspective of the neurodiversity movement and those who take issues with this movement, Simon Baron-Cohen in *a Scientific American* blog (blogs.scientificamerican.com) has argued that by taking a fine-grained look at the heterogeneity of autism, we can see that the neurodiversity model fits well, but also that the medical model can be a better fit for some. Baron-Cohen argues that an interrelationship between genetic underpinning, diagnostic criteria and co-morbidities means that we need to distinguish between four different concepts when describing autism. He defines disorder as a functional abnormality, but where the cause is unknown. Disease is then defined as a disorder because it is ascribed to a particular cause, such as epilepsy. Disability, in Baron-Cohen's definition, is defined as the person being below a standard measure of functioning and this can cause the person to find it difficult to cope in certain environments. Finally, he describes difference as a variation in trait.

Baron-Cohen argues that neurodiversity is a fact of nature in that all our brains are different. He argues that some of the genetic differences that have been found in autism can be seen as examples of neurodiversity. He says, for example, that about 10–50% of the variance in autism can buted to common genetic variants that simply reflect individual nces or natural variation. He also argues that about 5–15% of the ce within autism can be attributed to rare genetic variants, many of which can cause both autism and severe developmental delay. In relation to studies of the brain, some regions of the autistic brain are larger and some are smaller. These are evidence of difference not disorder whereas structural differences in the language part of the brains of people who are minimally verbal are likely to be a sign of disorder. He describes conditions such as epilepsy as being a sign of disease.

This formulation is an attempt to reconcile the arguments of the neurodiversity movement with those of its critics, and as such, it provides food for thought. There is nevertheless a need to stay tuned to the fact that the concepts of disorder, disease, disability and difference are all laden with social meanings and are defined and approached very differently by different people. These words say something about how someone is perceived in society, and they influence how people view that person. It is this perception of being portrayed as the 'disordered other', as Milton describes it, that many autism advocates object to, because they argue it leads to stigma and pathologising, with a focus on the individual as being the person that is 'broken' rather than dealing with societal barriers.

Implications for education

As a result of autistic people speaking up, there is now greater recognition of the importance of providing opportunities for autistic children and young people to have their voices heard. Listening to the voice of autistic people can be a first step towards developing teaching that is relevant to the child or young person's interests and needs. By capturing the perspectives of autistic children and young people, education staff can better understand how school experiences impact the development of self-esteem and identity (Norwich, 2002).

Autistic narratives and the neurodiversity movement have made researchers and educators more aware of the importance of active participation of autistic children and young people in education. This includes ensuring that pupils on the autism spectrum are effectively engaged in decision-making and in planning for after the school years.

This is essential for helping individuals gain belief in their own cap abilities and to gain the knowledge and skills needed to make healthy choices and develop their independence.

That said, researchers, policy makers and education staff need to know more about how to effectively consult with children and young people, in particular those with significant learning or communication difficulties (Jones et al., 2008). Providing opportunities for children and young people to have their voice heard and to express their thoughts, feeling and ideas requires modified or creative methods. This includes finding sensitive and imaginative ways of understanding a child's experiences, such as modifying questions and using other scaffolding techniques.

Understanding and acceptance of autism can increase by listening to autistic people and by becoming more familiar with their experiences. Greater knowledge of autism has been found to coincide with lower stigma towards autism (Gillespie-Lynch et al., 2015). Positively reframing thinking around autism can also help autistic individuals and their parents manage their difficulties and provide a more resilient outlook of what is ahead (Kapp et al., 2013). The main implication is that professionals and parents should not try to change a child or an adult with autism into a 'normal' individual but should appreciate their perspective and provide strategies for them to function and manage within situations in which they need to participate, such as their families, schools and workplaces. Such strategies might include teaching them ways of understanding others, communicating effectively, and managing situations that they find stressful.

The importance of conducting research on autistic experience without neurotypical preconceptions was illustrated in a consultation of 16 autistic UK higher education students about their experiences of success (MacLeod et al., 2018). Participants became co-analysts of their data and provided counter-narratives to deficit-based interpretations of autism, giving accounts of making themselves as 'extra-visible' as autistic students to assert their rights. The autism diagnosis was perceived both as an aid to self-understanding and a cause of additional barriers. In raising awareness of their own needs, participants contributed to broader understandings of autism within their academic communities, inadvertently becoming educators and role models.

utistic narratives and the autistic rights movement, one
nces is that there is much greater acceptance that the
people should be central in terms of the successful
design and delivery of education services as well as in the design of
research studies (Parsons & Cobb, 2014; Guldberg et al., 2017; Long
et al., 2017). This is seen as urgent given that autistic people and their
families are rarely involved in making decisions that shape their lives
(Milton & Bracher, 2013). It signals the need for education research to
deliver real partnerships, including the autistic voice, to design quality
research that is relevant to autistic children or young people. In fact,
autistic inclusion in the research process can enrich it by: 'increasing
the epistemological integrity of studies that seek to explore important
questions relating to the wellbeing of autistic people' (Milton & Bracher,
2013: 63).

Recommended reading

Grandin, T. (1995) *Thinking in pictures and other reports from my life with
autism.* New York: Bloomsbury.
Jackson, L. (2002) *Freaks, geeks and Asperger syndrome: A user guide to adolescence.* London: Jessica Kingsley.
Williams, D. (1996) *Like colour to the blind.* London: Jessica Kingsley.

6 Contributions from the social sciences

Key question

What do the contexts in which people live and learn tell us about some of the challenges and barriers faced by autistic people and their families?

Introduction

This chapter uses ecological systems theory to frame some of the key social issues that currently need to be prioritised in the education of autistic children and young people. Ecological systems theory is a way of examining an individual's relationship with communities and wider society. In this theory, development is conceptualised as being shaped by interactions in specific environments. Addressing the needs of autistic children and young people, and their teachers, means understanding the individual and how they relate to the people around them as well as the contexts in which they live and learn.

In Bronfenbrenner's (1979) original ecological systems theory, he argued that the ecological systems model focuses on understanding a child or young person's development within environmental systems. These consist of the *microsystem*, which includes the context closest to the individual, such as direct interactions and interpersonal relationships within the family. The *mesosystem* captures the interconnections between various parts of the microsystem, such as between a child or young person's family and school or between a child or young person's peers and their family. The *exosystem* is the part of the environment that does not affect the child directly but includes aspects of the structures of microsystems. It involves links between settings in which the child does not have a role. For example, a parent might be influenced by something in their life such as losing their job.

The *macrosystem* refers to sociocultural circumstances, patterns and events that affect the child or young person. These cultural contexts can differ according to geographical location, ethnicity or socioeconomic status, for example. This can include such issues as growing awareness of autism in the media or the growth of social media, for example. Bronfenbrenner's model sees these systems as all having an effect on the child's development.

Bronfenbrenner (1979) initially put forward his ecological systems theory as a way of understanding the contextual factors that are relevant to learning and development. At the time that he developed his original theory, there was a strong focus on children's psychological development, but this often ignored context. Later, Bronfenbrenner revisited his theory because he drew the conclusion that academics focused too much on context. As we will see in the next chapter, current studies in autism tend to focus on individual children or groups of children being studied separately from the context and environments in which they live. This highlights the importance of re-instating context as an important factor in people's lives.

In the chapter, I move from key issues relevant to the outer *macrosystem* through to the inner *microsystem*, and give an overview of key developments in autism studies related to each of those systems.

The macrosystem

Policy shifts

As stated above, the *macrosystem* refers to sociocultural circumstances, patterns and events. This highlights that policy shifts, values and ethos on inclusion are important because they impact in indirect ways on children's lives. The Salamanca World Conference on Special Needs Education brought together representatives from 92 different governments in 1994. The policies proposed by the conference were an important watershed because of the commitment made to promote inclusive education. The guiding principles that emerged were that ordinary schools should accommodate all children.

Through the statement and framework for Action on Special Needs in Education, the Salamanca statement noted that:

> Schools with inclusive orientation are the most effective means of combating discriminatory attitudes, creating welcoming communities, building an inclusive society and achieving education for all; moreover, they provide an effective education to the majority of children and improve the efficiency and ultimately the cost-effectiveness of the entire education system.
>
> (UNESCO, 1994, Article 2, p. ix)

This concept of inclusion encompasses universal involvement, access, participation and achievement. UNESCO (1994), for example, defines inclusive education as:

> an ongoing process aimed at offering quality education for all while respecting diversity and the different needs and abilities, characteristics and learning expectations of the students and communities, eliminating all forms of discrimination.
>
> (UNESCO, 1994: 3)

These principles of inclusion are also embedded in the United Nations Convention on the Rights of the Child, which states that children who are disabled should be educated in a way that their disability is understood and that works towards them achieving the fullest possible social inclusion (United Nations, 1989). This means enabling them to participate effectively in economic, social, political and cultural life, as well as living in a society that promotes equality and diversity.

More recently, the UN Sustainable Development Goals (2015) have made a strong commitment to 'ensure inclusive and equitable quality education and promote lifelong learning opportunities for all' (Goal 4), with clear direction given to the international community to address the exclusion of people with disabilities in all areas of life.

Writers on inclusion have highlighted that philosophical thinking is necessary for the foundations of our moral values (Clough & Corbett,

2000). Inclusion bases these moral values on social justice, equity of opportunities and freedom (Singal et al., 2017). Furthermore, all children and young people have a right to a good education, to feel valued, to have the opportunity to fulfil their potential and to take part in educational opportunities with their peers.

There is considerable variation in how this right to inclusion is interpreted. The concept of inclusive education is understood and implemented in different ways across different contexts, and varies with national policies and priorities. Social, cultural, historical and political issues influence the way inclusion develops in different countries. So, to fully understand reality of life for pupils with disabilities, one needs to understand the social conditions, cultures and contexts in which they live (Mercer & Littleton, 2007). This includes understanding the wider field of policy-making and institutional change (Jones et al., 2008), or even the culture of the country (Alexander, 2000).

The wider context of legislative changes and policy foci in the field of special educational needs will affect the lives of children and young people. In fact, as Alexander's (2004) research into mainstream schooling found, the classroom, school and wider culture all interrelate and should not be seen in isolation from one another. Actions and challenges will be situated within educational philosophies about what schools can or should accomplish (Gøranson & Nilholm, 2014). When aiming to understand the inclusive practices of a country, it is therefore important to have some understanding of the infrastructure, resources and processes required for successful implementation. Social, cultural, historical and political issues all influence how inclusion is implemented.

That said, children with autism continue to face barriers in the education system in many places in the world, and children with disabilities represent more than a third of the 60 million children worldwide who are excluded from school. If inclusion is to value everyone and enable participation, then public awareness is important, as the notion of being treated fairly needs to permeate throughout society. Public perceptions can nevertheless be both a route to inclusion and a barrier to it, and the general awareness of autism in society will vary from country to country.

Across the world, many countries have established laws, policies and other provisions. Countries are addressing how to improve autism

provision in a number of different ways. In England, the Aut
was introduced in 2009, whilst Wales and Scotland have th
strategic plans. The Qatar National Autism Plan was launched in _
and focuses on six pillars of awareness: early recognition and screening,
diagnosis and assessment, interventions, education and transition into
adolescence, adulthood and elderhood. A number of stakeholders and
ministries are involved in implementing this plan (Guldberg et al.,
2017). In China, there are no exclusive special education laws, for
example, whereas in India, there are acts and policies but no specific
laws, nor the structures or funding to implement the acts and policies.
In the Kingdom of Saudi Arabia, funding and teacher training is available, but procedural protections are not available. In the United States,
policies regarding identification vary from state to state and inclusion
is often not implemented in everyday practice.

In the UK, England, Wales, Scotland and Northern Ireland all have
established separate strategic plans for autism that have sought to introduce specific guidelines for local agencies, including local authorities
and health boards. The statutory guidance in the UK government's
Think Autism strategy (DfE, 2014), in England, for example, tells
various commissioning bodies what action should be taken to meet the
needs of people with autism living in their areas. The Scottish, Welsh
and Northern Ireland strategies also have a particular focus on detailed
planned improvements across services for children, young people and
adults in health, social services and education, with a focus on a 'whole
life' approach to the provision of services and support (DfE, 2014).

Public awareness, attitudes and culture

In most countries, awareness about autism is rising. Autism was the fifth
most common 'what is' question in 2014, according to an article by Carol
Povey in *The Independent* on 16 December 2014. Autism is nevertheless
often still viewed through a lens of stereotypes and misunderstandings.
These can include that autism is a childhood condition, that a large
proportion of autistic people have savant skills in certain areas, or that
autistic people lack empathy. Stigma varies from country to country.

Some of the myths around autism include that most autistic people
have a 'special gift' such as a special capacity for maths, music, drawing
or retaining knowledge. In fact, the true figure is 1:200. Other myths

include that autistic people do not feel love or have emotions. This is simply not the case as many have a strong desire to relate to others but might not know how to, and many autistic people can become overwhelmed with emotions. So there is a risk with raising awareness that it might just raise awareness of stereotypes.

Improving public understanding is nevertheless a key priority as it can improve every aspect of autistic people's lives. Educating the public about autism has been the focus of large-scale initiatives with millions spent on public awareness campaigns, with World Autism Awareness Day (2 April) and World Autism Awareness Month (April) being celebrated all over the world. Many landmarks are lit up in blue all over the world, from the United States to Japan. When these campaigns began, the goal was to make people aware of autism, and many people have now heard of autism. They are less likely to know how it affects people, so the notion of awareness raising has now shifted towards acceptance and education.

This includes understanding the broader social realities that have an impact on the lives of autistic people. *The Autism Dividend* (Lemmi et al., 2017) sought the views of people on the autism spectrum and their families in identifying clear research gaps in practice and provision. The report identified four consistent themes or principles that reflected the challenges most commonly faced by people on the autism spectrum. The report was broad in its scope, covering children and young adults across education, health and social care within the UK. The first principle, *Personalised Actions*, focused on the recognition of the individual characteristics and circumstances, different needs and individual preferences of people on the autism spectrum. The second principle, *Choice and Control*, highlighted the need to balance greater autonomy and agency for autistic people with effective support structures to meet their needs. The third principle, *Addressing Inequalities*, included the need to address inequalities in access to healthcare, education and employment. Finally, a *Life-long Perspective* recommended early identification and the use of evidence-based interventions during childhood or adolescence, and at all stages of life. These four principles led to more specific recommendations around practice, including early identification, providing evidence-based interventions, removing environmental and other stressors, ensuring better transitions and fighting stigma and discrimination.

Other key issues that are currently emerging from r
rising prevalence rates, the fact that outcomes for autis
poor all over the world, the continued existence of ex
society on a number of levels, and the way gender and cult
guistic diversity disadvantage children and young people. In
is a need to gain much better understandings of the intersecti
abilities and other disadvantages. Autistic people come from ⟨ ..erent
countries, have different ethnicities, are poor or rich, black or white,
and have different genders.

Prevalence

Children on the autism spectrum represent the fastest-growing group
of children with Special Educational Needs and Disabilities (SEND)
in the UK and internationally (Cimera & Cowan, 2009). Autism is no
longer considered a 'low incidence' condition, as it is the most prevalent developmental disability. The Centre for Disease Control and prevention in the United States, for example, found that 1 in 68 people in
2014 were on the autism spectrum (Baio et al., 2018) whilst the figure of
1 in 100 tends to be used in the UK (Baird et al., 2006). Most researchers
put the current estimates at around 1% but recognise that there is considerable global variation (Elsabbagh et al., 2012).

Most worryingly, long-term outcomes remain poor for autistic people
all over the world (Magiati et al., 2012). The concept of outcomes
includes 'measures of attainment, progress, absence, exclusions and
destinations' (DfE, 2016b: 35). The infographic in Figure 6.1 shows that
children and young people on the autism spectrum are more vulnerable to being excluded from education, services, socially or by their
peers, often leaving them isolated within their educational and wider
community.

Exclusion

Exclusion affects both the quality of life of individuals and the equity
and cohesion of society as a whole. In England this is now a serious
issue. In 2018, Amanda Spielman, the Chief Inspector of England's
schools, raised concerns in the Ofsted Annual Report about the high

At least

1%

of the population worldwide are autistic.

72%

of autistic pupils are educated in mainstream schools in England.

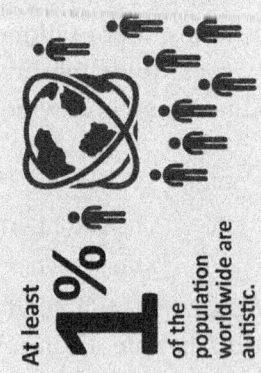

SCHOOL

The annual Ofsted report for 2018 highlighted that

27%

of pupils with SEND had a fixed-term exclusion last year.

The numbers of pupils with autism as their primary Special Educational Need

nearly doubled

between 2012 and 2018 in the UK.

Exclusions of autistic pupils from schools rose by

58.9%

between 2011 and 2016.

4 Million

is spent on research every year in the UK.

Only

16%

of autistic adults in the UK are in full-time paid employment

and only

32%

in some form of paid work.

The All Party Parliamentary Group for Autism (APPGA) survey found that fewer than

5 in 10

teachers felt confident supporting a child on the autism spectrum, and

over **half**

of parents of children with autism say they have kept their child out of school for fear that the school is unable to provide appropriate support.

Figure 6.1 Infographic about current realities for autistic people in England

exclusion rate for pupils with SEND. This report highlighted that 2/ of children and young people requiring Special Educational Needs (SEN) support had fixed-term exclusions the year before.

The topic of school exclusion was also the focus of the *We Need an Education* report by Ambitious about Autism (Cooke, 2018). This report found that autistic children and young people are three times more likely to be regularly and unlawfully excluded from school for a fixed period than children who do not have SEND (Cooke, 2018). In fact, the exclusions for autistic children and young people rose by 59% between 2011–2016 compared to a rise in overall exclusions of 4% over the same period (DfE, 2018). Every region in England has had an increase in the number of school exclusions for children and young people on the autism spectrum of between 45% and 100% in the last five years, whilst exclusion rates for the general school population have fallen in some regions such as the South East (Cooke, 2018).

When children and young people and their parents have been asked about what factors led to school exclusion, they have highlighted a lack of adaptation in sensory environments, conflict between staff and pupils, damaging peer relationships (including bullying), limited understanding of the needs of autistic children and young people, and a lack of transition planning when moving from their previous school (Brede et al., 2017; Sproston et al., 2017). In addition, mental health difficulties are a key factor related to school exclusion in the general school population (Parker, 2017) and we know that 70% of autistic children and young people meet the criteria for one mental health condition and 40% for two conditions (Simonoff et al., 2008). What is currently lacking is an understanding as to the reasons given for why autistic children are excluded, making it difficult to develop appropriate interventions.

The government's *Timpson Review of School Exclusion* (Timpson, 2019) highlights the importance of looking at the inter-sectionality of various factors which impact on the likelihood of a child being excluded, such as SEND, gender, ethnicity and social class. Whilst this report draws attention to the need for considering these factors, it does not provide specific, in-depth information on how these interplay in the case of children and young people on the autism spectrum. On 11 November 2019, Justice, an all-party law reform and human ion working to strengthen the human justice system, est working paper report on exclusions. This focused ; school leaders use to make and review decisions. This r significant change to the current system, including ir schools (Justice, 2019).

for Public Policy Research (IPPR) reported that from the general school population, those who have been excluded are more likely to be unemployed, develop severe mental health problems and be found within the criminal justice system later in life (Gill et al., 2017). They also report that there is a £2.1 billion cost to the UK economy for every cohort of excluded pupils. The outcome for autistic adults is often regarded as 'poor' (Howlin et al., 2004). They are more likely to be out of work (Howlin & Moss, 2012), with only 16% in full employment. They are often socially excluded (Howlin, 2013), experience mental health difficulties (Lever & Geurts, 2016) and many end up in the criminal justice system (King & Murphy, 2014).

A report based on qualitative data collected from nine autistic students in England who had attended mainstream schools said that exclusion had adversely affected their mental health and that the failure to include them in the school was down to limited teacher knowledge, a failure to make adjustments to the physical environment and little understanding of their specific needs (Brede et al., 2017). When girls on the autism spectrum were interviewed about their exclusion from school, they identified three aspects that would enhance inclusion. The first was adaptations to the school environment, with a preference for provision that was accepting of their needs and which sought to alleviate barriers. The second was the promotion of strong peer relationships to avoid social isolation. The third was to promote flexible, approachable and accepting attitudes of all staff (Sproston et al., 2017).

Gender

The autism research and practice field has recently started to seriously address the fact that there appear to be differences between males and females on the autism spectrum, but research into gender differences is still in its infancy. Historically there had been suggestions that females had more marked difficulties; however, recent data (Mandy et al., 2012; Loomes et al., 2017) suggest that these findings were a consequence of under-recognition of more able females on the autism spectrum. In fact, newer studies suggest that cognitive abilities are similar between autistic males and females (Mandy et al., 2012; Duvall et al., 2019).

Gender can influence both the expression of autism in individuals and educational needs. It does seem that females show less repetitive and stereotyped behaviours in childhood (Mandy et al., 2012) and fewer externalising and social problems than males (Mandy et al., 2012). Females have been found to have better social and communication skills than boys and their social difficulties may be overlooked by the wider social circle that girls typically have (Dean et al., 2014; Hiller et al., 2014). Recent studies have shown that females are likely to have fewer repetitive behaviours, more 'mainstream' special interests and can be more passive than males (Dworzynski et al., 2012).

As females often do not receive accurate diagnosis or appropriate supports in educational settings (Dworzynski et al., 2012), this can lead to different school experiences and decreased school engagement (Kreiser & White, 2014). Autistic girls may be less socially excluded than autistic boys but still face social exclusion or exclude themselves, as they do not identify with the interests and conversations of their neurotypical peers (Dean et al., 2014). This could be because there are gender differences in the way social interaction is constructed and the skills needed to gain access to social groups (Dean et al., 2014). Additionally, some girls and women report conscious attempts to fit in, either by copying the behaviours of non-autistic peers or by actively masking autistic traits (Bargiela et al., 2016).

The last few years have also seen a rise in studies of gender identity and gender self-esteem in autism. Studies have found that autistic people identified less with a gender group and perceived specific gender more negatively compared to non-autistic individuals (Cooper et al., 2018). There is also some evidence to suggest that autistic females have higher masculinity and lower femininity compared to non-autistic females (Cooper et al., 2018). It is important for educators to be aware of the rights of an autistic person who changes how they identify their gender and assist others in understanding this aspect of their life (Van Schalkwyk et al., 2015; George & Stokes, 2018).

Cultural and linguistic diversity

All cultures, races, ethnicities and genders are represented within the population of pupils diagnosed with autism. These factors influence both the expression of autism in individuals and also the educational needs of the population. Research on the needs of culturally and linguistically diverse pupils with autism and their families has found that minority populations are under-represented in research studies (Perepa, 2015).

As a consequence, there is little understanding of how different cultures and beliefs influence the unique educational needs of autistic pupils from diverse backgrounds (Davenport et al., 2018). In addition, culturally and linguistically diverse families find it difficult to access the information, help and resources they need and to navigate the education system (Lim et al., 2018). However, a growing area of research has been to explore how culturally and linguistically diverse populations access education.

Research has consistently shown across countries that rates of autism are higher in some ethnically diverse populations (Lehti et al., 2013; Bolton et al., 2014), and that those families may be more likely to have an autistic child with a learning disability (Bolton et al., 2014). A UK study of parents of autistic children from Somalia, for example, found that cultural attitudes, the presence of behaviours of concern and language differences were factors that influenced their understanding and acceptance of their child's difficulties (Fox et al., 2017).

Studies have reported on the negative impact of stigma on immigrant parents' perceptions, as well as their scepticism around services and how confusing these can be to access (Fox et al., 2017; Hussein et al., 2018). Some cultures do not have an equivalent word for autism and information is rarely translated. When it is, the translation may alter the meaning.

Intersectionality

In the chapter on biological and medical contributions to knowledge, we looked at the fact that there is high co-morbidity of autism with other conditions, including learning disabilities, depression and epilepsy. In autism studies, the notion of how to support individuals with

multiple conditions has been inconsistent. Having an aw
possible multiple challenges faced by autistic individu
families, including ethnicity, gender or class, is therefo
In fact, issues such as race, class, ethnicity, sexuality an
entangled (Goodley, 2013). O'Dell et al. (2016) have high
one of the limitations of autism research to date is the domi
United States in particular, with very little research coming from the
Global South, so that the knowledge being produced reflects specific
types of culture and community. This has led to the realisation among
research communities that it is important to understand how power
structures intersect in the lives of minorities.

The term *intersectionality* has been used to describe this. Kimberlé
Crenshaw, an American lawyer, civil rights advocate and scholar of
critical race theory, introduced this term. It captures the complexity of
being a person with multiple marginalised identities. Crenshaw's argument is that different aspects cannot be viewed separately because each
will influence the other, and an understanding of the potential impact
must take account of *how they intersect* rather than, for example,
considering autism and gender as two disconnected elements of an
individual.

Just as autistic people often argue that autism cannot be separated
from the individual as it is intrinsic to their personhood, the same is
true of other significant identities, which cannot be viewed and understood in isolation. The delicate balance to be struck is to recognise the
potential impact of autism on their sense of identity within its wider
context, rather than in a vacuum, giving consideration to the other
influences that might come into play. This means considering the individual in all their complexity.

The microsystem: the family, peers and school experiences

The microsystem takes account of both of the experiences of the individual within the family, and the experiences of the family within
society. Families will have different understandings of what autism is
depending on their background and context, and they will encounter
different challenges. In general, many studies have highlighted that

igher levels of parental stress are more likely for parents and caregivers of autistic children and young people and that this can negatively affect their own wellbeing and ability to engage and communicate with staff.

Stigma, the negative social reactions and beliefs of others regarding their child or their parenting, can increase stress and social isolation. As a consequence, families might isolate themselves to avoid difficult or embarrassing situations (Myers et al., 2009; Kinnear et al., 2016). Parents and caregivers of autistic children and young people are more likely to work fewer hours and earn less than other parents. This can have an impact on the economy of the household and it can impact on parental wellbeing and relationships.

In addition, issues with their child's sleep (Malow et al., 2012) and diet (Thullen & Bonsall, 2017) can affect family life, as can behaviours that challenge (Dykens et al., 2014), understanding and accepting their child's diagnosis (Zaidman-Zait et al., 2017) and financial burdens. Cultural factors can influence the extent to which a diagnosis of autism is sought or recognised by parents or caregivers (Perepa, 2015). In addition, some parents or caregivers may have autism or other communication needs themselves. They may find it more difficult to process information and to express their views.

More people are receiving a diagnosis of autism in adulthood, and many of them have children. Despite this, there is little research comparing the experiences of autistic and non-autistic parents. That said, the response of parents and carers to having an autistic child varies from family to family and at different times and stages of their child's life (Riddick, 2008). There has been a large increase in research on the emotional wellbeing of parents, particularly mothers (Giallo et al., 2013), and a suggestion that approaches such as mindfulness can be effective in reducing parental stress (Cachia et al., 2016). Evidence suggests that improving parental wellbeing can improve the long-term mental health of all members of the family (Cachia et al., 2016).

Practitioners and parents can find planning transitions, such as between home and school, from setting to setting and from school into adult life with young people on the autism spectrum stressful, with the lack of future options often being their greatest concern (Beresford et al., 2013). This highlights the need for transition planning and the importance of multi-agency working to lead to improved outcomes for autistic adults (Wittemeyer et al., 2011; Beresford et al., 2013). Parent reports of their children's transitions to secondary school suggest that there are a number of factors that impact on how successful this is. This includes the parents' level of anxiety, the quality of their social experience and the level of support they received (Peters & Brooks, 2016).

|The significant role played by siblings of people with autism has often been overlooked in terms of policy, practice and research. Having a brother or sister with autism can affect siblings in a number of ways. This can include finding it difficult to deal with their brother or sister's behaviour. They can sometimes face social isolation. They might feel that parents spend more time on the autistic child or young person than on themselves. Adult siblings may feel that their autistic brother or sister is a burden because as parents age, the care of individuals with autism may fall to siblings. Often siblings find themselves in the position of being a caregiver with no preparation and understanding of where to turn for support. There can be potential mental health issues and the need to have counselling to deal with the issues of living with a brother or sister with autism.

A review of the autism and friendship literature has suggested that autistic children and young people may have the lowest rates of friendship compared to both non-autistic children and other disability groups. They meet friends less outside of school and friendships are not maintained beyond school (Petrina et al., 2014). For autistic children and young people, the challenges in forming and maintaining friendships increase the potential vulnerability to social exclusion (Magnuson & Constantino, 2011; Kerns et al., 2015).

Friendships and peer relationships are a way to promote social and emotional development (Kendrick et al., 2012). The quality of these relationships has been shown to be a protective factor against social exclusion and feelings of loneliness and isolation (Skokauskas & Gallagher, 2012). The evidence for promoting social interaction is strong, and beneficial effects of this generalise to other areas as well (Watkins et al., 2015). However, it is important to note that the majority of this research is conducted with individuals in mainstream settings (Chang & Locke, 2016).

Developing friendships and peer relationships are ways to discourage bullying and promote social and emotional development (Kendrick et al., 2012). This needs to be a priority given that autistic children and young people experience a higher frequency of bullying than non-autistic peers (Sreckovic et al., 2014; Maiano et al., 2016). The long-term effects of this can be considerable as children and young people who are bullied are at higher risk of poor academic progress, non-attendance and mental health problems (Kloosterman et al., 2013). This includes physical, verbal and cyber-bullying. Figures for the number of autistic children and young people being bullied at school in the UK range between 40% and 82% (Bancroft et al., 2012; Rowley et al., 2012). That said, rates of bullying vary across studies and there are methodological differences. Notably, these figures may be an underestimate because some children might not report incidents as they might not be aware of what is happening. Equally, there might be a perceived lack of action by teachers to resolve issues (Humphrey & Hebron, 2015). In fact, studies have found that teachers may be less aware of bullying and victimisation compared to parents (Rowley et al., 2012).

Pupils who are included in mainstream settings without specialist support, who show a high number of autistic traits and co-occurring difficulties, are at the highest risk of experiencing bullying (Zablotsky et al., 2012), as are those children and young people on the autism spectrum who are seeking out social interactions (Rowley et al., 2012).

Summary

The broader social issues outlined here show the need to find better ways of supporting and educating autistic children and young people (Pellicano et al., 2014). Educators can play a significant role in improving the lives of autistic children and young people and their families. The interrelationship between the learner and the teacher will have an impact on learning. Motivation levels and how people feel about themselves and the learning environments are also likely to be factors that have a bearing on how they learn. So there are a number of dynamic and social processes involved in learning, and we ignore those at our peril in education.

The *process* of achieving an outcome is also crucial as the nature of the approach chosen and how this is delivered should be sensitive to the wishes and needs of the individual child or young person and their family. It should also be within the skill set of those who work with the

child or young person. There are therefore several ways (
the development and delivery of good autism practice
one solution or approach to an intended outcome.

Recommended reading

Hesmondhalgh, M. (2006) *Autism, access and inclusion on the front line: Confessions of an autism anorak.* London: Jessica Kingsley.

Jordan, R., Hume, K., & Roberts, J. (2019) *The SAGE handbook of autism and education.* London: Sage.

7

Evidence-informed practice

Key questions

What can we learn from research and how can research influence practice?

What evidence should we draw upon in the development of good autism practice in education?

What does it mean to be evidence-informed?

Introduction

The notion of evidence-based treatment was first highlighted in health by Archie Cochrane, a Scottish doctor when, in 1972, he found that only 20% of the work of clinicians was based on research (Shah & Chung, 2009). His research also showed that care based on evidence had better outcomes. Since then, the field of medicine has embraced the concept of Evidence-Based Treatment (EBT) and Evidence-Based Practice (EBP). These concepts are based on the notion that treatments or practice should emerge from peer-reviewed scientific evidence or theory, and from rigorous research. This evidence should then be used to bring about the best possible results in clinical practice. The difference between EBT and EBP is usually that the former is seen to cover traditional medicine whilst the latter term encompasses more fields of medicine, such as psychological approaches and techniques.

The concept of EBP has also been much discussed in educɩ
increase in publications focusing on communicating 'what ʍ
education illustrates this (Hattie, 2008). These publications aim
mote an educational culture in which teachers draw on evidenc
matter of routine (Goldacre, 2013). It is reflected in legislation toˏ
the United States, the No Child Left Behind Act (NCLB, 2001) requires
teachers to use scientifically proven practices in their classrooms, as
does the Individuals with Disabilities Education Act (IDEA, 2008).

In educational research, the 'what works' clearing houses, of which
there exist many, review and synthesise studies on educational
interventions. The idea is that these clearing houses should provide
practitioners with evidence of methods that are backed up by evidence.
In autism studies, for example, the National Clearing House for Autism
Evidence and Practice (NCAEP) has been set up to support staff to use
and implement practices. Current debates also emphasise the need
for education practitioners to ground their work in EBP (NAC, 2009).
The 'Research Autism' website, for example, is an information service
website set up by the National Autistic Society in the UK to provide
information about research findings related to different approaches in
autism. This website has summarised the evidence base for over 1000
interventions.

Research in autism education has historically tended to focus on using
particular methodologies to conduct research. When the US National
Research Council (NRC), for example, conducted assessment of intervention research studies in autism, studies would only be considered
an EBP if they used particular methodologies. These methodologies
were specified as randomised, quasi-experimental or single-subject
designs, showing a clear dominance of research designs modelled on
the natural sciences (Odom et al., 2005; Dingfelder & Mandell, 2011).
The most prominent methodologies in autism intervention research
are experimental designs (Dingfelder & Mandell, 2011; Kasari & Smith,
2013; Guldberg et al., 2017a).

However, the notion of trying to answer the question about 'what
works' and how we can attain goals and achieve the results we want
to achieve in autism education is more complex than it might seem
at first. This chapter therefore takes a critical look at research on
interventions in autism and the complexities associated with drawing
on research evidence to inform practice. It puts the case for focusing on

what matters rather than such an exclusive focus on *what works*. This is followed by discussion about how we can bridge the gap between research and practice.

The chapter provides a critical overview of research on interventions and approaches that have been developed for children and young people with autism and highlights some of the problematic issues with current research. The chapter then looks at what research can contribute to practice and what Evidence-Informed Practice entails for the teaching profession. This means critically examining what kind of evidence is important in autism education, what this should be based on, what we mean by practice, and how we consider the goals we should work towards, as well as what the causal factors might be in meeting those goals.

The evidence base from research studies

There has been a rapid expansion of research on autism interventions in recent years. This research tends to focus on therapeutic interventions coming from the field of psychology. These can include both Comprehensive Treatment Models (CTMs) and Focused Interventions. The former represents a prescribed set of interventions designed to achieve broad learning. These will be based on a manual, and will be intensive and address a range of outcomes. The latter occur within a shorter time frame and address a specific outcome. They cover fewer areas of functioning and behaviour such as specific targeted skills in areas of functioning. Research on interventions in autism studies has tended to concentrate on focused interventions.

The word 'intervention' can mean different things to different people, and can be understood in a variety of ways in different disciplines. In relation to the literature on autism interventions, the word 'intervention' tends to be used as a way of indicating that there is a particular model or way of working that will, in a causal way, lead to a particular result. It is this use of the word 'intervention' that will be used in this chapter as the chapter critically examines the evidence base for therapeutic interventions. This is how the word tends to be used in that research literature. In the chapters on pedagogy and principles of good autism practice, on the other hand, the concept of educational interventions will be used in a broader way. In that literature, the word 'intervention'

tends to denote a practice that aims to produce measur.
can include actions, strategies and methods of instruction.

In the past decade, a number of systematic internationa.
reviews have examined the evidence base for different inte.
and approaches for pupils with autism (Odom et al., 2010; .
et al., 2011; Wong et al., 2014). The main findings from the Na.
Council for Special Education (NCSE) review by Parsons et al. (2. 1)
were that most educational approaches and programmes had some evidence of their effectiveness, but varied in quality, and no approach had
been entirely successful in producing a methodologically sound evaluation. In fact, several reviews have found that there is no evidence to
suggest that a single intervention will meet the needs of all learners, or
that any single intervention or technique stands out from the others as
superior for a majority of children (Odom et al., 2010; Parsons et al.,
2011; Wong et al., 2014).

Furthermore, intervention research in autism is complex as it
involves many different strategies whilst simultaneously measuring a
limited range of outcomes (Howlin, 2010). This makes it very difficult
to make strong claims about a specific intervention or educational programme (Kasari & Smith, 2013). Many studies are not of high enough
quality to draw robust conclusions from. Research studies often have
limited sample sizes, focus on relatively short-term gains and sometimes struggle with isolating intervention effects from other variables
(Horner et al., 2005). Overviews of studies have indicated that there is
variation in inclusion criteria, inconsistencies in the actual intervention that is being implemented, different independent variables being
evaluated and a variety of research designs (Reichow, 2012).

Difficulties inherent in evaluating approaches for those on the
autism spectrum include gaining a clear description of the rationale,
aims and practices of an approach; as well as having confidence in
the diagnosis and in the assessment results for matching purposes and
for measuring change (Horner et al., 2005). The studies often address
narrow research questions and there tends to be a limited range of
outcomes measured (Parsons et al., 2011), whilst effects often impact
on a narrow range of skills. A programme that is designed to improve
non-verbal communication will narrowly focus on that without
examining its effect on broader cognitive functioning, for example
(Howlin, 2010).

The experimental studies that dominate the field often use standardised measures and statistical analyses but we know very little about how these reflect changes in everyday life. Statistical significance in controlled trials does not necessarily mean that pupils have improved in ways that are reflected in their everyday functioning (Mesibov & Shea, 2011). Many studies involving Early Intensive Behaviour Intervention, for example, have used IQ as a principal outcome measure, yet statistically significant increases in IQ do not necessarily lead to improvement in other, more practical day-to-day skills (Howlin, 2010).

We simply do not know whether variables that lend themselves to measurement and statistical analysis are important for some of the long-term goals and outcomes that people with autism care about, such as life satisfaction, community participation and personal relationships (Wittemeyer et al., 2011). Quite often studies focus on outcomes that are simpler to measure rather than outcomes that might be more important to focus on. It could be argued that the more fine-grained the measure of change, the more one would expect to be able to demonstrate change over a relatively short timescale. That does not necessarily mean that those fine-grained measures tell us much that is useful about the person's broader functioning. In other words, we might be able to draw conclusions about *what works* based on what these studies measure, but this does not necessarily mean that these are the outcomes *that matter* in education and for autistic people.

Studies have not tended to incorporate the aspirations, goals and personal qualities of autistic people and their families. Given that findings from studies indicate that autistic individuals place importance on outcomes that support choice and autonomy (Wittemeyer et al., 2011; Pellicano et al., 2014; Milton, 2014b), it is troubling that outcomes such as these, which can seem loose and fuzzy, are seldom focused on in autism research, with the consequence that interventions are limited to those whose goals can be measured. The dangers of this approach are summed up by Poplin, who argues that: 'When the human sciences use only quantitative data, we end up with a narrow, piecemeal view of reality' (Poplin, 2011: 150).

This is particularly striking when we take into account that very few studies take place in the school context. In classrooms, there are many variables that can influence outcomes and these can be difficult to pin down and measure. Autistic children and youn; be engaged in more than one approach and move in an during the research. In addition, most pupils receive n intervention at any one point in time, making it difficult t a particular element or type of approach (Parsons et al., 2 or young person may improve for a variety of reasons not related to the approach. This can include maturation, expectations, family input and other staff input.

Moreover, within all comprehensive interventions, large individual differences are reported with wide variability in response to treatment (Parsons et al., 2011). The research community understands little about why some children respond well to some interventions and others do not. As individuals on the autism spectrum are very different from one another in terms of their profile of needs and strengths, variation in individual characteristics means that more individualised approaches are often needed than can be delivered using manualised approaches (Reichow, 2012).

The research–practice gap

A further problem is that there is little overlap between what is known in research studies and what happens in real-life settings (Reichow et al., 2008). As a result, educational outcomes for pupils have not improved as a result of knowledge transfer from researchers to the classroom as it is still unusual for educators to change their practice by drawing on the evidence base from research (Lather, 2004). Many continue to use practices that are not based on evidence from research (Burns & Ysseldyke, 2009). In fact, teachers have reported that they view researchers as being out of touch with the realities of what happens in classrooms (Greenwood & Abbott, 2001).

There is therefore a gap between findings from research evidence and what happens in practice (Reichow et al., 2008; Dingfelder & Mandell, 2011), policy or service provision. This disparity between research and practice makes it a challenge to possess the full knowledge required to effect real change in classrooms (Thomas & Pring, 2004). As a result of this, the need to move Evidence-Based Practices into daily educational practice for learners with autism has been identified by many researchers as a research priority (Dingfelder & Mandell, 2011).

However, it is not as simple as this. *Efficacy studies* report the success or failure of interventions in 'ideal' conditions that are carefully controlled (Dingfelder & Mandell, 2011). Although efficacy studies are important, we need to stay mindful of the fact that even when there is evidence for specific interventions in the highly controlled contexts in which they were studied (Kasari & Smith, 2013), these might not be applicable to educational contexts where individual teachers make judgements based on available evidence. Studies in controlled contexts might not be relevant to educational contexts as they focus on what matters to research, not necessarily what matters to autistic people or to educators who are dealing with real-world scenarios in the classroom (Guldberg et al., 2017a).

If intervention research is to have both scientific validity in design and implementation as well as social validity within the broader community, the field needs to find better ways of ensuring interventions are evaluated in the area in which children are based, such as regular educational settings (NAC, 2009). This has led to calls for conducting a greater number of *effectiveness studies*. These focus on the benefits of an intervention in the real world, the sustainability of an approach and the importance of it to those participating in it in everyday conditions (Weisz & Jensen, 1999; Kasari & Smith, 2013).

It can be complex to undertake research in the school environment though. Educators have competing priorities, and it can be difficult to get the support of staff or find resources to support the implementation of interventions (Locke et al., 2014). Furthermore, those implementing the interventions need high levels of training, interventions can be intense and they often require high ratios of staff to children (Kasari & Smith, 2013). In addition, they are rarely implemented in the way they are designed (Stahmer et al., 2015), and do not take into account the school context (Parsons & Kasari, 2013). Sometimes, when interventions are implemented in schools, the intervention might have changed so much that it is different from the original intervention (Kasari & Smith, 2013). As a result, there is a lack of studies on how to best implement effective interventions in schools and communities (Morgan et al., 2018), despite the importance of understanding what happens naturally (Kasari & Smith, 2013).

Bridging the gap

The question then becomes how to bridge this gap. The first step in doing this is to question whether the methodologies used in intervention research are appropriate for drawing conclusions about what should happen in the classroom or school environment. The US Department of Education guide to educational practices (2003) states that Randomised Controlled Trials (RCTs) should demonstrate an intervention's effectiveness in contexts similar to yours before you can be confident it works. An RCT is a particular experimental research design that tries to reduce bias when testing 'treatments'.

Subjects are randomly allocated to different groups. These different groups are treated differently and then compared with respect to a particular measurable outcome. So, in a recent project that I was involved with, and led by the University of Hertfordshire, young children received an intervention to encourage them to develop their joint attention and turn-taking skills. One randomly allocated group of children received input from a therapist and the other groups from a therapist together with a robot called Kaspar. The difference between the groups was then measured according to the extent to which each group improved their joint attention and turn-taking skills (Mengoni et al., 2017).

The US Department of Education guide mentioned above uses the term 'similar to yours'. It is very difficult to know what this 'similar to yours' means though. School contexts differ from one another, parents differ, children and teachers differ. The assumption that an RCT has worked somewhere does not mean that it will work in every context. All interventions are inserted into an already existing practice and all practice exists in highly complex systems with many factors, causes, effects, values, interactions and relations. This makes it impossible for teachers to implement interventions in exactly the same way as they did when researchers implemented it. Yet if it is not implemented as intended, it may not produce the desired results and if it is implemented differently than described by researchers, we can no longer know exactly what it is that works.

Furthermore, we do need to ask the question about how teachers can control for the many factors that can interfere with or bias research results. In experimental designs, researchers need to control different factors in order to be able to show that the outcomes are the result of that specific intervention rather than being because the child has matured in that time, for example. In classroom settings, on the other hand, educators need to accommodate a number of factors and this includes taking account of both the context and the individual child or young person. Research can control for confounders and keep variables fixed, whilst in practice there is a need to accommodate different factors whilst taking into account contexts and individual differences. The evidence that research provides therefore does not necessarily tell the practitioner whether it will work in their particular context for their particular target group.

This highlights that there is a need to counter the narrow focus on experimental research designs as the only legitimate way of conducting research in the field (Horner et al., 2005; Reichow et al., 2008). Experimental research designs cannot necessarily capture and understand what happens naturally in practice, or arrive at practical real-world solutions (Guldberg, 2017). They lack the flexibility to reflect the pragmatics of learning–teaching interactions because they often deliberately strip away the contexts of unpredictable elements to remove any potential biases. It is difficult to predict all of the many and varied consequences of a particular course of action due to the context-specific nature of education. So much of what happens in the classroom depends upon chance and dynamic combinations of different starting points, teacher skills and understanding, the school context, and learning objectives (Biesta et al., 2014).

Cause and effect can also be based on a range of factors. Causal relations are context dependent and contexts should be expected to be different, as should people. One factor can make a difference to another factor in many different ways, by preventing it, contributing to it, enhancing it, delaying it, or producing undesirable side effects, for example. Human education is therefore complex and a given outcome will have several causes. How a child progresses on a given day, for example, can depend on how well they slept that night, the dynamics of the classroom, and also on whether the teacher slept well. The teacher might be intervening by providing an intervention that is based on developing the child's reading skills, but whether the child improves can also depend on a variety of factors, such as ability to decode letters in particular ways or recognise the shape of words, or motivation levels and the extent to which the child receives support at home.

There is a need to disentangle this notion that findings from research studies can necessarily be directly applicable to classroom settings, even if there has been evidence that an intervention has worked with a group of children at a particular time in a particular laboratory or clinic setting. This highlights the need to question the notion that rigorous research can give educators a step-by-step model for achieving progress in the classroom.

Rather, practitioners will need to gather a lot of different evidence, and make a judgement to bring about change in their own context and with a particular child or young person. Successful ways of drawing on the evidence therefore depend not only on rigorous research evidence but also on the steps taken to use an intervention to bring about desirable change in a context in which the intervention is as yet untried.

From Evidence-Based to Evidence-Informed Practice

Evidence-Informed Practice then becomes a very different concept to Evidence-Based Practice. In fact, Evidence-Informed Practice needs to take into account what it should work for and who should have a say in determining the latter (Biesta, 2013). This means taking into account important aspects of professional knowledge (Ryneset al., 2001) and the experiences and expectations of teachers and children in schools (Parsons & Kasari, 2013).

When autistic people themselves, schools and families are an integral part of the knowledge base, they are more likely to take note of research as they then have agency, and a sense of ownership of it rather than agency being in the hands of policy makers or researchers. The issue of agency is a crucial one in that it highlights the need to introduce methodologies that position not only teachers, but also individuals with autism and their families at the centre of inquiry and knowledge.

The history of intervention research has meant that autistic individuals and their families have had little say over what is researched and have tended to be excluded from research processes (Milton, 2014a; Pellicano et al., 2014). In a review of autism research in the UK, Pellicano et al. (2014) conclude that non-autistic theorists dominate research. They reflect that: 'There is a huge gap between the type of knowledge being produced by current UK autism research and the stated priorities of the autism community' (Pellicano et al., 2014: 202).

This highlights the importance of services and practitioners becoming better at developing 'interactive expertise' in caring for and working with autistic people, as well as the need for researchers and educators become 'more able to engage and interact with autistic language and communications' (Milton, 2014a: 796). Researchers and educators need to draw on the experiences of autistic people so that a positive relationship between educational research, the perspectives of autistic people and teaching knowledge and practice is generated (Parsons & Kasari, 2013). To identify the goals that are important for the autism community, for families and for practitioners, there needs to be recognition that meaning needs to be found in lived experiences, and research needs to invest in working *with* those stakeholders rather than *on* them (Freire, 1972).

It is difficult to see how education can be effective at generating improvement if we do not gain better understandings of the way that the world is viewed and experienced by autistic individuals themselves, as it is their experiences that can tell us how to optimise support and education for them, as well as identify what needs to change. This matters as autistic adults feel that 'research fails to speak to the reality of their lives in the here-and-now' (Pellicano et al., 2014: 5). Individuals with autism have simply not been involved in setting the agenda of working out what is important to focus on (Pellicano et al., 2014) and this has led to a large mismatch between what individuals with autism say they need in terms of what constitutes positive outcomes, and what research tends to focus on.

Researchers have therefore started to place more efforts on looking at the priorities of autistic people, parents and practitioners (Wallace et al., 2013; Pellicano et al., 2014; Fischbach et al., 2016). Wittemeyer et al. (2011) found that a good adult outcome needs to be considered within the context of individual needs and aspirations, enabling a person to make choices and giving them access to the right support when needed. Milton (2014b) has echoed this through advocating that care must be taken to ensure that structures are put in place to encourage the learner's autonomy and reduce their stress. Practitioners, autistic people and their families have called for increasing the amount of research into services, and for making research deliver practical change.

In short, there needs to be changes in the emphasis of current research, so that research, practice and lived experience can all contribute to the knowledge base. To this end, the American Psychological Association (APA) argued for: 'The integration of the best available research and clinical expertise within the context of patient characteristics, cultures, values and preferences' (APA, 2006: 273).

Kazdin (2008), who was at the time the chair of the APA, highlighted the dangers of taking a narrow view of seeing research as contributing to the knowledge base and practice as an application of research. He highlighted that this way of looking at things heightens the research–practice gap as it negates the contribution that clinical or educational practice can contribute to the scientific knowledge base.

This brings us on to an important critique of the way in which current debates around Evidence-Based Practice are framed. The debates indicate that there are hierarchies that privilege some forms of evidence over others, and that undervalue professional experience and judgement. The notion that research has come up with findings that show evidence that certain teaching methods lead to better outcomes for students is problematic because it is based on a top-down 'knowledge transfer' model that focuses on the need to transmit research to practitioners so that it flows from the journal to classroom practice (Greenwood & Abbott, 2001).

This model positions the researcher as the 'expert' and the teacher becomes the conduit for delivering the intervention (Trent et al., 1998). In this model, practice is viewed as a receiver rather than a creator of knowledge. The US-based National Professional Development Centre's focus on creating practitioner-friendly summaries that emphasise the translation of scientific results into intervention practices (Wong et al., 2014) are examples of such knowledge transfer models. This narrow view of knowledge transfer in which research is seen as contributing to the knowledge base and practice as an application of research does not take into account the contribution that educational practice and autistic people themselves can make to the scientific knowledge base.

The notion of implementation science is increasingly being used in relation to research on autism interventions. This is an example of the knowledge transfer model. Basically, at the core of implementation science is the notion that research-based practices need to be translated into an accessible form for teachers. As a consequence, the US Department of Education has developed resources and modules on focused interventions (Autism Focused Interventions Resources and Modules, 2015). These explain Evidence-Based Practices and steps for using them.

However, Thomas (2012) argues that we cannot say very accurately from research what will be a good way of teaching even though many evaluations have taken place. Thomas highlights that this is indeed the lesson that seemed to be emerging ten years after the No Child Left

Behind Act (NCLB) law in the United States. There is a legal obligation in this Act to use EBPs, but Thomas makes the valid point that teachers and administrators should have had their practices and policies determined solely by scientifically based research given that the legislation mandates them to. If they have been applying 'rigorous, systematic and objective procedures to obtain reliable and valid knowledge relevant to educational activities and progress' (US Department of Education, 2004: 30), he highlights that this is not evidenced in the PISA scores (the OECD's programme for international student assessment) (OECD, 2010) for the performance of American students for the period since the NCLB came into effect (Thomas, 2012).

As Thomas and Pring (2004) have argued, pointing out these tensions does not equate to saying that research evidence is not of value. Rather, it is about questioning the fact that so much focus is on the particular type of evidence that research represents. Also, in addressing how knowledge and conceptions of good autism practice develop, there is a need to understand that knowledge develops dynamically in relation to people, experiences and objects, and is also influenced by outside factors and contextual ways in which different knowledge bases are perceived in the wider context (Biesta, 2007). Unfortunately, the prevailing research culture of knowledge transfer in evidence-based research does not do enough to draw on the contributions of teachers, pupils and autistic people themselves.

This puts the case for multiple knowledge sources and types to come together to narrow the gap between research and practice. This needs to consider the fundamental importance of practitioner knowledge and their first-hand experience (Hammersley, 2005; Nind, 2006) rather than just the observations and reports of clinical researchers. Furthermore, it is built on the recognition that without the knowledge, understanding and experience of practitioners, research is unlikely to be fully meaningful, or have any real impact on practice (Nastasi et al., 2000).

The need for new methodologies

Given that there has been a notable lack of empirical evidence to inform practice and policy with regard to how effective and appropriate practice can best be achieved for autism-specific schools and services, much more research is needed into factors related to family, child and intervention factors that moderate outcomes (Morgan et al., 2018) as families are also different in their aspirations, goals and personal qualities. There is therefore a need to build a stronger evidence base regarding what good teaching is within the context of each individual setting and how it leads to learning (Sahlberg, 2010). This includes developing better insights into how teachers view good teaching, as well as how they eclectically sample from a variety of instructional or teaching models (Greenwood & Abbott, 2001).

There is a need to develop methodologies and methods that enable a focus on both what is meaningful *and* what is measurable (Hanney et al., 2007; Boaz et al., 2009). Such work is clearly complex as it needs to tap into all 'niches' of knowledge holders (Meessen & Bertone., 2012). As a result, several scholars have articulated the need to value qualitative methodologies on a par with quantitative experimental designs (Poplin, 2011).

This highlights the need for a broader range of methods that allow us to look at phenomena in ways that reveal many facets of human experience (Kazdin, 2008). The reason this is important is because evidence that is of value in education occurs in a number of different forms and it can also be gathered by diverse means. This can be via objective measures obtained from controlled trials, as well as through subjective perspectives grounded in professional understanding, experiences and interpretations of teachers. The issue to consider is how to ensure that these different forms of evidence can be combined to offer a more balanced insight into educational practices.

This necessitates broadening the concept of EBP beyond the knowledge transfer model to include a whole range of methodologies that enable this kind of study, from case studies to action research, phenomenology or narrative research (Gallagher et al., 2011). Nastasi et al. (2000) argued for participatory action research approaches that involve stakeholders in intervention efforts in order to focus on interventions that consumers find acceptable and to move towards a broad conception of integrity and effectiveness. Bronfenbrenner (2005) called for 'primarily generative' research designs that explore interactions between proximal processes and the developing person, environment, time and developmental outcome. He called this type of research the 'discovery mode' of developmental science. To best capture such dynamic processes, developmental research designs would ideally be longitudinal (over time), rather than cross-sectional (a single point in time), and conducted in children's natural environments, rather than a laboratory. Such designs would thus occur in schools, homes, day-care centres, and other environments in which proximal processes are most likely to occur.

Participatory research methodologies can be particularly powerful in advancing research in this field. They enable a focus on the context and culture of learning (Alexander, 2004). By working with stakeholders and involving them in decisions, such methodologies are based on the notion that people can benefit from one another's experiences, and critically engage in generating new knowledge (Anwaruddin, 2016). Knowledge co-creation is in this context defined as the collaborative process that brings together a plurality of knowledge sources and types to address a defined issue (Armitage et al., 2011).

Research methodologies focusing on participatory research are also often integrated into educational practice (Hammersley, 2006), and can therefore create bridges between types and areas of knowledge and move away from the 'silo mentality' that tends to characterise different knowledge bases. They challenge the dominant academic paradigm in which scholars define research agendas and produce research without directly engaging practitioners (Peters, 2010; Warren et al., 2016; Guldberg, 2017).

Such methodologies can support constructive engagement with stakeholders from the outset and can provide pathways to better prac-tice, and through this positively impact on the lived experience of the community members (Lather, 2004). New knowledge can then be more widely accepted in the context within which it is being applied (Bergold & Thomas, 2012; Gillespie-Lynch et al., 2017).

This recognises the importance of taking into account the unique knowledge bases of different actors in a field, such as policy makers, practitioners, researchers and the stakeholders themselves. As they all hold different types of knowledge, this can enrich understandings (Armitage et al., 2011). Participatory approaches to developing interventions should include competences that are relevant to the targeted culture, valuing naturalistic enquiry, real-life contexts and understanding, as well as the importance of describing phenomena from the population, thus facilitating culturally specific theory and intervention (Nastasi et al., 2000).

This type of project can take a number of different forms. An example of such a project is given in the case study below.

A case study of practitioner-based research: the Early Years Autism Project

In 2010 a multidisciplinary steering group was established to look at the current specialist support for Early Years children in Oxfordshire who had a diagnosis of autism. This was in response to concerns that current provision did not meet the needs of all Early Years children with autism effectively, consistently and equitably across the county.

As a result of reviewing current practice, the research literature on early autism educational approaches and consultation with other services and families, it was decided that Oxfordshire Local Authority should explore alternative methods of service provision. As a result, the Early Years Autism Project (EYAP) was initiated. The project was funded by a grant from the Oxfordshire Schools Forum and this expired on 31 March 2016.

The EYAP was a pilot of a multi-agency and multi-professional development team with supporting facilitators who worked with a limited number of Early Years children who had recently been diagnosed with autism. The team and support worker/facilitators working with the child's family and the existing Team Around the Child (TAC) trialled different ways of providing the most effective, specialist multi-agency support to Early Years children diagnosed with autism.

This included adapting approaches to different children and building evidence and practice about what worked. The project also supported the wider training and information needs around supporting Early Years children with autism, and on developing awareness across services of needs and approaches. The ethos and values of the project were to give information about autism and empower people, and to harness the passion and energy of those working with autistic children and their families.

To evaluate multidisciplinary practice within and across the EYAP, a researcher worked closely with the EYAP team to capture challenges, barriers and best practice from the project. This included considering how best to measure, capture and report on outcomes for children. The aims of the EYAP evaluation were separated into five key interrelated areas, which covered the objectives of the project. The aims were:

1. To evaluate the impact on the children, families, settings and staff.
2. To evaluate the multidisciplinary process itself.
3. To evaluate the approach, processes and tools that were implemented by the team in order to facilitate the interdisciplinary process.
4. To understand parental experiences of the project.
5. To understand staff experiences of the project.

In evaluating the impact of the EYAP on the outcomes of the children, settings and families, the project relied on diverse sources of information. This included:

- The evidence base for interventions.

- The needs of children and families.

- The values and preferences of children and families.

- The integration of pupils and families in decision-making.

Triangulation of data across these areas meant a rich and broad evaluation could be made that reflected both health and educational factors.

The following data were collected as part of the EYAP evaluation and formed a basis for answering the evaluation questions.

- SCERTS (this stands for Social Communication, Emotional Regulation and Transactional Supports) Assessment Protocol (Prizant et al., 2006) for each child including:
    - Questionnaire for determining SCERTS communication stage.
    - SCERTS Assessment Protocol (SAP) interview for parents and staff.
    - Video observation/assessment (using SCERTS criterion referenced assessment tool/coding framework).

- Parent questionnaire which included:
    - Likert-scale questions regarding perceptions of confidence and support.
    - Parental self-agency measure.

- Parent qualitative interview.

■ Staff exit interview at the end of the project or at transition to new setting.

■ Evaluation from training.

This evaluation therefore took a broad view of the evidence. The focus was on ensuring that the intervention was individualised according to the characteristics of the children, that it included real-life outcome measures and that these were generalisable to complex real-life conditions and multiple cultures and settings (Mesibov & Shea, 2010).

Summary

The issues outlined in this chapter highlight that the process of deciding on an intervention is more complex than the results of individual research papers can tell us. This is because the choice of intervention needs to take into account the child's characteristics, parental preference, staff expertise and the goals selected. Research therefore cannot give definitive answers about how to support an individual pupil in the classroom (Guldberg et al., 2011). Given the heterogeneity of autism, and the methodological difficulties with many studies, research findings from individual papers cannot give us clear models about how to support an autistic pupil at home or in education. What they can provide is robust information that can be of general value in autism education.

Research therefore needs to shift more towards ensuring that the field gets a better understanding about what good teaching is and how it leads to learning (Sahlberg, 2010). A teacher will need to be able to draw upon the evidence base for research, whilst also being able to reflect on how those strategies are being implemented and responded to in the interactions and relationships that are developing in the classroom.

As a result, good autism practice is based on adapting interventions to the individual and the context. This means taking account of the evidence that has emerged from research whilst keeping a focus on what is the best intervention for this person at this time and in this context. Academic knowledge is needed but this is not sufficient on its own. It requires the integration of the best available research *and* practitioner expertise within the context of a pupil's individual characteristics, and within the contexts of cultures, values and preferences. The range of sources when developing good autism practice in classrooms needs to include the perspectives of autistic pupils and their families, practitioner experience, research, school data, and the views of stakeholders.

Recommended reading

Biesta, G. (2007) 'Why 'what works' won't work: Evidence-Based Practice and the democratic deficit in educational research', *Educational Theory*, 57 (1): 1–22.

Thomas, G. & Pring, R. (eds) (2004) *Evidence-based practice in education*. Maidenhead: Open University Press.

PART II

Inclusive practice and distinctive pedagogies for autistic pupils

Part I of this book focused on the knowledge that can support educators to learn in order to make a difference. It put forward the bio-psycho-social-insider model and gave an overview of the knowledge that has arisen from the respective fields, and which in turn has relevance to educational practice. Part I highlighted that autism is based on neurodevelopmental differences, and it affects the way autistic people learn, process and make sense of the world. The second part of this book moves from the *know-that* of learning to the *know-how* of learning and teaching, from *learning in order to make a difference* to *learning to make a difference*. Whilst the first part of the book focused on what we need to know in order to make a difference, the second part focuses on how to make a difference through developing clarity about the ethos and values that will enable change, the teaching approaches and methods that need to be considered in the education of an autistic child or young person, the kind of professional development that can lead to genuine transformative change in the classroom, and finally what this requires of practitioners in the field in terms of scholarly practice.

8

Inclusion and inclusive pedagogy

Key questions

What is inclusive pedagogy?

What are the implications of inclusive pedagogy for practice, classroom teaching and the curriculum?

Inclusive education: more than a locational issue

As highlighted in Chapter 5, inclusive education sees the teaching of children with Special Educational Needs and Disabilities (SEND) as existing within an interacting and multi-levelled system in which individual children are situated in the class group, whole school, local authority, regional and central government policies and practices, and that these all interact and are interrelated with one another. Classroom pedagogy is nested within teaching programmes that are determined by school and then ultimately influenced by national programmes and commitments. To fully understand a country's inclusion, it is therefore necessary to examine policies and practices at different levels of granularity, whether those are at national level (policy), school level (practices, support structures) or individual level (Australian Research Alliance for Children and Youth, 2013). This shifts the debate towards seeing schools as closely linked with the development of the wider community and society, focusing on the potential to create a better society.

Inclusion pedagogy can mean different things to different people. For some, it might be learning in the same classroom as other children. For others it might be about care, respect and belonging. Ravet (2011) makes the case for an 'integrative inclusionist' model that enables multiple rather than binary possibilities for the inclusion of autistic children and young people within education. She argues that in current discourse, the 'needs-based perspective' tends to advocate for some separate needs-adapted provision for some children whilst the 'rights-based' perspective tends to advocate a single inclusive pedagogy for all, and sees no need for specialist provision.

The 'needs-based' perspective highlights the lack of research evidence for mainstreaming autistic students and the risk of exclusion this may cause. Key to this perspective is the availability of a range of schools and educational provisions to meet the distinctive group needs of autistic children who have identified additional support needs (Lindsay et al., 2013). This approach prioritises the rights of children to wide academic and social inclusion, and the requirement of schools and practitioners to adapt their practice to meet the needs of all students.

In contrast, the 'rights-based' perspective tends to argue for no educational segregation and the inclusion of all children and young people in mainstream schools (Allan & Slee, 2008). This rights-based perspective tends to adopt the social model whilst the needs-based perspective takes a more interactive stance of seeing a child's difficulties as an interaction between their disability and the environment, adopting a mix of the social and medical model, seeing labelling as useful and inclusionary as well as recognising the need for special pedagogies (Ravet, 2013).

Ravet (2011) argues that the needs-based and rights-based perspectives on inclusion have come to dominate the field of autism education and provide contradictory standpoints on the effective inclusion of children and young people on the autism spectrum in mainstream schools, but neither has a 'monopoly on the values of social justice, social democracy and social equality' (Ravet, 2011: 679). This shows that it may be useful to consider inclusion not as the binary opposite of segregation but to recognise that a variety of forms of provision may be needed.

Norwich (2013) highlights that the concept of Special Educational Needs (SEN) was first introduced in 1981 following the recommendations of the Warnock report (DES, 1978) and it was then seen as abandoning medical categories and focusing on individual needs. He argues that, at the time, the use of the term 'need' linked children's characteristics with provision that was required for learning and education and that this marked a different way of thinking about difficulties. Before that, discourse relating to children with disabilities was very focused on a deficit model. The term SEN focused the lens on thinking about individual children in terms of what kind of provision was needed in order to enable them to progress with their learning. He argues that it was therefore about individual functioning and needs, not about fitting children into a general category, such as a 'disorder' category.

As highlighted by Allan and Slee (2008), inclusion is a dynamic and evolving *process* in which different factors interrelate in a complex way. Therefore, inclusive education needs to be understood as a fluid process of identifying, understanding and breaking down barriers to participation and belonging (Guldberg, 2010). In fact, the real focus needs to be on social and learning participation and on the kind of pedagogic and social support a child might need in order to not be excluded from learning or the social life of the classroom. Flowing from this, the creation of societies that are tolerant, accepting of diversity, equitable and cohesive need to change individual beliefs and systemic practices towards greater acceptance of the rights of people with disabilities.

The degree to which individuals can and should be taught alongside typical peers depends on the severity of their unique needs, the expertise and attitude of the teaching staff, their access to additional support in mainstream settings and the adaptability and flexibility of the mainstream situation. The balance of advantage for one choice over another will always vary according to particular circumstances, although policy guidelines in different countries might move provision in particular directions. Some countries, such as Italy and Norway, have moved towards all children being educated in mainstream schools. In other countries there has been a move towards providing a balance of provisions, with recognition that both mainstream and special education can be needed because some children require specific measures to ensure their access or to facilitate participation (Hollenweger, 2014).

Whether a child is educated in special, specialist or mainstream provision, the core of inclusive practice is that children should not be excluded from education on the grounds of disability. The argument here is that the concept of inclusion is broader than where a child is geographically located, and what type of school they are in. In other words, whether they attend a specialist/special school or mainstream provision. It goes deeper than being about the physical presence of children and young people with disabilities in mainstream, special or specialist provisions. Inclusion is therefore about much more than geographical placement as inclusive thinking is about diversity and social justice as much as it is about mainstreaming and disability. This shifts the debate from questions about *where* inclusion takes place to a focus on the wellbeing and agency of all children (Terzi, 2014).

What does inclusion mean in practice?

In discussing inclusion, it is essential to consider the concepts of equality and equity. Equality relates to students achieving equal access to resources, whilst equity recognises that some students require more or additional resources to catch up and succeed. According to the World Health Organization (n.d.), equity is:

> The absence of avoidable or remediable differences among groups of people, whether those groups are defined socially, economically, demographically or geographically.
>
> (www.who.int/topics/health_equity/en/)

In education, equality is about treating every student the same whilst equity means that every student is provided with the appropriate support to give them an equal chance to succeed. Equality is therefore about taking a generic, group-focused approach which states that everyone should have the same rights, opportunities and resources, whilst equity is about providing resources to fit circumstances. Equity is about being adaptable, focused on the individual and fair.

So, in the UK, for example, all children have rights under the Equality Act to an education that meets their specific needs. This is a statement about equality. Equity is addressed through the concept of reasonable adjustment, which is encompassed in the Disability Act,

1995, in England. This is based on the notion of removing or minimising disadvantages faced by people with SEND. It requires educators to take positive steps to ensure that some kind of adjustment needs to be made for children and young people with disabilities. In most countries, Schools, Early Years and Post-16 settings have a duty to treat disabled children and young people as favourably as their non-disabled peers. They must make reasonable adjustments for disabled children and young people to ensure they are not disadvantaged.

Changing outcomes for vulnerable groups is unlikely to be achieved unless there are changes in the understanding, attitudes and actions of adults. Some have therefore argued that attitudinal barriers are the most significant (Finkelstein & French, 1993) as this is where the greatest opportunities lie for change and moving forward. Consequently, the starting point in education must be with practitioners by increasing their capacity to imagine what might be achieved, and enhancing their sense of accountability for bringing this about.

The development of inclusive practices requires all staff to work together to address barriers to education experienced by learners, as their beliefs, attitudes and actions create the contexts in which all children and young people are able to participate and learn. So, autistic pupils should all have equal rights to education but in order to have that, they need to be treated equitably, and that means that they need to be provided with the resources or pedagogy that addresses their needs.

One international model that has been developed to address these issues and to ensure equity at the levels of schools is the 'Response to Intervention' (RTI) model. The RTI process is generally defined as a three-tier (or three-step) model of school supports that uses research-based academic and/or behavioural interventions. The principle is that every RTI can provide a school-wide framework for efficiently allocating resources to improve pupil outcomes. It is principally a teacher-led process, but may involve other professionals and services throughout three tiers of support.

The RTI model of identifying difficulties and disability in education (Vaughn & Fuchs, 2003) has as its starting point that a commonality of strategies should be used as far as possible. Such a commonality of strategies should promote an improved school system that is more inclusive, with better staff training, improved school ethos, promotion of positive images of disability and encouraging more mixing with peers.

In this model, primary intervention is high-quality general education; secondary intervention is fixed intervention programmes and tertiary intervention consists of specialised programmes. Tier one is based on the notion that all pupils should receive teaching to meet their needs. Pupils are screened on a regular basis to establish baseline measures for academic and behavioural progress. Pupils who do not make adequate progress at this stage are then moved onto Tier 2 support. In Tier 2, pupils are given increasingly targeted and intensive support matched to their needs and rates of progress. The level of training of the professionals providing support at Tier 2 may differ along with the frequency and duration of intervention. Generally, Tier 2 support is provided in addition to the standard curriculum, often in small-group settings.

In Tier 3, pupils are considered for more intensive support if there are still concerns regarding their progress after Tier 2 interventions. This requires a comprehensive multidisciplinary assessment of the pupil's educational needs, including the identification of any specific learning or developmental disabilities. In this tier, individualised, intensive interventions are used to target the needs of pupils. This involves more intensive teaching methods and may mean the placement of the pupil outside the classroom.

The terminology varies, and there are different types of terminology used for very similar concepts to RTI. These include the concepts of 'universal', 'targeted' and 'specialist' provision. In England, for example, the graduated response of assess-plan-do-review is a way of identifying, assessing and recording the needs of children with disabilities. In this model, class and subject teachers should identify children that need additional support and the first response to this should be high-quality teaching targeted at their difficulties. The term 'quality first' teaching is generally used to encompass the notion of having high expectations, but it is not very clear what exactly is meant by the concept. It appears to cover the need to have focused and well-planned lessons, engagement of participation of pupils, high levels of interaction, appropriate use of questioning, learning through dialogue and ensuring pupils take responsibility for their learning.

The graduated response is tied in with the 'wave model'. 'Wave one' is what should be on offer to all children. This has been described as 'universal' services, and they are those services provided to all children, young people and their families. 'Wave two' is described as targeted provision to help children and young people who are struggling to catch up and 'wave three', or specialised services, consists of deeper interventions offering more personalised solutions. Specialist provision is often considered to be for students with more complex disabilities across areas of development.

Norwich (2013) argues that the RTI model is a causal modelling framework that takes account of the interaction between biological, cognitive, behavioural and environmental factors. It takes seriously that additional needs are based on an interaction between the learner and their environment. It does not, however, address how social and cultural processes affect the child in his or her immediate context. The RTI is also about the allocation of resources and the intensity of input the child receives, rather than necessarily identifying whether children need distinctive or specialised pedagogies. This brings us on to what kind of pedagogy is needed in order to have equity for autistic children and young people.

Pedagogy

Pedagogy can be summarised as the values and purposes of education, the nature of the teacher and the learner, and the processes through which learning takes place. It includes the theory, methods and practice of education and teaching, the approach a teacher or school takes to their teaching or the ideas people hold about knowledge, skills and understanding that lead to the growth of learners. Inclusive teaching or pedagogy is often taken to being about meeting the needs of all learners, being friendly and welcoming, and about participation. Pedagogy therefore needs to ensure it takes account of context, the kind of learning we are looking for and those who are being taught.

Alexander (2009) states that pedagogy is a complex field of practice, theory and research in its own right. In discussing pedagogy, he highlights that we cannot really separate the world inside and outside of the school because there is a close interrelationship between social structure, culture and human agency. He argues for combining macro and micro-level theories to provide a comprehensive understanding of human behaviour. Florian and Black-Hawkins (2011) also argue that inclusive pedagogy is multi-level in that it is about national, local authority, school and class levels, but that it is also multi-dimensional in that it is about presence, participation, achievement and belonging.

Lewis and Norwich (2005) took pedagogy to mean the broad cluster of decisions and actions taken in classroom settings that aim to promote school learning (encompassing pedagogic strategies and, more narrowly, teaching actions). Alexander (2000) discusses the multi-factorial nature of pedagogy, which includes organisation, discourse and values.

The big question, then, is whether there needs to be such a thing as special pedagogies for different groups of children. In other words, are particular values, methods and practices of teaching children and young people with SEND needed? In the UK, there is no such thing as specialist initial teacher training for teachers who want to specialise in working with children and young people with SEND, for example. In Norway though, 'special pedagogues' have a different level of education than other teachers. This is also the case in Italy.

In the UK, there are also strong debates questioning whether there is a need for specialist pedagogy for autistic pupils. Some have argued that it is not possible to differentiate enough to talk about having a separate SEND pedagogy (Davis & Florian, 2004). Rose (2009) argues that all students have different learning styles and that this should be a starting point rather than the notion that children with different disabilities require different pedagogies. This is echoed by Slee (2010) in the argument that teachers should be helped to include all children and by Florian (2007) in the suggestion that schools should develop an ethos whereby what is generally available is extended to all children.

An extension of this argument, and one of the principles that have emerged from debates around inclusion, is that an inclusive curriculum should be made available to everyone from the outset rather than have to add to or adapt a non-inclusive curriculum to include all children (Jordan, 2005). This approach to pedagogy is echoed in Universal Design for Learning (UDL). UDL is an educational framework that it is about improving and optimising learning and teaching based on scientific insights into how people learn. It is referred to by name in US legislation. It has an emphasis on equal access to the curriculum. The argument is that education should be inclusive from its inception. This therefore negates the necessity for a specialist curriculum, and argues that the curriculum should from the outset be designed to meet the needs of all learners.

UDL is designed to support all learners regardless of age, gender, ability, cultural and linguistic diversity and disability. In particular, it is a response to addressing the barriers of inflexible one-size-fits-all curricula and it guides the development of flexible learning environments that accommodate individual learning differences. UDL places a strong emphasis on the notion that there is not one universal method that will work for all pupils but that there is a need to use a variety of teaching methods, to remove barriers to learning and to give all children and young people the opportunity to succeed. As a result, it focuses on the importance of differentiating the ways that students can express what they know, gives flexibility in the way students access materials, and adjusts teaching for all students' strengths and needs.

A strong aspect of UDL is that it aims to create a community that welcomes all. The focus is therefore on context rather than on a narrow differentiation for the individual. Its philosophy is to support inclusive learning environments so that they do not necessitate removal of the child from the classroom. It is about working towards an education system that values difference and that makes all children and young people valued members of the community. The argument is that it can benefit many learners because the principles within it are designed for universal use.

The framework has three principles. The 'why' of learning includes engagement and motivation and is about stimulating interest in learning and the notion that there are multiple ways to engage and motivate students. The second is the 'what' of learning. This includes presenting content in different ways and offering information in more than one format. Action and expression is based on the notion that there is more than one way to interact. For example, teaching can be based on whole-class teaching, on group work or on one-to-one teaching. They call this the 'how' of learning.

The curriculum has four parts. This includes instructional goals, methods, materials and assessments. The argument is that by using the principles, teachers can effectively instruct diverse groups of learners as it is designed to reduce cognitive, material, intellectual and organisational barriers to learning. So, UDL is achieved through having flexible curricular activities that provide alternatives for diverse pupils.

Dimensions of pedagogy

Lewis and Norwich (2005) proposed an alternative to this perspective when they suggested that there are three dimensions of pedagogy. One dimension is that which is common to all learners. Another is that particular groups of children and young people have group differences. A child with a visual impairment will need teachers who understand how having a visual impairment is likely to impact on their learning, for example. A child with hearing impairments will have very different needs. This dimension therefore relates to the notion that there are specific teaching principles, different tasks and outcomes relevant to specific sub-groups of learners.

The third dimension is that which is unique and personalised to individual learners. In other words, learners share needs or requirements with all other children and there are some common needs shared by all learners. Group differences apply to whether they belong to particular categories of learners, such as learners who have visual impairment or learners that have hearing impairment. Within those group differences, individuals will also have unique needs. These unique needs or requirements will be distinct from all others.

Whilst I find Lewis and Norwich's (2005) model very useful for thinking about good autism practice in education, I find the notion of having common needs with other children places the focus too strongly on the individual learner and on the notion that we all have common ways of learning, rather than learning being situated in a particular context at a particular time. Assumptions about children's learning needs to be tested in particular instances of practice. If we take the position that particular pedagogies are relevant for all pupils, then the notion of common pedagogy needs to be considered in terms of principles that are wide enough and flexible enough to enable group and individual variation within a wide framework. The notion of having 'common needs' could therefore better be framed as 'principles of inclusive practice' as this takes the focus away from the individual learner to the context in which the learner exists. It also puts the onus on the educator to consider the values and principles that should guide them, rather than the danger that 'common needs' could be interpreted as seeing learning as something that can be fixed into a set of common attributes that we all share.

For children and young people with autism, Ravet (2011) argued that the term 'distinctive pedagogy' is preferable to the terminology 'specialist or specialised' because it preserves a pedagogy that is different and distinct, but it does not have to be confined to those with difficulties or disabilities. In general, concepts around specialist or specialised teaching have tended to focus on the learner's difficulties, either to circumvent them or to reduce them fully or to some extent. This again puts the focus too strongly on the individual learner rather than on the educator or the context. Again, it embodies within it the danger of seeing learning in a static way rather than as being situated in a particular context at a particular time, and in a specific community of learning (Lave & Wenger, 1991).

Rather than using the terminology of specialist or specialised for children with SEND, the preference here is to use the terminology 'distinctive' group needs because the word 'distinctive' also takes away the connotation that a specialist teacher is required in a separate class or withdrawal setting. The notion of specialist or specialised often has connotations with withdrawal from the regular classroom, or with the notion of specialised or separate provision.

This distinctive dimension, then, is about taking account of needs that are specific to a group of learners that share a characteristic and recognising that autistic pupils have some core strengths and difficulties in common that mean that there are certain teaching approaches and methods that can potentially be useful for them as a group. Most importantly, their distinctive group differences mean that they need teachers who have knowledge and understanding of autism and of how autism might impact on the development and learning of the child or young person.

Knowledge and understanding really needs to be the first step in the development of a distinctive pedagogic dimension for autistic children and young people. Having some knowledge and understanding about autism, and how autism might impact on the child, is paramount. Therefore, part of what is needed is to incorporate insights about autism into teachers' practical theorising and teaching. This implies that common curricular needs or aims need to be formulated in general and very flexible terms (Lewis & Norwich, 2005).

The distinctive pedagogy for autistic children and young people emerges from the knowledge that educators need to have about autism and how this can affect the autistic pupil. So, specific knowledge is needed about autism as a distinctive neurodevelopmental condition and about how biology might have an effect on that person. Diagnostic classification gives pointers to the kind of difficulties the person might have whilst the pedagogy requires a principled approach to teaching and learning that focuses on extending what is generally available to all children in a class, whilst taking into account that there will be differences between learners.

Going back to Ravet's (2011) integrative model, this recognises the need to balance the rights to both a similar and different pedagogy. This logically leads us to the notion that there is a need for an autism distinct pedagogy to complement an inclusive pedagogy, and that we need autism-friendly schools and teaching practices.

Good autism practice therefore needs to be approached in a systemic fashion with a focus on both the environment, on teaching and on the needs of the individual learner. It needs to be based on the integration of the best available research and practitioner expertise within the context of a pupil's individual characteristics, as well as cultures, values and preferences. Autism-friendly education demands adjustments and clarifications, not only in surroundings or educational material but also in the way teachers understand their autistic pupils and their own teaching approaches.

Summary

Approaches should be sensitive to the wishes and needs of the individual child or young person and their family. They should also be within the skill set of those who work with the child or young person. Educators need to use their professional judgement to adapt practice to their own settings, as all settings and the needs of individuals are different. In terms of the practice in UK schools, including those specific to autism, it is extremely rare for a school to adopt and follow just one approach or intervention. An eclectic approach is usually adopted and practice is influenced and develops as a result of the experience and expertise of the staff and visiting professionals such as speech and language therapists, educational and clinical psychologists, paediatricians, occupational therapists and physiotherapists.

Recommended reading

Lewis, A. & Norwich, B. (2005) *Special teaching for special children? Pedagogies for inclusion.* London: Open University Press.

Inclusive pedagogy for autistic children and young people

Key questions

Can differences between learners (by special needs group) be identified and systematically linked with learners' needs for differential teaching?

Does autism lead to a particular way of learning that requires different pedagogical and organisational processes?

Introduction

This chapter gives an overview of policy in England as an example of how inclusive principles emerged in this country in relation to Special Educational Needs and Disabilities (SEND). In England, the pedagogy for pupils with SEND is encompassed in the SEND Code of Practice (2014), the Teachers' Standards and the Department for Education strategy documents. Expectations for teachers are also clearly articulated in the Office for Standards in Education, Children's Services and Skills (Ofsted) guidelines, and a new Ofsted framework (2019) was launched in September 2019. These documents provide statutory guidance regarding the expectations on all teachers, at the level of settings, schools and leadership, classrooms and individual teachers.

The Children and Families Act (2014) established a new SEND support system, covering education, health and social care. This included a SEND code of practice that provided statutory guidance for organisations that support children and young people, including those on the autism spectrum, aged between 0 to 25 years. The SEND Code of Practice states that:

> Public bodies, including further education institutions, local authorities, maintained schools, maintained nursery schools, academies and free schools are covered by the public sector equality duty and, when carrying out their functions, must have regard to the need to eliminate discrimination, promote equality of opportunity and foster good relations between disabled and non-disabled children and young people.
>
> (DfE/DoH, 2014: 17)

Central to this was the involvement of children, young people and their families and a recognition that provision should be based on:

> Individual strengths and needs and should seek to address them all, using well-evidenced interventions targeted at areas of difficulty and, where necessary, specialist equipment or software. This will help to overcome barriers to learning and participation.
>
> (DfE/DoH, 2014: 85)

Two broad levels of support were established: SEND support, and Education, Health and Care Plans (EHCPs). SEND support is support given to a child or young person in their pre-school, school or college. The type of support provided might include extra help from a teacher, help communicating with other children, or support with physical or personal care.

EHCPs are for children and young people aged up to 25 years who need more support than is available through SEND support. In England, an EHCP is a legal document that describes a child or young person's special educational needs, the support they need and the outcomes they would like to achieve. The Code of Practice states that where a child has SEND but does not have an EHCP plan they must be educated in a mainstream setting, except in specific circumstances. As such, all local authority-maintained mainstream schools and academies in England are expected to admit children and young people with SEND, including those on the autism spectrum, whether they have an EHCP or not. Autism is currently the most prevalent primary type of need for both boys (32%) and girls (17%) with an EHCP (DfE, 2018).

In schools, the Code of Practice highlights the class teacher's responsibility for the teaching and learning of all children with SEND in their class. This builds on the requirement that all newly qualified teachers and Early Years educators must have a clear understanding of the needs of all children and young people, including those with SEND, and be able to use and evaluate distinctive teaching/learning approaches appropriately as part of the Teachers' Standards (DfE, 2011).

The Teachers' Standards were introduced in September 2012 to set a clear baseline of expectations for the professional practice and conduct of teachers and to define the minimum level of practice expected of teachers in England. Leadership and management are expected to use the Teachers' Standards (DfE, 2011) to improve standards of teaching, by setting minimum expectations and assessing performance against them. Teachers are expected to have a clear understanding of the needs of all pupils, including those with SEND. They need to demonstrate an awareness of the physical, social and intellectual development of children, and know how to adapt teaching to support the education of pupils at different stages of development.

In July 2016, the Department for Education published a new framework for Initial Teacher Training (ITT) content (DfE, 2016a). The framework is available for training providers to use and has specific content on training in SEND, including autism. This means that all trainee teachers should learn how to adapt their teaching strategies so that pupils on the autism spectrum are fully included and helped to succeed.

The Department for Education document, *Strategy 2015–2020 – World-class Education and Care* (2016), outlines the government's vision to 'provide world-class education and care that allows every child and young person to reach his or her potential, regardless of background' (DfE, 2016b: 3).

Although there is no specific reference to the education of children and young people on the autism spectrum in the document, the Department for Education recognises that:

There is more to be done to improve educational outcomes and experiences for children and young people with SEND. There is a very wide spectrum of types and scale of need, but taken together, outcomes are generally poor across measures of attainment, progress, absence, exclusions and destinations.

(DfE, 2016b: 35)

The Department for Education states they will address these issues, under the priority of supporting and protecting vulnerable children, by reviewing the current strategy for SEND provision and ensuring SEND reforms are embedded within the education system to empower children and families and improve outcomes.

In addition to this, the All Party Parliamentary Group on Autism (APPGA, 2017) investigated how decisions are made about the provision that children and young people on the autism spectrum receive, what support they receive in school and how effectively the reformed SEND system is working for them and their families. This included conducting a national survey and interviewing children and young people on the autism spectrum, their families and practitioners. Several key recommendations emerged from the report.

Firstly, the report recommended that the government should develop a national autism and education strategy by the end of 2019. This should include a focus on measures to promote inclusion, reduce bullying and ensure that reasonable adjustments are made for children and young people on the autism spectrum in schools. The second recommendation focused on embedding autism understanding throughout the education system via training for all teachers, including head teachers and senior leadership. Finally, the report highlighted the need for local authorities to collect data on the number of children and young people on the autism spectrum together with a profile of their needs to better inform provision.

Meanwhile, Ofsted, the inspecting body for education in England, has recently revised its frameworks for Early Years, School and Post-16 settings and these were implemented from September 2019. The Education Inspection Framework sets out how Ofsted inspects maintained schools, academies, non-association independent schools, Further Education and Skills provision and registered Early Years settings in England. The quality of education is a key judgement area for Ofsted. Across all settings, inspectors will consider how well leaders and teachers promote high expectations for achievement and progress through the systems they use to monitor and develop the quality of provision for learners, including those with SEND.

There is a strong emphasis on leadership and that leaders are responsible for ensuring that all learners, including those with SEND, get the information, advice, guidance and support to achieve their next steps and progress to positive destinations. Leaders are expected to provide the support for staff to make this possible. When assessing leadership and management, inspectors will consider the school's use of performance management and the effectiveness of strategies for improving teaching. This will include the extent to which professional development is based on the identified needs of staff and the needs of teachers at an early stage of their career.

For Post-16 settings, Ofsted inspections will focus on the extent to which learners with SEND have independence in making decisions about their lives. Across the settings, reference is made to the need to measure outcomes and to show evidence that there are high expectations of children and young people with SEND and that they are achieving well and are prepared for the next stage of their education or adult life. Given this, the question then becomes how this can be achieved.

Teaching as interconnection between curriculum (*what*), pedagogy (*how*) and rationale (*why*)

Teaching is the interconnection between curriculum, pedagogy and knowledge (Lewis & Norwich, 2005; Norwich, 2013). Curriculum refers to *what* is being studied and taught, pedagogy is *how* one teaches, and *why* in the heading above relates to the rationale for the kind of pedagogy and curriculum. In examining the question of to what extent the learner needs of children with a visual impairment can be considered as being distinctive, Douglas and McLinden (2005) highlight that this can be difficult to unpick. Curriculum, knowledge and pedagogic strategies are closely intertwined and interdependent. They go on to argue that the distinctive needs of children with visual impairments have given rise to a number of curriculum areas that are considered to be either 'over and above' the mainstream curriculum or areas that are outside the mainstream teacher's expertise and require input from professionals with specialist training.

Treating all children fairly might require educators to sometimes treat them differently; these differences should be seen as both natural and valuable. Distinctive knowledge will be needed by teachers to support children to learn the common curriculum. This can include teachers needing specialist knowledge about the implications of particular disabilities on individual children. A visually impaired child will therefore have very different challenges to a child with autism, despite the fact that some challenges might overlap, but the teacher will need knowledge about the accommodations that need to be made in order for the child or young person to have access to learning (Douglas & McLinden, 2005).

In autism education, teachers' choices of educational programmes tend to derive from a combination of educational, behavioural and developmental research and theory (Howlin, 2010). In reality, and particularly in the UK, this means that teachers tend to employ an eclectic mix of strategies (Guldberg, 2010) from a variety of instructional or teaching models (Greenwood & Abbott, 2001). In special education, behavioural approaches have been used a lot. So, a teacher might draw on behaviourism for teaching certain skills. Teachers are also likely to be informed by developmental approaches.

If a child is at a one-word level in terms of language development, the teacher might be working on increasing their vocabulary to more words, or might be moving on to teaching the use of two words in combination. In other situations, teachers are likely to draw on sociocultural approaches. Examples of this are activities in which students learn from one another. Being eclectic is therefore a natural part of being a teacher, as is the notion of drawing on a range of different strategies, approaches and interventions and implementing them differently in different teaching contexts and according the needs of the individual child (Guldberg, 2010).

Having said this, autism education cannot be about the simple matter of identifying missing skills. The value and purpose of teaching that skill must be thought about very carefully and should be included in planning. Autistic people themselves and their caregivers have indicated that they would rather focus on functional skills rather than academic goals (Wittemeyer et al., 2011). This includes the skills that are needed to live independently, and those needed to function in work and social environments.

Current guidelines in autism education

In the autism education field, many guidelines and principles have been developed for the therapy and education of autistic pupils. These have led to recommendations that distinctive approaches are needed for autistic children and young people. Guidelines take into account the research evidence and are usually created to encourage consistent understanding and practice within health, education and social care, and across the country (Jones, 2019). Many of these guidelines contain principles that can in their broadest sense be considered to represent good practice in SEND generally.

The Australian guidelines (ARACY, 2013) for autistic children and young people, for example, identify that the key principles in education provision need to include better co-ordination and collaboration between agencies, more equitable funding and provision across states for children with autism and their families, a continuum of provision with an emphasis upon inclusion, a comprehensive planning approach to meeting needs, and consideration of evidence-based approaches and training in order to increase capacity for school staff.

Guidelines in Ireland have emphasised that approaches should be selected for individuals using a team-based approach and based upon knowledge of the person, and parental preference, matched to the needs of the child, family and education setting. Ensuring sufficient capacity to deliver the intervention effectively has also been emphasised in guidelines from the National Council for Special Education in Ireland (NCSE, 2015).

In the UK, the Department for Education in England identified principles of 'good autism practice'. These focused on the importance of practitioner understanding of autism, the need for policy and planning at all levels, for supporting families and working in partnership. These guidelines also highlighted the need to involve children and young people in decisions affecting their education (Jones et al., 2008). Guidelines emerging from New Zealand similarly argued for the importance of adopting models to fit the particular pupils, to focus on social progress, to target individual teaching to the needs of the individual child, and to offer positive behavioural support (Ministry of Health & Education, 2016).

Furthermore, a number of authors have emphasised the need to adapt the environment to the needs of children and young people; including parents and caregivers in educational planning and goals; teaching in a natural setting; using visual strategies and involving peers (Guldberg, 2010; Jones et al., 2008; Charman et al., 2011). Charman et al.'s (2011) study identified the elements of good autism practice as:

- Having high aspirations for pupils.

- Monitoring progress.

- Adapting the curriculum.

- Involvement of other professionals.

- Emphasis on staff knowledge and training.

- Effective communication processes.

- Engaging in broader participation in the community.

- Building strong relationships with families.

Authors have emphasised the importance of working in an ethical way, with values such as appreciating, respecting and accepting autistic people (De Clercq, 2019). There has also been a strong emphasis on the fact that practitioners need to combine their knowledge from academic study with practical knowledge and common sense in order to develop effective practice (Jordan et al., 2019).

The distinctive group differences of autistic children

Guidelines emerging from policy, coupled with research undertaken by different researchers who have a particular interest in developing understandings of educational provision and practice for autistic people, have also highlighted that autistic children and young people require distinctive types of supports and assistance to be successful in their local schools (Ravet, 2015; Jordan et al., 2019). As a result, there is a need for transformation in how autistic pupils are taught by exploring new ideas and ways of working that can lead to change in the classroom and to better outcomes for autistic pupils. This entails the necessity to focus on the importance of, and strategies to support, agency, choice and empowerment for autistic pupils, promoting the active participation of the learner as the primary aim.

It has been argued that the values inherent in the 'curriculum for all' approach are problematic when it comes to autism, where it is important to consider education as the acquisition of culturally approved skills, knowledge and attitudes *and* a more therapeutic model of education that can support the pupil to access learning and participation (Jordan, 2005). Traditionally, there has been a divide between education and therapy in autism studies. Therapeutic and psychological interventions tend to focus on skills and behaviour that are needed to access education. This can include learning to work in a group, taking turns, developing friendships, and so on. Most of these fall outside the statutory curriculum (the National Curriculum in England), and often fall within what Lewis and Norwich (2005) call the 'uncertain interface between teaching and therapeutic interventions that are learning based' (Lewis & Norwich, 2005: 11).

However, education is more than treatment in that it is the way citizens are taught the values, understanding, knowledge and skills that will enable their full participation in their community (Jordan, 2005). Education is about helping individuals to develop their potential for a fuller and more productive life. It is about enabling individuals to appreciate meaning in situations and to achieve their own ends. Education focuses on the acquisition of academic and functional knowledge and skills by facilitating learning. The autistic child is, like any other child, entitled to a broad and relevant curriculum to meet his or her needs.

In order for autistic children and young people to have true access in education, however, there is a need for educators to understand the needs of autistic children and young people, and to create classrooms that circumvent barriers, provide opportunities for positive and reciprocal social interactions and foster the development of social understanding. This dual approach of focusing on both context and the individual learning needs of children and young people is core to the concepts developed by McLinden et al. (2016) regarding 'access to learning' and 'learning to access' for children and young people with visual impairment. 'Access to learning' is ensuring that the environment is structured to promote learning and 'learning to access' is supporting the child to learn distinctive skills in order to afford more independent learning.

To that end, authors have stressed the importance of teachers having knowledge of autism and the learning needs of autistic pupils in order to be able to offer autistic pupils an appropriate educational environment and teaching (Jordan, 2005; Guldberg, 2010; Parsons et al., 2011; Ravet, 2015). As Norwich (2013) notes, there is a need to have knowledge about the unique ways that autistic people process the world when we teach autistic children: 'The key point is that this kind of knowledge is not covered by general knowledge about teaching and learning as it represents knowledge of atypical responses' (Norwich, 2013: 78).

That does not mean that by knowing that a child has autism, practitioners will know exactly what his or her difficulties are, nor necessarily how to teach, but it provides a signpost for starting the journey of how to best meet that child or young person's needs. The teacher will still need to observe the child as an individual, but knowing about autism will guide those observations in more fruitful directions (Jordan, 2005). The point being made here is that children with autism have unique needs, which are recognised through, and derive from, group differences but are not fully determined by group membership (Jordan, 2005). For autistic children and young people, this trajectory manifests itself differently for every child with autism but inherently includes the need for support to develop social, communication and adaptive skills directly related to autism.

Implications for the curriculum

Given the nature of autism, and taking individual abilities and needs into account, autistic children and young people will therefore require support in a range of areas outside of the national or universal curriculum. In other words, they need a 'therapeutic' curriculum (Jordan, 2005) that can support the 'learning to access' process. The characteristics of autistic learning and thinking need to underpin and inform the approaches used and these characteristics indicate areas that will be a priority for a child with autism. This is because in autism, learning and developmental patterns are different, with four key areas of difference impacting on how a pupil might learn. These four key areas of difference are closely interrelated with one another and include communication and language, social understanding, interests and information processing and sensory processing differences.

Notably, the research literature highlights that the social challenges that autistic children and young people face are key. Educators need to understand that autistic children and young people might not have the instinctive understanding and responsiveness to social signals that other children and young people have. Autistic children and young people will have different responses to social stimuli and are therefore likely to find it difficult to intuitively and instinctively understand their teacher (and vice versa). Autistic children and young people therefore require education for those aspects of development that other children acquire instinctively or intuitively (Jordan, 2005). Much teaching is intuitive and happens through social interaction and guidance but the child on the spectrum is deprived of that social guidance and needs help to acquire skills in understanding the world.

The distinctive group needs of children with autism therefore arise both directly from their developmental difficulties and also indirectly from the fact that having autism prevents autistic children from participating in the socialisation process through which development usually takes place. As autistic pupils are often responsive to social stimuli in a different way to non-autistic pupils, this has implications for all aspects of learning and teaching. It means that they have a unique need for explicit teaching of social and emotional understanding (Jordan, 2005). A key implication of this is that those with autism require education for those aspects of development that others acquire intuitively (Jordan, 2005).

The need for a therapeutic curriculum is highlighted most clearly in relation to the issue of mental health. Currently, there are high rates of anxiety, depression and suicide evident in autistic adolescents and adults (Hirvikoski et al., 2016). Children and young people on the autism spectrum are at much higher risk of mental health difficulties, particularly anxiety and depression, than people who do not have autism. Good mental health and wellbeing therefore needs to be prioritised. The curriculum for autistic children and young people should be diversified to work on emotional understanding and regulation, and mental health.

This will include the need for support to reduce anxiety and to increase self-esteem. Confidence to interact with the wider world is absolutely crucial. Many studies highlight that autistic people struggle to identify and regulate their emotional response to environmental changes and have extreme reactions that are harder to control than for their typical peers (Gotham et al., 2015). This approach therefore includes working with students to teach them about their emotional state and to use appropriate coping strategies, whilst promoting a calm, caring and positive whole-school environment (Morewood, 2019).

This approach is aligned with the use of a low-arousal approach. The low-arousal approach responds to the fact that individuals on the autism spectrum have extreme reactions to their sensory environment (McDonnell et al., 2015). It highlights the need for educators to teach autistic children and young people to identify the messages their body is giving and then to use strategies to regulate their emotions. This includes the need to work on developing introceptive skills. In other words, the capacity to notice and give meaning to internal bodily sensations, enabling the person to connect to themselves and self-regulate.

Furthermore, given the impact having autism has on communication, it is crucial to support the development of communication. NICE guidelines, for example, highlight that Early Years should remain a priority and that interventions that focus on early communicative behaviours are particularly important (NICE, 2013). These guidelines also recommend the use of social communication interventions, which focus on the core difficulties such as developing joint attention through play.

Ability to communicate effectively provides the meaningful foundations through which social relationships are built. Educators therefore need to explore and value multiple modes of communication and expression, whilst developing environments that foster communication and collaboration. Children and young people on the autism spectrum will have difficulty with joint attention. This can make it difficult to get the person to attend to the things the teacher regards as important as the child or young person will have difficulties in all aspects of joint attention. There is good evidence of the importance of prioritising spontaneous communication and play; interventions in naturalistic settings; and the importance of monitoring and adapting those interventions as needed (Ministry of Health & Education, 2016).

As we saw in previous chapters, interests and information processing will also affect how the pupil with autism understands the world and processes information, and can also affect planning, generalising and predicting as well as transitions and passions or interests. Sensory sensitivities can lead to low or high sensitivity in any of the senses. The kind of adaptations that might need to be considered regarding this are dealt with in the next chapter.

Methods

The 'how' of what is being taught refers to how to provide the child or young person with both 'access to learning and 'learning to access' (Douglas & McLinden, 2005). It refers to the *ways of* teaching, which in turn can support autistic children and young people to learn. Organisational factors that have been identified as important are systematic instruction, individualised instruction, structured environments, specialised curricula, a functional approach to problem behaviours, family involvement and planned transitions (Jordan et al., 2019). Furthermore, it has been highlighted that is important to make adjustments to the social and physical environment, to support families, and to focus on the development of life skills (NICE, 2013).

The methods that can be used to support the autistic child or young person have been highlighted in the literature. The National Professional Development Centre (NPDC) in the United States, for example, stressed the importance of foundational practices as these can set the framework for core support. Emphasis has been placed on the importance of focusing on working on the foundational skills that are necessary for more complex academic skills. For example, communication abilities impact on reading; social skills are needed for group reading and writing; executive functioning is needed for solving maths problems. Focusing on these skills can set autistic children and young people up with the necessary building blocks to access the curriculum.

Generally, there is consensus that visual supports can be helpful for many children and young people on the autism spectrum. Visual supports can be photographs, symbols or the written word, and what a teacher chooses to use should depend on the developmental level of the child. Visual supports can give the child or young person concrete cues to give key information regarding the environment, can be used to teach a new skill, and/or can give the child or young person access to the school environment and support with transitions.

Summary

Regardless of which country they are working in, teachers need to be aware of the difficulties autistic pupils might face, and compensate for those in providing learning opportunities by using other ways of making learning accessible. This will mean drawing on distinctive pedagogy. Meanwhile, every child is different so strategies and approaches need to be based on the individual needs of that particular child. To address processing needs, for example, one person might need extra time to complete assignments. Another person might need assignments to be modified by being provided with multiple choice rather than short essays, for example.

The needs of autistic children and young people mean that practitioners should place a strong focus on supporting the child or young person to learn and develop through and with other people. More broadly, it includes enabling the child or young person to develop the skills, knowledge and understanding necessary to be able to com-municate effectively in social situations and develop and maintain relationships, as well as predict and manage change. Good autism prac-tice needs to start with the individual and what is best for the pupil and their family, take account of the context and it needs to look at the evidence for different approaches whilst integrating consultation with autistic pupils and their families.

Recommended reading

Ravet, J. (2015) *Supporting change in autism services: Bridging the gap between theory and practice*. London: Routledge.

Eight principles of good autism practice in education

Key question

How can principles of good autism practice capture general inclusive principles, as well as the distinctive group needs of autistic children and young people, whilst emphasising individual needs?

Introduction

This chapter articulates how inclusive principles, distinct group differences and the individual needs dimensions of pedagogy interrelate with one another to provide a framework for defining good autism practice around a set of eight principles of good autism practice. The eight key principles emerged from an examination of the current evidence base from research and practice, as well as key policies, statutory guidance and messages from the autistic community.

They are presented within the themes of 'understanding the individual', 'positive and effective relationships', 'enabling environments' and 'learning and development'. These are the four overarching themes of the Early Years Foundation Stage in England (DCSF, 2008). The themes provide a framework for highlighting the key areas to prioritise when working with autistic children and young people. They highlight the need for sound understanding of autism and of 'understanding the individual'. 'Positive and effective relationships' focuses the lens on the importance of developing secure and loving relationships for children and young people, and that these are formed though interaction and emotional connection. As autistic children and young people have particular developmental differences in these areas, working on this needs to be prioritised.

'Enabling environments' encompasses the notion that both the ethos and physical space in which people exist and learn has an impact on learning and wellbeing. This therefore includes both the physical and the emotional environment. There are particular issues that educators need to attend to in order to create enabling environments for autistic children and young people, and these changes can be helpful to all children. 'Learning and development' highlights the need to understand specific ways in which autistic children learn and develop in a different way by identifying the characteristics of effective learning and teaching (DCSF, 2008).

These themes and principles are based on the assumption that there is no 'one-size-fits-all' solution as it is about making decisions based on sound professional judgement and understanding how autism can impact on the learning needs of the child or young person. They situate teaching within the development of an ecological curriculum that looks at the whole context in which the child or young person exists, taking into account education, health and wellbeing. The starting point is the individual child, young person or adult, rather than the 'model' or 'intervention' (Guldberg, 2010).

Each theme has two key principles that have emerged as important for both a broad inclusive pedagogy and for the distinct implementation of such pedagogy for autistic children. Taken together, they highlight key elements of inclusive practice and provide guidance for practice in the education of autistic children and young people (see Figure 10.1). The principles are listed here:

1. Understanding the strengths, interests and challenges of each individual.
2. Enabling the voice of the pupil to contribute to and influence decisions.
3. Collaboration with parents and carers.
4. Workforce development.
5. Leadership and management that promotes and embeds good autism practice.

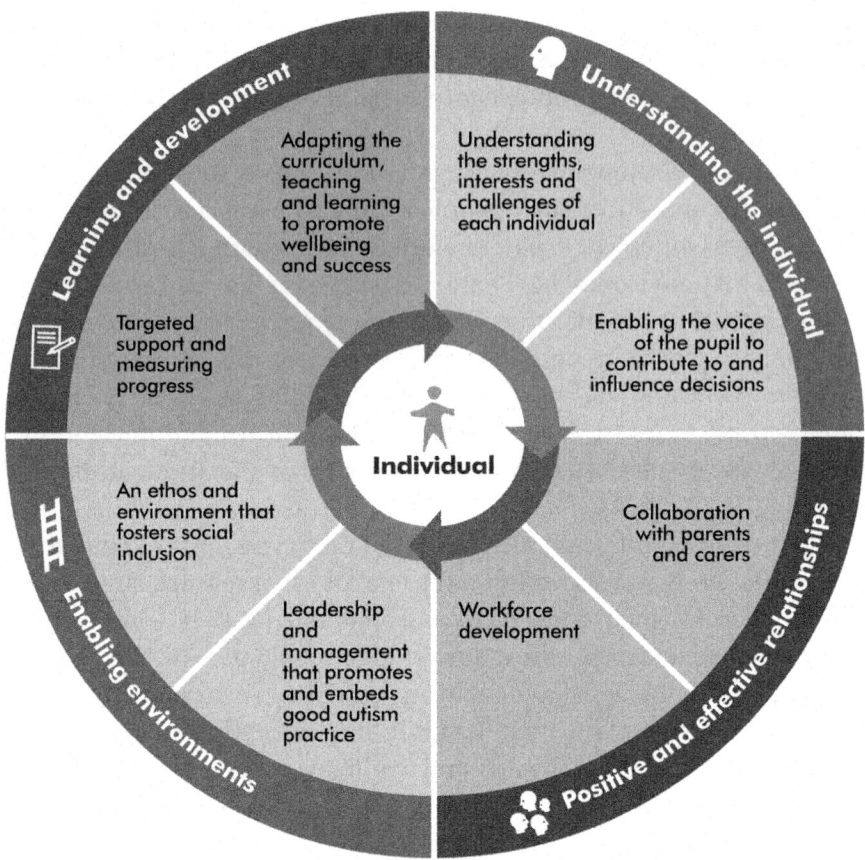

Figure 10.1 Eight key principles

6. An ethos and environment that fosters social inclusion.
7. Targeted support and measuring progress.
8. Adapting the curriculum, teaching and learning to promote well-being and success.

Although the principles are presented in numerical order above, they do not indicate an order of importance. They are all closely interrelated. Equally, the themes could be applied to the education of any child or young person. All children and young people are different and all children are unique. They learn and develop in different ways. This highlights the need to respond in a way that takes into account their unique developmental pathway, and should be based on building upon strengths.

That said, although the themes and principles outline general inclusive principles that apply in education to any child or young person, this chapter focuses on the *distinctive* ways in which these inclusive principles need to be implemented in order to meet the needs of autistic children and young people. For each principle, the chapter looks at why this principle is important, what it says about the curriculum, and the key considerations practitioners need to take into account to implement the principle.

Principle One: Understanding the strengths, interests and challenges of each individual

Good autism practice requires an understanding and awareness of how the main areas of difference impact on the learning, participation, independence and emotional state of the individual autistic child or young person. It means being committed to an ethical way of working by appreciating, accepting and respecting the child or young person (De Clercq, 2012).

Whilst a diagnosis gives a signpost to the needs of a child or young person, full identification of their needs can only arise from understanding how the condition impacts on the individual at a particular time and in a particular learning environment. Given that autistic children and young people will be very different from one another, it is crucial to take into account the child or young person's individuality. Individualised assessment should identify a profile of relative strengths and weaknesses that can inform educational programming (Ravet, 2015).

Autistic children and young people need to be able to generalise, so this makes it crucial to undertake assessments that take into account functioning both in school and in other places, such as the community. There may be significant differences between the home and the setting in the way an autistic child or young person communicates, interacts and expresses their emotional state, as the demands made are often very different. Being aware of these differences and acknowledging these are important for both parents and staff, and for the wellbeing of the child or young person. In the SCERTS™ (2006) assessment protocol, for example, the guidance states that observations and assessments need to be undertaken in at least four different contexts.

Information can be gathered through observations and communication with the individual, discussions with their caregivers and other professionals who have worked with them, and from reports and supporting documents from previous settings or from other professionals. Importantly, parents and caregivers should be consulted and have an input into identifying the goals they think are important to work on for their child. Families know their child or young person and it is vital that they are listened to.

Assessments need to be nuanced enough to identify uneven profiles of abilities. Autistic children and young people will often be more or less advanced in different areas of academic, social and emotional functioning. In addition, and as we have seen from previous chapters, other conditions often co-occur with autism and knowledge of these conditions should influence educational planning. The effect of potential disturbed and erratic eating and drinking, sleeping and personal care routines need also to be taken into account.

Furthermore, the sensory processing issues of the child or young person need to be considered. Going through a sensory profile with the child or undertaking a sensory profile by observing the child in different circumstances is crucial. Consideration must be given to the impact of the sensory environment and the identification of ways to reduce and manage this. This might include conducting an audit of the sensory environment. There are different ways of measuring outcomes, so bear in mind that there are many tools to assess sensory issues. Always take account of the fact that all autistic children and young people are likely to experience increased levels of anxiety and stress compared to their peers and this will impact on their learning, participation and wellbeing.

Following this, educators need to prioritise the strengths and interests of children and young people on the autism spectrum to support their engagement, learning and motivation. Allow children and young people to develop their talents whilst recognising their difficulties. Being able to pursue their interests and strengths can have a number of benefits for children and young people, including improved communication, greater independence and better motor skills. Andy McDonnell and Damian Milton, an autistic academic, write about the state of *positive flow* that ensues when engaged in activities that one enjoys and loves and how essential this is to all humans and particularly to those who have challenges in life (Milton & McDonnell, 2014).

Approaches and interventions need to be based on the needs of the child or young person, and be developmentally appropriate. The person-centred planning approach can help in this. The key features of person-centred planning are that the individual is at the centre of the planning process and plans are made according to their needs. Family, friends and caregivers are included as partners in this process. Planning reflects what is important to the individual now and for the future, and takes into consideration the support the child or young person requires. The plan helps the individual to be included in a community, and supports the community to include them.

The Communication Autism Team (CAT) at Birmingham City Council developed the 'All about me' tool to support the person-centred planning process. 'All about me' is a computer-based tool to obtain information directly from the pupil on their strengths and interests (Houlahan, 2019). It is now used in the 420 local schools the local authority team works with. It supports the development of goals and progression and complements information given by parents and teachers. All person-centred plans should be ongoing in putting into action what the individual wants for their life. They should be reviewed and amended as necessary.

The child or young person's needs and the resulting accommodations that are needed will often be expressed through the development of an Individual Education Plan (IEP). One very helpful tool for supporting teachers in building up a picture of the child's needs, strengths and interests is to develop an individual passport or a person-centred workbook, which can sit alongside the IEP. A person-centred workbook can include photos, drawings, written text or symbols depending on the individual's understanding. It can have a section entitled 'All about me' in which the child, young person or teacher outlines how the person communicates, what their interests are, what makes them happy, sad, anxious or angry, and things they need help with.

Other sections can include the person's hopes and dreams for the future, how they like to spend their leisure time, where they live and whom they live with, and their thoughts on what work they would like to do after completing school. Sections on advocacy can be helpful too. This can include what the child or young person can do independently and what they need help with. The workbook can list people who support them. Other ways of easily communicating a child's likes or dislikes is to have a board marked with activities and strengths in which boxes can be ticked or marked and completed with statements such as 'I like', 'I am good at', 'I can', and so on.

Importantly, person-centred workbooks need to be put together in a way which is appropriate to that particular child or young person. This needs to take into account the age of the person and their ability level. Key information about a child or young person should be regularly updated and shared through appropriate means. Pupil profiles or passports can be shorter, more condensed versions of the person-centred workbook, and these can be used to share and regularly update key information about a child or young person.

In short, teaching needs to be planned and conducted in the knowledge that individual pupils will respond differently and require different types of support to do the task. A flexible educational approach should be adopted, based on an understanding of the individual requirements of the child or young person on the autism spectrum within their setting. On a system-wide level, settings need systems in place to identify the individual strengths, interests and challenges of individual children and young people as a starting point for understanding and meeting their needs. High-quality programmes are therefore those that provide individualised services and supports whilst addressing core characteristics of autism through effective teaming and in partnership with families.

Damian Milton (2012b) provides a set of five key points to consider:

- Respect the individual learning style of the pupil and work with it, not against it.

- Always consider sensory issues.

- Consider that how you process information may be very different to that of the pupil you work with.

- Remember that stress is a key issue and reduce i are over-stressed.

- Collaborate for consistency in support.

Principle Two: Enabling the voice of the contribute to and influence decisions

The participation of all children and young people in decision-making has been an important issue in education since the United Nations Convention on the Rights of the Child (UNCRC; UN, 1989) established the right of all children to express their views, and to have these views listened to and taken seriously when decisions are being made that affect them:

> Children have a right to receive and impart information, to express an opinion and to have that opinion taken into account in any matters affecting them from the early years onwards. Their views should be given due weight according to their age, maturity and capability.
>
> (UN, 1989, Articles 12 and 13: 20).

The UN Convention on the Rights of Persons with Disabilities (Article 7.3) also states that children with disabilities should be able to express their views freely, on an equal basis with other children, and according to their age and maturity. They should be provided with the appropriate assistance to realise that right. The Convention also recognises that children who are disabled should be taught at school in a way that understands their disability and works towards achieving their fullest possible social inclusion and individual development (Article 23).

These rights have been embedded into legislation and policy initiatives in England since the ratification of the UNCRC by the UK in 1991, with the SEND Code of Practice (2014) highlighting the need for the full participation of children and young people with SEND in decisions that affect their lives. Involving children and young people in decisions can benefit their emotional health and wellbeing and enable to feel in control of their lives, to develop their decision-making ils and make them feel a valued part of their educational setting and the wider community.

Schools and other professionals need to ensure that autistic students have a say over the decisions that ultimately affect their lives, especially at key transition points. Listening to the pupil is an essential competency. In the Autism Education Trust's National Standards, for example, one of the Standards states that:

> Your setting ensures that pupils with autism are effectively and regularly consulted on all aspects of their education and experience at school.

(www.autismeducationtrust.org.uk)

Lundy (2007) highlights that there are four key components to the process of ensuring that children and young people are given a voice. The first is space. This means giving them the opportunity to express a view. The second is voice. Children and young people will need support to express their views. The third is that they need to have an audience. In other words, their view should be listened to. Finally, a person needs to feel that they have influence. In other words, their view must be acted upon, as appropriate.

Although there have been some substantial advances in autism education and the importance of pupil voice is recognised, the field is still in its infancy. Others can easily make inferences about the opinions of children and young people and subsequent decisions might be made on the basis of those inferences.

Another issue is that research that is available on pupil voice and pupils' experience of inclusion in mainstream settings seems to come largely from pupils who do not have significant language difficulties, and who have been able to express themselves effectively using language-based tools such as interviews, questionnaires and diaries (Humphrey & Lewis, 2008).

This highlights the importance of finding mechanisms to enable *all* children and young people to have their perspectives and experiences taken into account. For some children and young people, the most appropriate and developmentally relevant means need to be identified and used to enable them to communicate their views. This might involve the use of alternative and augmentative forms of communication. One approach, for example, is a photo-voice approach where children and young people take photographs of the places where they felt listened to and the people who they felt listened to them.

Educational approaches need to consider the preferences of children and young people on how they can best be supported in their day-to-day activities. Staff should proactively listen to the child or young person across the range of activities in which they engage, not only at points of transition or review meetings. It can include talking to the child or young person about their understanding of autism if this is appropriate, and about the social aspects of their education, such as working as part of a group and peer relationships. Discussions can also include the nature and level of one-to-one adult support, as well as planning, organisation and time management. It is particularly important to support the child or young person to understand and manage their emotional state, their sensory needs and the need for time alone.

Some useful information about how autistic children and young people see their experiences of school can be found in research. A review of 17 qualitative studies reported on the experiences of autistic children and young people in school. The focus was in particular on how this related to their sense of feeling different or isolated from their non-autistic peers (Williams et al., 2019). The authors concluded that there were three key issues that shaped these young people's experiences. They said that the things that made them feel different related to their autism, the quality of interpersonal relationships and the accessibility of the school environment. The review identified the importance of listening to their voice and making them feel more included, thus reducing the risk of social isolation which may cause mental health difficulties.

Despite the growing evidence of the importance and value of the autistic voice in research and educational practice, there is still a need to know more about how to meaningfully consult autistic children and young people around lesson planning, producing individual passports and finding out what they want to achieve in terms of outcomes from education (Wittemeyer et al., 2011).

As long as parents and the young person consent to this, including and consulting the child or young person in decisions about their education will mean working with the child or young person to develop their understanding of the way autism affects them. It can include building up knowledge of day-to-day activities and tasks, social preferences, review meetings and transition planning. Regular discussions about current and future needs and wishes with the child or young person can be enabled by arranging times to discuss the support they receive and what might help, and reviewing their pupil passport or profile together with them.

It is also important to find ways of involving the child or young person in decision-making in the school, if that is something the child or young person wants and can contribute to. Children and young people can be involved in their school councils, for example. This can take different forms. It could be that the council gathers feedback from students and informs them of decisions that will be made at the school. Alternatively, it could involve including pupils with autism in the school council so that they can help to create a more autism-friendly environment. Regardless of what form the involvement takes, it is important to be clear about the aims and the potential outcomes of the pupil's participation so as not to create unrealistic expectations. Practitioners should provide sufficient information so that the child or young person can make a decision on whether or not to engage with the process. Sensory processing difficulties or any other issues that might impact on the pupil's full participation need to be considered.

In summary, autistic learners need environments in which they can have agency, where they have a voice and are listened to, where they can make choices and influence what happens, and where they can build relationships based on trust. Personal agency is crucial to this. Studies have shown that students with disabilities need a range of skills for transition beyond school, for example. These include self-determination, self-advocacy, resilience, understanding of their own strengths and weaknesses and study skills (Moriña, 2017).

Principle Three: Collaboration with parents and caregivers

Teachers are expected to work with parents in the best interests of their pupils, and partnership with parents is crucial in education. In England, the SEND Code of Practice states that:

Local authorities, Early Years providers and school
enable parents to share their knowledge about the child
them confidence that their views and contributions ar
and will be acted upon. At times, parents, teachers an
may have differing expectations of how a child's needs
met. Sometimes these discussions can be challenging but it is in
the child's best interests for a positive dialogue between parents,
teachers and others to be maintained, to work through points of
difference and establish what action is to be taken.

(DfE/DoH, 2014: 21)

Staff should actively seek ways of engaging with parents and caregivers
of all autistic children and young people to share concerns, ideas and
strategies, as they play a key role in influencing children and young
people's progress in learning, independence, emotional health and wellbeing. Parents and caregivers have lived through successes and failures
and can provide useful information on the child or young person's
preferences and needs, as well as how best to address specific issues.
They can also provide information about co-existing conditions, the
young person's awareness of their diagnosis and what it means to them,
and factors that are likely to cause anxiety or stress.

Good communication is critical in helping the child or young person
to prepare for transitions and changes, to support wider curriculum
events and trips, homework arrangements, developing independence
skills and preparing for adult life. There should therefore be planned
opportunities for informal communication and more formal review
meetings. Parents and caregivers should be asked what the priorities
are for their child and agree effective ways in which to communicate
and to whom. Positive partnerships, mutual respect and good communication are likely to lead to more effective support. In working with
parents, practitioners need to consider whether they should adapt the
way they communicate with individual parents and carers to enable
them to fully participate and engage in their child's education. One way
can be to provide written confirmation of any actions agreed verbally.

Staff members need to be mindful of the impact of stress on
parents and caregivers as they will often be going through a whole
range of emotions related to having a child with autism. High levels
of parenting stress can counteract the effectiveness of early teaching

interventions (Osborne et al., 2008). Parents of children with autism, especially mothers, report a greater amount of stress and depression than do parents of children who have other developmental conditions. Following a child's diagnosis, it is quite common that parents experience depression, anger, shock, denial, fear, guilt, grief, confusion and despair (Boucher, 2009: 310). Feelings of emotional stress are quite common as there can be worries about the future, or about potential negative responses of the extended family, friends and the public.

Many parents and caregivers highlight that the most stressful part of being a parent is when professionals do not listen to them. Being involved with numerous professionals can also be very difficult, as can finding an appropriate school for the child. They might have another child with SEND and may have other difficult family issues to address in addition to autism. Practitioners can help parents by providing them with good-quality, positive information about diagnosis. They can advise parents on what they and others can do to help their child as well as support them to have a good quality of life within the family. This can include advice about how to support siblings, and giving parents and caregivers information about organisations that support siblings of children and young people with disabilities, such as the organisation 'Sibs' (www.sibs.org.uk).

The range of support that parents and professionals can give one another includes advice on communication strategies and on managing behaviour. Information about school placements is important. The Autism Education Trust developed a parent and carers guide designed specifically for this purpose – *Working Together with Your Child's School* (see www.autismeducationtrust.org.uk). This recognises that parent and caregivers' concerns are often as much about their child being safe, secure, accepted, respected, valued and nurtured as they are about curriculum issues.

Support is often needed at important points of transition between year groups or educational settings. Providing timely support and information to parents and caregivers on possible Post-16 options can help to reduce anxiety around transition into adulthood for their child, for example. Signposting parents and caregivers to appropriate services and support and, if they are seeking diagnostic assessment, informing them about the referral pathway in their local area through the Local

Offer, is also important. The parent might need support in knowing how to get help outside the education setting. It could be that educators have concerns about a child, but that parents find it difficult to accept this concern. This might need sensitive handling, building a relationship of trust with the parents and sensitively handling how to raise issues with them.

Sometimes parents might need the opportunity to meet with other parents and attend support groups. Creating a wider network of support and help can be beneficial for addressing parental stress and isolation for families. Settings can also provide a forum where parents and caregivers can meet together to share information. This can happen through training events or signposting to parent groups and other services via their Local Offer. This can be particularly helpful for parents or caregivers of newly diagnosed children and young people.

It is important to understand the needs of parents and caregivers who themselves may have autism, as well as families from a diversity of cultural and religious backgrounds. Being aware of the needs of the family as a whole, including siblings, can lead to more effective support. It is vital to co-ordinate and disseminate important information from all key stakeholders and ensure this information is shared with all, including the child and young person.

Principle Four: Workforce development

Enhancing people's understanding of autism, targeting personal and professional development and creating time for staff to reflect on, discuss and evaluate their practice is crucial given that there is a direct link between unqualified and under-confident teaching staff, school exclusions and poor adult outcomes for autistic children and young people (Gill et al., 2017). Research has shown that a lack of autism knowledge in teaching staff can negatively impact on the school experiences of autistic children and reduce pupils' opportunities to succeed (Humphrey & Symes, 2013).

Studies and accounts have shown that outcomes for children may be undermined because many staff lack professional development and supervision (Lemmi et al., 2017). Unfortunately, educators often feel ill-prepared to support the complex needs of neurodiverse learners in their classrooms. Lack of knowledge, particularly in mainstream school settings (Dillon et al., 2016; Goodall, 2018), still negatively impacts on the school experiences of autistic children and their opportunities to succeed. In these settings, without an understanding of autism, teachers are likely to apply their knowledge of mainstream or general education to autistic learners, rather than basing teaching on the different needs of the autistic learners.

In fact, fewer than five in ten teachers in a recent study said that they are confident about supporting a child with autism (APPGA, 2017). In England, the All Party Parliamentary Group on Autism report on *Autism and Education in England* (APPGA, 2017) found that 41% of 308 teachers surveyed were confident in supporting a child who had an Education, Health and Care Plan (EHCP), but this dropped to 33% where such a plan did not exist. This suggests that there is less detail and knowledge available on children who have not had a formal statutory assessment. It is vital that staff members are given key information on all autistic children and young people and that they consult with children without EHCPs, who are likely to be in the majority, to identify their needs and how these are best addressed.

Staff development is clearly critical in terms of enhancing practice and outcomes for autistic children and young people, and in reducing exclusion rates (Parsons et al., 2011). Professional development can include a wide range of activities such as self-directed learning, mentoring and coaching, discussion and collaboration with colleagues, internal and external training courses, and studying for accredited qualifications. Settings need to provide access to professional development on several levels to meet the range of needs of autistic children and young people and the staff who work with them. The starting point should always be to enable staff to develop an understanding of autism and how this might affect the learning of individual autistic children and young people.

It is essential that all those working within a setting receive professional development that gives them a basic awareness about autism, given that having autism affects the way in which children and young people understand and interact with their environment and other people. Flowing from this, staff development should provide staff with pointers regarding specific approaches that can address one or more areas of development. Effective engagement and partnership with parents and caregivers needs to be emphasised. This should be included as part of the induction programme for new governors and all staff. This would mean that all staff that are new to the workforce participate in professional development on autism as part of their induction.

At a specialist level, professional development should support the skills and knowledge needed for staff to take a lead role in co-ordinating the support of children and young people in their setting. In England, many settings have a lead autism practitioner or autism champion, for example. Having an identified lead for autism can enable a more co-ordinated approach between staff, children and young people, families and other services whilst providing ongoing opportunities for identifying and meeting professional development needs within a setting.

The SEND Code of Practice states that settings should use a graduated approach to meet the needs of children and young people. Support should arise from a four-part cycle of assess, plan, do and review, where earlier decisions and actions are revisited, refined and revised, leading to a growing understanding of individual needs, progress and strategies to support a child or young person. Settings can use this approach to identify strengths and where gaps and barriers to learning currently exist for children and young people on the autism spectrum. Too often this stage is missed out, leading to either no or inappropriate interventions and a lack of understanding of how needs could be met through high-quality and suitably differentiated teaching within the classroom.

Continued professional development programmes should focus on the wellbeing, good mental health and resilience of children and young people on the autism spectrum. This will support staff to prevent, identify and meet needs through effective practice in settings. It will also support their work with children and young people, their families and specialist services, such as Educational Psychology, Autism Advisory Teams and Child and Adolescent Mental Health Services.

Research indicates that education staff should receive professional development on how to reduce bullying (Schroeder et al., 2014) whilst facilitating quality and lasting peer relationships. Attention needs to be focused on playground supervision, classroom management and being consistent in enforcing anti-bullying rules, as well as carefully restoring relationships between pupils when bullying occurs (Schroeder et al., 2014). A comprehensive approach including peers, teaching and support staff and the broader ethos of the school are needed in order to support children and young people on the autism spectrum who are experiencing bullying at school.

In England, progress has been made in providing professional development to 240,000 educators to date through the AET programme. Among numerous positive outcomes from the AET training, in particular, staff feel more confident in their abilities, there is a reduction in the risk of autistic children being excluded and staff are more able to construct assessments that more accurately reflect the child's strengths and needs. A report on five case-study schools where staff had completed the AET Schools Programme across three modules highlighted that the professional development had been important in enabling the schools to provide good autism provision. The next chapter will provide more detailed information about the AET programme, as it encapsulates the values and ethos outlined in this book.

Principle Five: Leadership and management that promotes and embeds good autism practice

Numerous studies have highlighted the significant role that leadership plays in increasing educational effectiveness. A key task for leaders is therefore to develop education systems within which staff members feel supported to enable the inclusion, participation and achievement of autistic children and young people. This will often mean restructuring the cultures, policies and practices in settings so that they respond to the diversity of children and young people in this group.

A consultation with teachers (Lindsay et al., 2013) highlighted that in order to create an effective inclusive environment, staff needed:

- More resources and training.

- Teaching methods tailored to each child.

- Greater teamwork within the school.

- To build a rapport with the autistic child.

- Whole-school awareness of disability and acceptance of differences.

Effective leadership strategies can have a significant impact on pupil outcomes (Hallinger & Heck, 1997) by unifying organisational vision and values, and developing the skills, support and resources available. Leadership and management need to have a commitment to inclusive values and to meeting the needs of all children and young people on the autism spectrum within their settings. This includes a responsibility to establish an inclusive culture and ethos towards autism through influencing the attitudes and beliefs of staff, children and young people, their families and the wider community.

There is also a need to have a commitment to provide ongoing professional development in autism to update the knowledge, skills and practice of their workforce. The AET National Standards and Competency Frameworks can help leaders to identify the professional development needs of all staff. Many settings regularly audit staff confidence levels, understanding and knowledge of autism and link this to Continuing Professional Development (CPD) and the Performance Management system. For example, settings can use the AET Competency Framework to audit staff skills and identify areas for staff development.

Having high expectations for all learners and a strong commitment to equal opportunities means that leadership and management can enable staff to proactively meet the needs of autistic children and young people through making reasonable adjustments in their practice. It includes the importance of exploring effective ways of facilitating the learning of all children and young people. Specific consideration needs to be given to the management and reduction of exclusions. Given that making reasonable adjustments is a statutory obligation in disability law, leadership and management do need to ensure that this is applied to autistic children and young people.

To ensure that actions are integrated, sustained and monitored for impact, it is important that a commitment to addressing the needs of autistic children and young people is referenced within improvement plans, policies and practice. Leaders and governing bodies must be aware of the different forms of disability discrimination and their setting's legal duties under the Equality Act (2010). This could include, for example, sharing and discussing the AET document, *A Guide to Help Governing Bodies Comply with Equality Law When Considering a Headteacher's Decision to Exclude an Autistic Pupil*, at a full Governors' meeting.

In considering whether exclusion is an appropriate and propor-
tionate measure and whether alternatives have been explored, leaders
will need to understand how autism affects an individual child or young
person, including levels of anxiety and stress, and whether reasonable
adjustments have been made to support them. Leaders can use the AET
National Standards to identify areas of good autism practice and areas
that need development. Early Years, School or Post-16 settings can use
this information as part of the development plan for the setting.

Principle Six: An ethos and environment that fosters social inclusion

Settings need to be aware of the increased risk of social exclusion for
autistic children and young people and have proactive strategies in
place to support their inclusion and to develop peer understanding and
friendships. This requires a multi-layered approach based on improved
autism awareness for everyone within the setting, strong partnerships
with parents and the local community, and implementing strategies
that enable autistic children and young people to engage socially and
be better understood by their peers. Social inclusion requires settings
to make reasonable adjustments and to adapt systems and structures to
remove barriers to participation.

Staff should consider the accessibility of the learning environment
for autistic children and young people by taking into account potential physical barriers and sensory processing difficulties as well as
social demands of working with or being with their peers. Reasonable
adjustments need to be made to remove barriers to participation and
to enable autistic children and young people to access the curriculum,
break and lunchtimes, extra-curricular activities, residential trips, work
experience or exams. This includes providing a clearly organised environment, a variety of means to communicate with children and young
people on the autism spectrum, and an environment that encourages
and facilitates communication.

Learning environments need to be structured, understandable and predictable. Structured teaching, such as having clear, consistent routines
and an environment that is understood by the autistic child or young
person, has been shown to be crucial. Autistic children and young people

have suggested that the design of classrooms is particularly important in terms of their ability to learn and that modifications to the environment may be related to the frequency of behaviours of concern and increased participation. An organised environment with visual cues can enable access to the learning environment. Guidance on elements to consider when designing a school or classroom include proper placement of the visual timetable, reducing visual distraction and controlling lighting, creating spaces that provide a sense of calm, having a quiet room or space for time alone, and adequate storage for possessions.

Environmental accommodations that take into account the potential sensory processing difficulties of a child or young person are also essential, but these accommodations will depend very much on the sensory differences of the particular child or young person in the classroom. Undertaking a sensory audit is therefore crucial in the education of autistic pupils. All teachers should consider whether scent-free and odourless craft supplies might be needed. If a child is tactile sensitive, the classroom seating can be organised so that there is adequate distance from others. If the child or young person has tactile hyposensitivities, then weighted pencils or fidget toys might be needed.

Children or young people with hypersensitivities related to sight or sound might react to classroom stimuli such as lights, colours, noise from fans or air conditioners. There is therefore a need to minimise auditory and visual distraction. Earmuffs can help and softening chair legs with underlay can make a difference. Vestibular issues (balance and movement) can make a child or young person fearful, cautious and anxious about movement as these difficulties can lead to the person having motor difficulties and low muscle tone. It can lead to clumsiness when undertaking tasks or bumping into things. Jumping on a trampoline can be helpful as can other physical exercise.

Autistic children and young people need support to develop positive relationships with their peers. The last ten years have seen an increase in research demonstrating the effectiveness of interventions to promote peer relationships. There have been five key areas which peer intervention approaches have addressed. These include building the social understanding and skills of autistic children and young people, improving the attitudes and knowledge of peers, addressing the support structures implemented by teachers, improving school-wide efforts and knowledge, and engaging families in the process.

Strategies can include developmentally appropriate autism awareness sessions with peers to increase understanding and promote a supportive attitude to the child or young person on the autism spectrum. A whole-setting priority could be around the development of effective anti-bullying policies and practice. Anti-bullying policies are most effective when all school staff understand the principles and the purpose of the school's policy, its legal responsibilities, how to resolve problems, and where to seek support.

The implementation of approaches to develop the mutual understanding, communication and support between the child or young person on the autism spectrum and their peers will help promote social inclusion and lessen the risk of bullying. This can include introducing peer-mentoring programmes, autism awareness sessions or setting up lunchtime clubs based on shared interests. Leadership and management should ensure that staff members are given information and training to raise the profile of this issue for autistic children and young people and integrate it into their practice. This could include using the Anti-Bullying Alliance materials on bullying and autism to inform the setting's anti-bullying strategy (www.antibullyingalliance. org.uk). Autistic children and young people themselves will also need specific guidance on how to recognise the signs of bullying and what they should do if they feel they, or others, are being bullied, including information on cyber-bullying and how to stay safe online.

Another recent research trend has been the growth of research looking into the beneficial effects of exercise in autism and the reduction in obesity, both clear indicators of improved physical and mental health. There is a growing need for practitioners across school settings to focus on exercise, nutrition and weight in autistic children and young people, given the increased likelihood of a sedentary lifestyle and a more restricted diet.

Principle Seven: Targeted support and measuring progress

There is increased awareness about the need to adapt assessment methods to reflect the particular strengths and learning processes of autistic children and young people. A range of assessments is likely to be needed in order to inform individual planning (Charman et al., 2011). Research studies on outcome tend to measure attainments, severity of autism and intellectual ability but rarely ask if the intervention has led to increased wellbeing or happiness. This highlights the need to include assessment tools that can measure wellbeing and family quality of life, and that this needs to be monitored and prioritised alongside academic progress (McConachie et al., 2015). This is particularly important given that anxiety has been reported as the overriding emotion experienced by autistic people, and anxiety is a major inhibitor of learning.

Teachers need to have a secure understanding of how a range of factors can inhibit pupils' ability to learn, and how best to overcome these. This includes making use of formative and summative assessment to secure pupils' progress and using relevant data to monitor progress, set targets and plan lessons, as mentioned in the SEND Code of Practice:

> Early years providers, schools and colleges should know precisely where children and young people with SEND are in their learning and development. They should ensure decisions are informed by the insights of parents and those of children and young people themselves; have high ambitions and set stretching targets for them; track their progress towards these goals; keep under review the additional or different provision that is made for them; promote positive outcomes in the wider areas of personal and social development, and ensure that the approaches used are based on the best possible evidence and are having the required impact on progress.
>
> (DfE/DoH, 2014: 25)

There needs be a focus on identifying and addressing barriers to learning in areas such as communication, play, social understanding and sensory issues. Many of these may be addressed through quality first teaching and making reasonable adjustments, whilst others may require 'small-step' planning and more personalised support. This may involve the use of specific interventions or approaches identified through the 'assess' stage of the graduated approach. Staff should draw on the latest research about the likely impact of particular interventions and consider the views of children and young people as part of this process.

A priority should be to develop children and young people's sense of agency and ability to carry out tasks with lessening support from adults whilst providing appropriate scaffolds and strategies to achieve this. Technological advances have opened up many new possibilities in this regard. Educational applications on iPads can be adapted to accommodate different ways of learning, for example, whilst the number of repetitions of material to be learnt, the quantity and type of scaffold to support learning, and the level of difficulty can all be adjusted based on the learner's response.

As part of the graduated approach, settings need to embed effective assessment processes to identify progress for children and young people on the autism spectrum across non-academic areas as well as on attainment in academic areas. A graduated approach and the 'Assess, Plan, Review and Do' cycle should ascertain the process and quality of the learning experience, as well as outcomes, from the perspective of the autistic child or young person. When assessing progress towards learning goals, data needs to be collected on social and emotional awareness, communication, social understanding and inclusion, daily life skills, independence and autonomy.

The AET Progression Framework (Farrell et al., 2017) can support this process. The AET Progression Framework is divided into seven main areas. The seven areas relate closely to what is known about the distinct challenges and learning needs of autistic children and young people, and the impact of these on their social, emotional and learning needs, their independence and community participation. The main areas it focuses on are social communication, social interaction, social imagination and flexibility, sensory processing, emotional understanding and self-awareness, learning, and independence and community participation.

A key feature of the AET Progression Framework is a focus on the individual child or young person and the facility to set specific priorities and evaluate progress based on individual learning needs. A key aim of the AET Progression Framework is to provide a starting point for identifying individual priorities in consultation with key people, including parents and the children and young people themselves. This highlights that rather than focusing solely on outcomes, staff should actively involve autistic children and young people as part of the 'Assess, Plan, Review and Do' cycle to improve understanding of the learning experience from their perspective. This process will be enhanced through engagement with parents, caregivers and other services such as Speech and Language Therapy, the Autism Advisory Team and Educational Psychology.

Principle Eight: Adapting the curriculum, teaching and learning to promote wellbeing and success

In England, the Department for Education provides statutory requirements for the curriculum delivered in School and Early Years settings, and non-statutory guidance for providers of 16–19 education. The guidance recommends providing a balanced and broadly based curriculum that should promote the spiritual, moral, cultural, mental and physical development of all children and young people. This recognises the need to promote teaching and learning that gives children and young people the full range of knowledge and skills that provide the right foundation for good future progress through education and prepares them for the opportunities, responsibilities and experiences of later life.

The way in which autistic children and young people are understood by others has implications for the approaches taken in Early Years, School and Post-16 settings. The performance and actions of an individual child or young person depend very much on the context, in addition to their profile of skills and understanding. The type of environments created for typically developing individuals are often very difficult for autistic children and young people to operate within. Without knowledge of this fact, and of autism generally, teaching staff and others can unwittingly create serious problems for autistic children and young people.

It is undoubtedly the case that many autistic children and young people can achieve academic success, but without addressing wider developmental needs, their participation in broader community life, further or higher education, or in employment, can be compromised. Currently there is a strong emphasis on academic attainment as a measure of a school's effectiveness, yet the research evidence indicates that in order to meet their potential academically, autistic children and young people need a focus on communicative competence, social understanding, physical and emotional wellbeing and independence skills (Parsons et al., 2011).

Settings need to provide a flexible curriculum that promotes social inclusion and wellbeing, and that prepares autistic children and young people for transitions between educational stages and into further education or the workplace. This should ensure that all learning environments and teaching methods are adapted to enable learners on the autism spectrum to participate and succeed in both academic and non-academic areas. The concept of 'autism friendliness' is often used, and this concept is about moving away from trying to change the person to changing environments and interventions to make them more supportive. Being 'autism friendly' therefore suggests adaptations to contexts, activities and resources that enable autistic children and young people to access learning. This includes modification of the physical, sensory, social and communication environment.

A national survey and follow-up interviews undertaken with a wide variety of stakeholders in Australia, focused on the educational needs of students on the autism spectrum aged 5–18, highlighted the needs of school-age children that would influence their learning (Saggers, 2015). Stakeholders identified the importance of focusing on the social and emotional needs of autistic children and young people and emphasised the critical role of this in developing motivation, connection and engagement. Other factors identified by the survey were executive functioning and attention to task, managing anxiety, comprehending what was required and change and transition. In a different set of guidelines, a particular issue for secondary students has been transition support within the school environment and planned transition for adult life and community activities (Ministries of Health and Education, 2016).

Making reasonable adjustments for children and young people on the autism spectrum includes providing clearly organised environments. Structure is therefore important and this includes organisation of time, space and sequences of events so that the child or young person can be supported to understand learning activities better (Mesibov & Shea, 2011). A structured learning environment also involves the organisation of the physical and sensory environment. This is important because change can be difficult for autistic children and young people, and difficulties with social understanding can make it hard for autistic children to understand many aspects of the context they are in.

Structure can enable the child or young person to navigate the context more easily. Adjusting the timetable, where the child or young person sits in class, how and when they do their homework, and facilitating their inclusion with peers in a way that respects their preferences, as well as reducing social demands, are some of the ways in which children and young people can be helped to feel comfortable in an educational setting (O'Brien, 2018).

There is much evidence to indicate that structured learning can improve communication skills, independent functioning and self-help skills. This is particularly so when visual support is provided. Many autistic children and young people are visual thinkers and will benefit from augmentative visual support. This can include using written information, symbols and objects of reference to communicate transition between activities, what happens when during the day, and to provide sequences of instructions. Visual methods can be very helpful for children and young people on the autism spectrum, regardless of their level of language. This is because most autistic children and young people will have difficulty ordering and organising information.

Many will also have difficulties in making sense of verbal information. Visual structure can remove the reliance on verbal input and can reduce the cognitive demands on the person, as sensory, social and cognitive demands can be overwhelming. Visual strategies include use of a variety of cues and supports, including tactile, visual and auditory, to help children with autism understand and navigate the learning environment. Guidance on elements to consider when designing a school or classroom (McAllister & Maguire, 2012) includes proper placement of the visual timetable, reducing visual distraction and controlling lighting, as well as using a space to create a sense of calm.

Schools, colleges and Early Years settings have an important role in promoting positive wellbeing and good mental health for all children and young people (NCB, 2017). The Green Paper *Transforming Children and Young People's Mental Health Provision* (DoH/DfE, 2017) details ambitious, transformational proposals to provide earlier support for children and young people's mental health, working closely with schools and colleges. This indicates the importance of staff needing to work with children and young people, their families and other services to identify triggers for anxiety and stress. This will involve observing and assessing potential sensory challenges, and considering how to address these. Adaptation of learning environments will therefore need to take into account the potential sensory processing difficulties as well as social demands of working with or being with other pupils.

Children and young people on the autism spectrum will need support with how to identify, understand and regulate their emotional state. This highlights the importance of establishing a safe and stimulating environment based on mutual respect. It also means that settings will need to have systems to identify, monitor, build and maintain the mental and emotional wellbeing of children and young people on the autism spectrum. This can include programmes of social and emotional learning that have the potential to help children and young people acquire the skills they need to have good mental health and wellbeing, as well as benefitting their academic progress. Targeted learning opportunities should focus on emotional understanding and regulation across all ages. This will include setting aside time to develop and promote social and emotional skills through dedicated relationships and sex education; personal, social, health and economic education (PSHE), as well as the wider curriculum.

A UK survey showed that autistic adults were more sexually naive than non-autistic adults, possibly as a result of reduced social networks. They were therefore more likely to be exposed to sexual victimisation and abuse (Brown-Lavoie et al., 2014). Children, young people and parents can benefit significantly from programmes designed to improve knowledge on sex and relationships, and these should be proactive rather than reactive (Corona et al., 2016). There is no empirical evidence in support of a particular curriculum for sex education, and practitioners are typically using training programmes or their own knowledge to deliver this education. In addition, there remains little guidance on how to adapt existing sex education curricula to make it more accessible and relevant to autistic children and young people. There is a growing literature on the issues involved in sex and relationships written by autistic individuals (Lawson, 2005; Hendrickx, 2008) and by those who have led groups for autistic young people (Henault, 2005).

ICT (Information and Communication Technology) can be a powerful tool for communication and leisure for autistic children and young people, and for enhancing their learning experience. In recent years, there has been a significant increase in the amount of autism technology research (Grynszpan et al., 2014). Findings indicate that autistic people enjoy and may have a particular affinity with technology (Putnam & Chong, 2008; Wei et al., 2013). This can be seen in the adoption of technology tools in educational settings (Putnam & Chong, 2008).

There are of course a number of different technologies that are being used. These range from virtual reality to robotics and wearable devices. They include mobile technologies and applications. Positive findings have included that technologies can support beneficial outcomes on a number of areas of development, including social cognition, communication, planning and emotional health.

Autistic children and young people have been found to show a preference for using non-social media (such as video games or television) over social media (Mazurek et al., 2012). The preference shown by autistic children for using non-social media could be related to an increased risk of cyber-bullying (Kowalski et al., 2011) and, as with all people who may be more vulnerable to the risks of engaging online, additional support may be needed. Guidance on this issue has been developed by the UK charity Cerebra (Archer, 2012). On the negative side, excessive playing of video games is reported as a problem by parents (Mazurek et al., 2012) and may impact on the quality of their child's sleep (Engelhardt et al., 2013).

Summary

The eight principles are designed to give those working with autistic children and young people in Early Years, School and Post-16 settings the opportunity to develop their understanding of autism and to make adjustments in their current settings to the teaching as well as the physical, sensory and social environments. This means adapting what they offer and how autistic children and young people are supported. The principles give an overview and a framework for guiding practitioners to decide how they might move forward. As stated in the introductory chapter, more detailed guidance and resources can be found in the frameworks, and the manifold resources and tools that are available through the Autism Education Trust website (www.autismeducationtrust.org.uk). By implementing the principles and identifying the development needs of settings and individual practitioners, it is hoped that the principles can provide a framework for enabling autistic children and young people to succeed.

Recommended reading

Guldberg, K., Bradley, R., Wittemeyer, K., Briscombe, J., Phillips, C., & Jones, G. (2019) *Good autism practice report*. London: Autism Education Trust.

Readers are recommended to download the free materials available on the AET website: www.autismeducationtrust.org.uk. These offer useful materials and guidance and come with a range of practical resources, which can be adapted to different contexts and countries. For this chapter, the following are particularly recommended:

- The Parent Guide

- The Progression Framework

- The Local Authority Guide

Professional development

Key question

How can Continuous Professional Development (CPD) lead to real change in the classroom and be transformative?

Introduction

Many reports have recognised the importance of high-quality professional development in the education of autistic children and young people. Furthermore, as knowledge of autism is constantly being developed, there is a need for professional development to regularly update the knowledge, skills and practice of the educational workforce as a whole, and not just for new staff.

Unfortunately, the experience of many teachers is that the provision of professional development intended to improve teaching and learning is often inconsistent in quality. Effective professional development needs to be strategically planned and implemented, focus on Evidence-Informed teaching practice and it needs to properly evaluate its impact. The discipline of creating quality professional development requires careful thought and planning (DfE, 2016a) to be meaningful.

This chapter explains the Autism Education Trust (AET) professional development programme because that programme shows the possibilities of changing ways of thinking and the practice of practitioners through collaboration and partnership. The chapter provides an introduction to the AET before explaining the pedagogy of the programme, its collaborative nature, the underpinning content and finally the changes to understandings and practice that have been brought about as a result of the programme.

The Autism Education Trust programme

The AET was launched in November 2007 with support and funding from the Department for Education, England. It is a unique partnership working specifically on autism education across the voluntary, public and private sectors. It was founded by Ambitious about Autism, the Council for Disabled Children and the National Autistic Society. The AET is dedicated to co-ordinating, supporting and promoting effective education practice for all children and young people on the autism spectrum.

The AET received funding from the Department for Education in 2011 to develop three tiers of training materials, a set of National Standards and a Competency Framework for primary and secondary schools in England based on the findings and recommendations from their three commissioned reports on the state of autism education (Jones et al., 2008), good practice in autism education (Charman et al., 2011) and good outcomes for children and young people with autism (Wittemeyer et al., 2011). Since then, the Department has continued funding the programme bi-annually.

The conceptual framework, distinctive pedagogy and empirical research outlined in this book underpins the AET's Continuing Professional Development (CPD) programme, which was co-created between members of the Autism Centre for Education and Research (ACER) and the AET partnership. This is now known as the 'AET programme' and will be referred to as such. In 2011, researchers in ACER were commissioned to develop each strand of the AET programme, which consists of a set of Autism Standards (for educational settings to assess autism practice in education against a recognised set of principles which are evidence-informed); an Autism Competency Framework (guidance on the knowledge, skills and competencies needed by practitioners) and autism professional development for educators.

The AET professional Competency Framework sets out the key understandings and knowledge required by staff working with children and young people on the autism spectrum. Staff can use this to audit the skills they feel they have and to identify any gaps. It has resources online that illustrate how staff can provide evidence for competencies and is designed for staff appraisal in a positive way, acknowledging strengths and areas for development. The AET Standards enable whole-school development through establishing the key factors common to good practice for pupils with autism. The modular part of the professional development programme includes modules for Early Years, School and Post-16 staff. Module 1 is entitled 'making sense of autism' (general awareness); Module 2 is 'good autism practice' (for staff working with children and young people with autism on a daily basis), and Module 3 is 'leading good autism practice' (for specialists such as Special Educational Needs Coordinators).

The three components of the professional development (modules and materials, the Competency Framework and National Standards) are all closely interlinked with one another (see Figure 11.1). In Module 2 of the training, for example, practitioners engage in practical activities linking what they have learnt with their continuing development needs by highlighting two or three competencies that they wish to work on as they go back to their practice. In Module 3, which focuses upon those in leadership positions, the training links practitioners in a practical

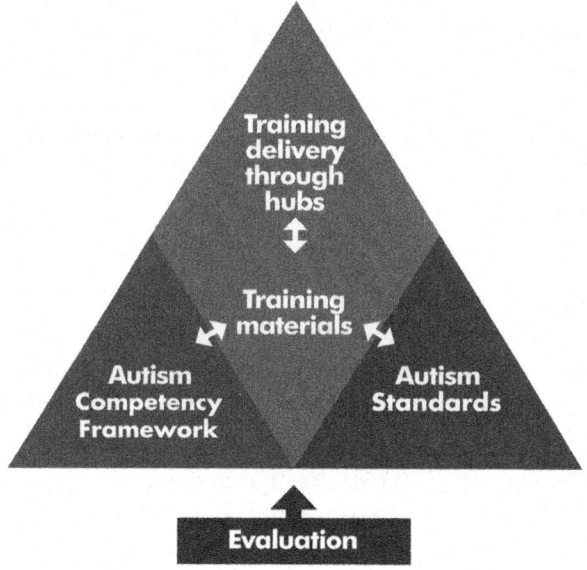

Figure 11.1 The components of the AET training programme

way with the National Standards in order to enable settings to identify their development needs.

The Birmingham Local Authority team highlight the strength of this integrated module and that the uniqueness of the professional development programme lies:

> in the way that the training, National Standards and Professional Competencies provide a package, with the combination of those providing a consensus on what an enabling environment is for pupils with autism, informs schools how to create a safe and secure environment and identifies the social and emotional needs of pupils with autism and how these should be addressed.
>
> (Simpson et al., 2015: 28)

This integration between the three different components (the three modules of training, the Competency Framework and the National Standards) ensures that the professional development goes beyond giving practitioners new knowledge, tools and strategies to think about, and enables them to follow through their learning into practice. It situates the learning within the practitioners' current practice and considers how the practitioners can be actively engaged in developing and embedding good practice themselves.

The National Standards can also be used to evidence good practice against other professional and educational values such as the Ofsted Common Inspection Framework: Education, Skills and Early Years (Ofsted, 2019), and the Professional Standards for Teachers and Trainers in Education and Training – England (DfE, 2014).

Pedagogy

As the AET programme aimed to arrive at real change in education, it was informed by the theoretical orientation of seeing autism as a transactional condition that requires mutual adaptation on behalf of the person with autism *and* those who live or work with that person (Jordan, 2005; Prizant, 2015). As a consequence, materials engage practitioners in thinking about what they can do to change their own practice. Therefore, rather than viewing autism as an impairment, with the difficulties being located within the pupil (Hughes,

2000), materials encourage practitioners to reflect on the dynamic relationship between the person with autism and those around them. The materials and activities aim to support practitioners to become more adept at observing and learning through reflection on their own practice, as well as on the practice of others (Schon, 1987). The everyday experiential knowledge of practitioners provides a focal point for learning, promoting reflection, processing, thinking and understanding (Kolb, 1984).

The content moves educators from a focus on disability to a conception of difference, away from language which presents autism as a deficit towards a language in which autism is presented as a different way of being. Rather than overly focus on the difficulties and problems presented by pupils with autism, the materials encourage educators to look at the strengths of people with autism. Equally, rather than research dominating thinking about what is considered 'good autism practice', the voice of autistic people and practitioners is included in the materials, with the perspective and experiences of autistic people embedded in all aspects of the professional development.

Materials support practitioners to develop knowledge of the individual, to try to see the world from the perspective of the person on the spectrum, to develop their abilities to be reflective, to observe and to change their practice accordingly. Rather than provide practitioners with a set of models or interventions, the focus is on developing professionals as autonomous and strong professionals who can problem-solve and make decisions.

Learning is seen as 'expanding involvement' with a system over time, both in a social and intellectual way (Russell, 2001). This represents a broadly sociocultural approach to learning (Vygotsky, 1978; Engeström, 1987) rooted in social theories of learning (Lave & Wenger, 1991; Wenger, 1998) that focus on participation in community life as a basis for learning and identity construction (Lave & Wenger, 1991). Language and culture are seen as social products rather than as products of the individual mind, with learning being mediated by tools such as language and physical artefacts. This theoretical approach sees knowledge as at its strongest when it develops dynamically in relation to people, experiences and objects (Biesta, 2013).

The AET programme promotes a strengths-based approach to differentiation. It enables staff to think more flexibly about the need for a distinctive curriculum for children and young people on the autism spectrum and to take account of social, emotional, sensory, physical and communication needs. This stands in contrast to a focus on discrete skills or particular models of intervention, which is often the bedrock of many professional development programmes.

The materials therefore give participants the opportunity to learn through discussion and role play, to discuss strategies with others, and to then take this back into their settings. They can also tie the professional development they have received with the AET professional Competency Framework, so that they can use this to identify their own development needs. The AET National Standards help practitioners examine the broader action plans for their settings.

The professional development is research-informed, but rather than promote particular interventions and examine the evidence base for those, it draws upon a much wider evidence base than is normally conceived in current discussions around 'Evidence-Based Practice'. This broader evidence comes from the autistic community itself, from parents and families and from practitioners and policy makers as well as from experimental studies.

Bringing different elements of the community together

The model of delivery for the AET programme has been central to it success. The AET partnership gathered a community of researchers and practitioners to meet common aims. The work represents a successful collaboration between universities, voluntary, statutory and private-sector organisations, with all partners having different roles within the partnership. Dr. Steve Huggett, former Director of AET, stated (personal communication, Autism Education Trust National Conference, 2015):

> This interactive relationship between the AET and its stakeholders drives the organic growth of the AET's products and outputs, which is a key feature of the AET model. Feedback from users of the AET offer drives revision and improvement of the training and materials with the schools training materials having already benefitted from an interim revision. Feedback from professionals, families and people with autism themselves also drives the programme

into new areas of work. The 2013–15 expansion into the Early Years and the Post 16 sectors was first requested by AET users and partners. Recently published AET guidance for parents on schools was both instigated and developed by parents themselves.

The collaborative model has enabled the AET programme to become the largest professional development programme on autism in England for education-based staff. Whereas professional development in the field was previously piecemeal and localised, this is now a national programme in which training providers (called 'hubs') work together to deliver it. Hubs consist of a range of organisations, including local authorities, the voluntary sector and schools.

The collaborative model has also been crucial to the long-term success of the programme as it has been significant in shaping the flexibility of the materials to be used by the hubs in a range of educational settings (mainstream, special and specialist) and with a wide range of school-based professionals across England. The researchers at the Autism Centre for Education and Research (ACER) led the initial development of the materials, for example, whilst the AET appointed regional hubs to deliver it, with the training hubs being involved in the development of the materials from the outset. This meant that those delivering the professional development had a strong sense of ownership of the materials, and contributed feedback on the content that was developed. They also shared and adapted their own resources for use on the programme. This in turn helped ensure that the materials connected with the participants undertaking the training.

When the AET programme was launched, seven hubs were involved in delivering training between 2011 and 2013. In 2019, 73 out of a total of 150 local authorities (LAs) across each of the nine regions of England were involved in the AET programme. The professional development is therefore reaching approximately 50% of the 24,281 schools in England. Case studies of four of the LAs that deliver the programme found that over 85% of schools are involved in the programme in those LAs and it constitutes part of the Local Offer in each of those LAs. The programme has been delivered to over 240,000 people in over 100 LAs in England to date. It has been extended to other sectors, with a Parent Guide, an Early Years and a Post-16 programme having been launched, as well as the development of special modules for children with significant learning difficulties. With evaluation built into the professional development from the start, it has robust quality assurance procedures.

The AET partnership shows the value in generating a 'learning partnership among people who find it useful to learn from and with each other about a particular domain' (Wenger et al., 2011: 2). This approach to creating professional development has cohered practitioners round a set of values that build on their current knowledge and practice in a way that connects them with others, whilst also challenging them. The partnership illustrates a community in which mutual engagement improves the skills, knowledge and competencies of educational practitioners.

The programme has supported the development of a strategic and collaborative approach that enables a whole-school response to meeting the needs of children and young people with autism. As stated by Pam Simpson, AET Lead in Birmingham City Council: 'we now have a structured and consistent response, based on research principles and aligned to key legislation, supported by the DFE' (Simpson, 2017: 15). As a result of using the AET programme to improve workforce planning and professional development for school staff, LA training providers state that it has led to a shift in the culture of those LAs and that the greatest strength of the AET programme is that it gives a different perspective on autism. A trainer stated that it has 'changed the way we conduct training for staff. We now focus on the differences and strengths of pupils with autism rather than their deficits'. Case studies of four local authorities found that those in leadership positions in schools are now better informed by evidence, more able to address the professional development needs of staff, have a framework for auditing existing practice, as well as providing a good local offer for pupils with autism. This has in turn been highly effective in raising the capacity of schools to meet the needs of children and young people on the autism spectrum.

Outcomes

The AET programme has led to new conceptualisations of how to effectively teach pupils with autism, and staff members feel more confident in their abilities, with the knowledge to make reasonable adjustments

(Cullen et al., 2013, Cullen, 2016). Results of pre and post questionnaires to participants in the professional development (n=21,867) found that Module 1 participants reported enhanced understanding of autism, more inclusive attitudes towards pupils with autism, greater confidence about working with pupils with autism, and the training stimulated whole-school developments to enhance the educational experience of pupils with autism (Cullen et al., 2013).

The Cullen et al. (2013) evaluation found that Module 2 participants reported significantly increased confidence about having the know-ledge, understanding and skills to support the education of pupils with autism compared to before the training. They tailored their interaction with pupils with autism to reduce anxiety and stress, and improved their teaching approaches for pupils with autism. They improved the learning environment and the communication across the school about the needs of pupils with autism. Module 3 participants reported sig-nificantly increased confidence about having the knowledge, skills and understanding needed to improve the education of pupils with autism through enhanced practice in their school or setting compared to before the training. They used what had been learnt to support colleagues working with pupils with autism, sought the views of parents of pupils with autism and used pupil profiles to identify strengths and challenges for pupils with autism.

This has in turn led to the uptake of new teaching approaches, from Early Years to Post-16. One participant, for example, reported:

> The child now uses the visual systems I developed for him every day in the classroom. As a result, he is more successful, he doesn't argue as he used to, he collaborates with the teacher and peers, he listens to instructions and he has reduced his meltdowns.
>
> (Guldberg et al., 2019b)

Staff in four hubs stated that the framework of the AET programme has enabled them to develop their knowledge and skills to deliver universal, targeted and specialist support within their settings, thereby meeting the needs of all children (Guldberg et al., 2019a). Staff, including head teachers and senior leadership, have adopted more inclusive attitudes towards autistic children and young people and have implemented whole-school developments. As a result of improved knowledge and understanding, educators now construct assessments that accurately reflect the child's strengths and needs, obtain the views of children and young people and use these to make reasonable adjustments in schools (Cullen et al., 2013; Cullen, 2016).

The uptake of new teaching methods has resulted in positive and lasting changes to daily practice in the classroom, enhanced the educational experiences of autistic pupils and increased their opportunities to succeed (Cullen, 2016; Guldberg et al., 2019b). Work with five case-study schools, for example, provided detailed accounts of day-to-day support for children and young people in three different types of school setting. In one school, the Lead Practitioner noted that the first module, undertaken by all the teaching and Teaching Assistant (TA) staff, had established a baseline of knowledge across the school and had enabled planning for change at school level:

> so, we've looked at how we can change the environment, how we can change the curriculum, and how we can monitor that. This resulted in a planning framework for continued improvements to autism provision in the school.
>
> (Cullen, 2016: 43–44)

International implications: case studies from Greece and Italy

The experience and lessons learnt via the AET programme have been applied to the creation and delivery of professional development programmes in Greece and Italy. 'Transform Autism Education' was a European Union (EU) funded project that built on the underlying pedagogy, values and approach of the AET programme. It adapted this programme to the contexts of Greece and Italy by firstly gaining new understandings of the 'state of the art' in autism practice and then using this research as a basis for informing the design of professional development programmes for school staff in Greece and Italy.

The partners involved in this development consisted of two universities, a non-profit organisation, and a school district, with researchers and practitioners learning from one another through a collaborative partnership. The aims of the project were to share educational practices in the professional development of teachers who work with children with

autism aged between five and ten; adapt the AET professional development programme to create ecologically valid materials for these educational contexts and standards of practice; develop the skills, knowledge
and understanding of educational professionals in each country; create
a framework for international collaboration and a method of delivery
that could be applied to other countries to research and develop their
own educational practice in autism, as well as to create a website with
Open Educational Resources to support the education of pupils with
autism internationally.

The research, and the subsequent professional development programme, was translated, adapted and delivered in Greece to 110 schools,
and to 200 staff in Italy (Guldberg, 2016; Guldberg et al., 2017b). The
Greek Ministry of Education endorsed the provision of the translated
and adapted professional development programme throughout Piraeus
and Athens. Case studies of two schools in Greece and Italy undertaken
two years after the professional development took place highlighted
that teachers continued to take account of the distinctive learning
needs of autistic pupils, they implemented appropriate communication
strategies with those pupils, and adapted the classroom environments
to make these more enabling (Guldberg et al., 2019b).

The Transform Autism Education (TAE) project challenged medical
conceptions of autism in those countries and generated debate about
the consequences of viewing autism as a different way of being rather
than a disorder. As stated by a Greek participant:

> It changed the way I understood autism, the way I understood
> intervention, and it changed my expectations of people with
> autism – not less but different. The approach was very different
> from the Greek medical model of understanding autism. I felt very
> excited thinking that autism needn't be considered a tragedy (as it
> commonly is perceived in Greece).
>
> (Guldberg et al., 2019b)

Drawing on the experience of people with autism in the video and audio
content of the materials was central to the participants' understanding
of autism. This was further enhanced by the use of activities in the professional development that showed what it might be like for a child or
young person with autism in school:

I think that it's about making sense of what we are calling the autism lens that actually is key to making that training effective. You can do training and training and training but it's about seeing it from the child's perspective, isn't it? And that's a real key focus.

(Guldberg et al., 2017b: 251)

Engagement with autistic people led participants to gain insight and develop deeper understandings of autism as well as how to work with autistic people. Participant satisfaction surveys found that practitioners understood the needs of autistic pupils better and enhanced their adaptations of the environment. Their changed practices led to improved outcomes for pupils (Guldberg et al., 2017b).

Summary

This chapter has outlined the importance of considering underpinning pedagogy and values when creating and delivering professional development that aims to support practitioners to understand the learning needs of autistic pupils, to increase their knowledge of the curriculum, and to support them to develop strategies (Norwich & Lewis, 2007). The design of the AET professional development programme was firmly rooted in notions of 'good autism practice' in education. It emphasised the importance of focusing the lens on the individual child, young person or adult, rather than the 'model' or 'intervention' (Guldberg, 2010; Wittemeyer et al., 2011). It was based on the premise that the inclusion of any child needs to start with understanding the nature of autism as well as understanding the individual child (Jordan, 1999; Guldberg et al., 2011).

Through the pedagogy of the programme, practitioners are encouraged to consider teaching strategies within the context of individual needs and aspirations, enabling a person to make choices and giving them access to the right support when needed (Wittemeyer et al., 2011). Practitioners are also encouraged to focus on the nature of the environment they provide (Jordan, 1999; Guldberg, 2010) with schools needing to be welcoming places that work to develop community participation of all the students (Thomas 2012). Milton (2014b) has emphasised the importance of this when advocating that care must be taken to ensure that structures are put in place to encourage the learner's autonomy and reduce their stress.

The work of this project shows how powerful collaborative communities and community-based projects can be. Collaboration between individuals with autism, practitioners and researchers enables knowledge co-creation, a process that brings together a plurality of knowledge sources and types to address a defined issue (Kazdin, 2008). This can in turn enable change in practice at local, national and international levels (Macdonald, 2002). The Transform Autism Education (TAE) project is an example of how the lessons learnt from the AET programme can be useful to other sectors or countries, for example.

The mixed constituencies involved in the development of the AET programme have required the community to think about what was happening both at the intersection of people's practices and in moving across them. Lave and Wenger (1991) identify this as a place in which a great deal of learning can take place. This collaborative approach has been essential in the process of enabling inclusion and improved outcomes for individuals with autism in England.

Recommended reading

Readers are recommended to download the free materials available on the AET website: www.autismeducationtrust.org.uk. These offer useful materials and guidance and come with a range of practical resources. These can be adapted to different contexts and countries. For this chapter, the following are particularly recommended:

■ The AET National Standards

■ The AET Professional Competencies

The scholarly practitioner

Key question

How do we create educational practices that are grounded in both research and practice?

Introduction

This chapter looks at the ways in which both research and practice need to change to meet the ultimate goal of aiding educators in their understanding and support for individuals. As outlined in Chapter 6, there tends to be a one-way relationship between research and practice in autism education, with practitioners being given a secondary role as appliers rather than contributors to knowledge. Practice-based evidence is not valued as highly as research-based evidence and has been downplayed by the scientific community. The chapter on Evidence-Informed Practice highlighted that expanded forms of evidence to include practice-based evidence are needed and that models of practice-related evidence and rules for evaluating practice-based evidence need to be articulated.

In the autism field, participatory and inclusive research is still in its infancy, with studies dominated by experimental research designs, but the autistic community itself has campaigned strongly for 'nothing about us without us'. Thankfully, recent inclusive research scholarship has focused on frameworks, strategies and technologies to support the active participation in research of people with intellectual disabilities (Morgan et al., 2015).

In fact, in the area of Special Educational Needs and Disabilities (SEND), inclusive research with people with learning disabilities has developed rapidly in recent years. As argued by Walmsley, this genre of research is an extension of emancipatory and participatory research and supports democratic processes (Walmsley, 2010). The characteristics of inclusive research in learning disability are that disabled people own the research problem, the research should be in their interests, they are involved in the conduct of the research, they control the research to some extent and the research is accessible to them (Walmsley, 2004). It is conducted to further their interests and it should lead to improved lives for them (Nind, 2014).

The question posed is therefore how, not if, people with intellectual disabilities can be active participants in research production. The basic premise is that research on inclusion is meaningful only when embedded in understandings of community and society. Essentially, in such projects, school and community need to be seen as equal partners in establishing communities of learning and practice, with action that encourages cooperation, sharing and debate and focuses on the development of deep, lasting and collaborative partnerships aimed at addressing real-world problems (Harkavy & Hartley, 2009). Collaboration and dialogue are considered to be fundamental features of research that recognises the culturally specific and situated nature of knowledge and, therefore, creation of evidence (Houston et al., 2010).

Community-engaged scholarship and research

Phillips (1993) warned a long time ago that as long as science is narrowly defined, researchers will:

> tend to confine themselves to a limited class of problems, using research approaches that are not well suited to the examination of actual practice problems and the uncertain contexts of practice.
>
> (Phillips, 1993: 29)

Given that advances in educational equity require the dedicated collaboration of researchers, educators and community members, the civic responsibility of universities has garnered increased attention in educational scholarship in recent years. This requires community-engaged scholarship, which represents an alternative to the dominant academic paradigm in which scholars define research agendas and produce research without directly engaging practitioners (Peters, 2010; Warren et al., 2016). Community-engaged scholarship is defined by its explicit attention to community and to promoting equity in education.

It involves working with community partners and researchers to design the research, in order to produce findings directly relevant to advancing social change agendas. It includes addressing community needs and ensuring that communities provide a real-world context for research and practice (Campano et al., 2015). It involves researching alongside rather than on. It values the forms of knowledge based on lived experience and understanding. It accommodates differences in cultures, and it requires consensus in decision-making.

Community-engaged scholarship is about the interrelationship between research and practice and it challenges assumptions that expertise is located solely within university contexts (Campano et al., 2015). It entails expanding the methods that are used in both practice and research. It highlights the need to respect and value the processes and knowledge gained through practical activities, and to draw upon knowledge from multiple sources.

Warren et al. (2016), for example, describe a project in which doctoral students were engaged in a community-engaged scholarship project. The project arose out of a recognised need for graduate students to see community engagement as a way of being a scholar as graduate students across the social sciences expressed a desire to do work that connected their passions with the needs of society (Austin & McDaniels, 2006).

The study demonstrated the value of moving beyond drawing on research evidence to grasping the power of a collective approach to learning. They found that communities can be collective vehicles for forging new identities. The specific skills the students developed were to be able to articulate their values and tell their stories of self; build horizontal and collaborative relationships; and to interrogate researcher positionality by embracing their own diversity and identity as a community-engaged scholar. Learning to conduct research with, rather than on, communities led to greater equality and mutual respect.

Flowing from this, Thomas (2012) argues that it is contextual, case-based research that researchers should be focusing on. He argues that the landscape of inquiry does not exist at the level of the big 'what works' questions but at the level of personalised questions posed locally. This is because practitioner work happens within institutional settings that provide continual challenges that research knowledge can guide only at a very general level. When a practitioner works with a child or an adult, their learning is situated within the context of sharing practical experiences of working in a particular domain (Wenger, 1998), with identities dependent on the discourses and practices within the contexts of teaching and working with autistic children and young people.

This acknowledges that the knowledge of practitioners is rooted in immersion and reflection, resulting in cumulative knowledge arising from an accumulation of understandings (Thomas, 2012), and that it is often practical and tacit, based upon personal experience and learning from the experience of others (Wenger, 1998). It exists in the dynamic of teachers' work, in everyday judgements. Practical knowledge, the everyday practice of teachers' work, and therefore inquiry about that knowledge, needs to take into account that practices will vary, and they will change over time. So, Thomas (2012) sees knowledge gained as part of practice as tentative and provisional. It will be constantly developing and will need to be repeatedly reviewed. It therefore requires flexibility. It is characterised by revision and informal experiment, by the flexibility and changeability that are the hallmarks of local practice.

It is essential that the personal and tacit knowledge that educators possess should be taken into account when we think about the knowledge that matters in education. The knowledge gained about what works, therefore, has an important predicate. It is 'what works for me'. So we should accept rather than deny insights that emerge from learning, including our knowledge of failure, acceptance and success. And we should accept that there are no startling insights or magic fixes.

Most traditional research methods, on the other hand, attempt to control or isolate what are considered confounding factors, such as background characteristics of children and young people, in order to judge efficacy of treatment. They can therefore draw conclusions about what works in the research context. They cannot, however, dictate the choices that might be made in someone's life situation because the practitioner has to accommodate, not control, a variety of factors, as well as account for contextual and setting differences, individual differences and cultural variation.

It is not that research is not useful or important, nor that research is too complex or confusing. Most of us would probably agree that the idiosyncrasies of particular children and their difficulties mean that they are not likely to be amenable to a simple application of a manualised treatment. However, this should not become an excuse to rely primarily on practical judgement or authoritative prescriptions. Relevant research findings and careful evaluation of outcomes should still be emphasised. In autism studies, for example, many children and young people have been responsive to specific approaches (Parsons et al., 2011; Bond et al., 2016). In addition, there is some evidence for the efficacy of a range of interventions for specific types of problems for both children and adults (Reichow et al., 2008).

Ignoring this research in favour of only relying on professional experience is risky and also unethical. It is unethical because research and practice knowledge together can provide a more complete understanding and basis for action, and both can contribute to improving quality of life for autistic people. In fact, all sources of evidence have the potential to contribute to the understanding of phenomena, so the conjoining and interconnection of teaching and research is crucial.

Without this interconnection, there will continue to be a gulf between research and practitioner communities. The press for the disseminative, top-down, model of educational inquiry can distance inquiry from the work itself. It uncouples research, inquiry and scholarship from the practice of the teacher (Thomas & Loxley, 2007). Relevant and rigorous research can indeed inform practice. But it needs to start with the formulation of what the problems in educational life are that we should be studying. It needs to be focused on what research questions are applicable to practice.

In this respect, 'citizen science' can be of value to the scientific community. Citizen science is the involvement of the public in scientific research. It offers the opportunity for the public to get involved in collecting, sharing and acting on data they care about. It is a tool for global scientific empowerment, education and action. Citizen science projects vary in themes, scale and types of activity. They can be initiated or led by researchers or government institutions. The idea is that the information and data that is analysed should be relevant to local conditions and institutions. It should educate and engage the public, and enrich people and communities.

What is needed in such projects is the ultimate marriage of scholarship and practice. Both research and practice have in common that they require data gathering, hypothesis testing, control of variables and outcome evaluation. Bringing the practical and theoretical together with a data-driven and science-based approach, whilst focusing on research that matters and that has a connection with the real world requires a balance between the two.

The scholar-practitioner

This brings the discussion on to what this means for practitioners and how they might need to change their orientation. Reid and Valle (2004) make insightful points about the ways that such deliberative pedagogy may actually be built out of, and integrated with, personal, tacit knowledge. They argue that teachers need to approach their work as scholar-practitioners, and in so doing, sharpen the tools of critical inquiry.

Concepts of the scholar-practitioner have in part emerged from the scientist-practitioner model, also called the 'Boulder Model'. This is a training model for applied psychologists and was based on giving them a foundation in research and scientific practice. It was initially developed by the American Psychological Association (APA) in 1949 and focused on ensuring that graduate programmes engaged and developed the ability of psychologists to engage in psychological theory, fieldwork and a range of research methodologies. The scholar-practitioner model urged clinicians to allow empirical research to influence their applied practice, whilst also allowing their experiences during applied practice to shape their future research questions.

This model has been extended in different forms to education. McClintock (2003), for example, made three key points in defining the scholarly practitioner. These were that the work of the scholarly practitioner should be grounded in theory and research, in experiential knowledge, and be driven by personal values, commitment and ethical conduct. The scholar-practitioner model of Reid and Valle (2004) argues that teachers must approach their work as scholar-practitioners and that they need to pick up the tools of critical enquiry through a variety of means. They give the examples of observation, conferencing and taking and analysing field notes, among others (Reid & Valle, 2004).

Furthermore, the scholar-practitioner needs to be committed to well-being, to learning new ways of being effective, and to conceptualising their work in relation to broader organisational, community, political and cultural contexts.

Sorensen (2004) states:

> As a member of both cultures the practitioner–scholar is able to translate and create meaning between the two cultures. The scholar–practitioner has an appreciation of the norms, appropriate behavior and values embodied in both.
>
> (Sorensen, 2004: 160)

The acceptance of both cultures leads to someone becoming a scholar-practitioner. Scholar-practitioners conjoin the strategies and knowledge gained through meticulous academic endeavours with experiences and knowledge inherent to membership in their craft to form the basis of effective, change-centred practices. In fact, scholar-practitioners seek social change and view current educational practice through a 'critical lens' in an effort to quell the cultural politics 'associated with inequality, control, resistance, and identity' (Anderson, 1996: 6).

Throughout the process of developing an understanding of attributes that frame scholar-practitioner identity, there is recognition that this needs to embody the overarching qualities of compassion, caring and acceptance. Those qualities include a commitment to diversity. In addition to these guiding principles, the scholar-practitioner possesses a duty to look critically at educational systems and expose practices that facilitate the production or reproduction of oppressive societies.

What skills do scholar-practitioners need?

Planned interventions such as policies, programmes and projects need ways of capturing the social change processes arising from those interventions by 'analyzing, monitoring and managing the intended and unintended social consequences, both positive and negative, of planned "interventions"' (Vanclay, 2003: 6).

Theory is nevertheless important for the scholar-practitioner because it serves at least two purposes. First, it enables the community to interpret and learn from its experiences by situating those experiences in an organising schema that infuses them with meaning (Håkanson, 2007). In this way, shared theoretical assumptions create a common basis for the interpretation of practice among practitioners who might otherwise arrive at very different conclusions. Theory, in this context, can entail a scientifically validated set of causal relations but can also include a set of commonly held understandings, or 'rules of thumb', about the nature of practice.

This highlights the need to develop methodologies and methods that enable a focus on both what is meaningful *and* what is measurable (Hanney et al., 2007; Boaz et al., 2009;). It means challenging narrow conceptions of science that are rooted in a positivist philosophy. Both scientific thinking and competent practice rely on observation, inference, formulating and evaluating hypotheses, and selecting and evaluating interventions.

Training in scientific theory and method, in addition to empirical research, can prepare practitioners for the highest level of practice. The scholar-practitioner should therefore be supported, through professional development, to identify a problem, gather relevant data, formulate hypotheses, and test these hypotheses in a systematic manner. This means taking a scientific approach to evaluating effectiveness beyond promotional hype, or what appears to be the latest intervention that is celebrated in terms of 'what works'. Otherwise, practitioners risk becoming disciples of the most recent fad rather than systematically studying the learning and teaching process.

As a consequence, the aim should be to nurture flexible interpretative and emotional capacities in scholar-practitioners that support examination of tacit assumptions, exploration of cultural diversity, integration of varied intellectual perspectives and incorporation of unifying aspirations. The attributes needed are therefore to become innovators and problem-solvers, to be able to abstractly, efficiently and creatively interpret information from everyday work. Involvement in reflection and action fosters new awareness of the social reality and the transformation of such reality. It supports the scholar-practitioner to address what they should do in the here and now given the particular circumstances facing this particular child or young person at this time.

Towards communities of practice

Thomas and Loxley (2007) argue that the 21st century needs inclusive educators that reject the deficit-oriented history of exceptionality and who mesh instead with contemporary currents of thinking on the way children learn or fail to learn. They argue that there are two theories of learning that inclusive educators fail to engage with. The first is the model of learning that stresses the centrality of community and the second are models of learning that take on board the 'psychology of difference'. These shine the light on the strong connection between how students feel about themselves in communities, and how they learn. Thomas and Loxley (2007) argue that the focus now needs to be on communities of learning and how children and young people's identities are constructed as part of those.

Wenger's social learning theory proposes that participation in community life provides the basis for learning and identity construction (Wenger, 1998). This perspective also emphasises that learning is a social process and human beings are intrinsically social. People participate in different social experiences in various communities throughout their lives. This participation in communities leads to learning because it contributes to the construction of identity. Glazer and Peurach (2015) use the concept of an epistemic community to identify the mechanisms that unite practitioners into a community of practice extending beyond the borders of local work environments. Underlying this is a shared set of theory, codes and tools that govern interpretation and practice and, in their interaction, facilitate the continuous generation of knowledge.

In education, Reid and Valle (2004) urge us to 'focus on redesigning the context' of schooling rather than 'on "curing" or "remediating" individuals' impairments' (p. 468). They offer a 'sociopolitical vision of the classroom' (p. 474), which includes the notion that pedagogy should be student-centred, authentic and focused on strengths. They also focus on the need for classrooms to become communities of learners in which everyone works together. That community-building must be a conscious and evolutionary process which supports 'cooperative learning, differentiated instruction, and the formation of positive classroom relationships and talk' (p. 474). They also argue that teachers should intentionally create classrooms that 'engender a sense of safety and belonging, value for diversity, shared responsibility for the community and an overall atmosphere of support and caring' (p. 475).

How can we move forward?

Apparently, a teacher typically makes upwards of a thousand 'on-the-spot, evaluative decisions' on any given day (MacBeath, 2012: 17). This sums up the complexity and the skill involved in teaching. It also begs the question of how teachers make decisions about how effective different aspects of practice are. How do teachers know what is useful and what needs to be discarded when implementing interventions? These are all crucial questions because they get to the core of what the nature of learning is and how one draws conclusions as to whether the children and young people we teach are learning and developing, or whether they are failing to learn.

This book has put forward the case for framing understandings of autism in broad and holistic ways, drawing on a number of knowledge bases and evidence in a different way compared to current discussions about Evidence-Based Practice and the notion of 'what works'. It has put the case for being Evidence-Informed. The notion of being Evidence-Informed accepts that evidence exists in a number of forms. This includes findings that have emerged from research, drawing on data from the classroom and using this data to evaluate processes and impact. It includes drawing on the insights and experiences of autistic people, and listening to the voice of the child or young person.

It might seem that the shift from being Evidence-Based to being Evidence-Informed is a subtle one, but it is not. It represents two very different framings and mindsets. If teaching is Evidence-Informed, teachers are in the driving seat, rather than the evidence. The evidence should be there to help the teacher make judgements. The concept of Evidence-Based Practice, on the other hand, tends to make teachers follow rules and can curb a teacher's judgement.

Shifting from being Evidence-Based to being Evidence-Informed therefore re-instates the importance of teachers' agency. Bandura (2006: 164) states that being an agent means: 'to influence intentionally one's functioning and life circumstances'. In this context, agency is taken to mean the capacity to make choices, to impose those choices on the world, and to act on them in environments.

This book has stated the need to develop individual and collective agency to make a difference in autism practice. On an individual level, moving forward and embracing change means risking our own practice being challenged. It means being open, keen, exploring our learning and evaluating how best to support the learning, development, progress and achievement of the children and young people with whom we work. Engaging with the notion of thinking about how to make a difference is grounded in how we frame the way we understand autistic children and young people, the way we work with them and their families, and the way we see our own role in this. It entails being able to envision the possibility of making a difference.

Although the concept of 'making a difference' is often referred to as grand ideas and big changes in the world, it can be small and incremental too (Wenger-Trayner & Wenger-Trayner, in press). It can be about making a child's day better than it would have been without the teacher taking time to talk to them. It can relate to developing an excellent peer-mentoring programme that leads to an autistic child becoming more included with his classmates and in the community, or it can be a grand vision of creating a society that values diversity and embraces equality. The possibilities are many, and making a difference is often about making a difference through small everyday interactions in the classroom.

Bigger societal changes require a community response and need to be a joint endeavour. Educators, schools and communities need to be equal partners in learning by creating communities of learning and participation (Thomas & Loxley, 2007). Researchers, autistic people, families, school leaders and practitioners need to work together to move forward. Autistic children and young people need to be part of their communities, with those communities embracing difference. That is the big change we want to see. There may not be a clear path to get there but if you reach out, connect with others in your community and hold on to your aspirations to make a difference, you will make a difference.

References

Alexander, R.J. (2000) *Culture and pedagogy: International comparisons in primary education*. Oxford: Blackwell.

Alexander, R. (2004) *Towards dialogic teaching: Rethinking classroom talk*. Cambridge: Dialogos.

Alexander, R.J. (2009) *Towards a new primary curriculum: A report from the Cambridge primary review. Part 2: The future*. Cambridge: Cambridge University Faculty of Education.

All Party Parliamentary Group for Autism (APPGA) (2017) *Autism and education in England: A report by the All Party Parliamentary Group on autism on how the education system in England works for children and young people on the autism spectrum*. London: The National Autistic Society.

Allan, J. & Slee, R. (2008) *Doing inclusive education research* (Vol. 1). Rotterdam: Sense Publishers.

American Psychiatric Association (2013) *Diagnostic and statistical manual of mental disorders (DSM-5®)*. Washington, DC: American Psychiatric Publications.

American Psychological Association Presidential Task Force on Evidence Based Practice (2006) 'Evidence based practice in psychology', *American Psychologist*, 61: 271–285.

Anderson G.L. (1996) 'The cultural politics of schools: Implications for leadership', in Leithwood, K., Chapman, J., Corson, D., Hallinger, P., & Hart A. (eds) *International handbook of educational leadership and administration* (Vol. 1). Kluwer International Handbooks of Education. Dordrecht: Springer.

Anwaruddin, S.M. (2016) 'Language teachers' responses to educational research: Addressing the 'crisis' of representation', *International Journal of Research & Method in Education*, 39 (3): 314–328, doi:10.1080/1743727X.2016.1166485

ARACY (Australian Research Alliance for Children and Youth, 2013) *Inclusive education for students with disability: A review of best evidence in relation to theory and practice.* Available at: www.aracy.org.au/publicationsresources/command/download_file/id/246/filename/Inclusive_education_for_students_with_disability_-A_review_of_the_best_evidence_in_relation_to_theory_and_practice.pdf.

Archer, E. (2012) *Learning disabilities, autism and internet safety: A parent's guide.* Carmarthen: Cerebra.

Armitage, D.R., Berkes, F., Dale, A., Kocho-Schellenberg, E., & Patton, E. (2011). 'Co-management and the co-production of knowledge: Learning to adapt in Canada's Arctic', *Global Environmental Change,* 21: 995–1004.

Arnold, L. (2010) 'The medium is the message'. *Autism, Ethics and Society.* Conference, University College London.

Asperger, H. (1944) 'Die "Autistischen Psychopathen" im Kindesalter' (Autistic Psychopathy of Childhood). *Archivfür Psychiatrie und Nervenkrankheiten,* 117: 76–136.

Austin, A.E. & McDaniels, M. (2006) 'Preparing the professoriate of the future: Graduate student socialization for faculty roles', in Smart, J.C. (eds) *Higher education: Handbook of theory and research* (Vol 21). Dordrecht: Springer.

Autism Education Trust (2018) *A guide to help governing boards comply with Equality Law when considering a headteacher's decision to exclude an autistic pupil.* London: Autism Education Trust.

Autism Focused Interventions Resources and Modules (2015) Available at: https://afirm.fpg.unc.edu/afirm-modules (last accessed 7 December 2019).

Baio, J., Wiggins, L., Christensen, D.L., Maenner, M.J., Daniels, J., Warren, Z., ... & Durkin, M.S. (2018) 'Prevalence of autism spectrum disorder among children aged 8 years—autism and developmental disabilities monitoring network, 11 sites, United States, 2014', *MMWR Surveillance Summaries,* 67 (6).

Baird, G., Simonoff, E., Pickles, A., Chandler, S., Loucas, T., Meldrum, D., & Charman, T. (2006) 'Prevalence of disorders of the autism spectrum in a population cohort of children in South Thames: The Special Needs and Autism Project (SNAP)', *The Lancet,* 368 (9531): 210–215.

Bancroft, K., Batten, A., Lambert, S., & Madders, T. (2012) *The way we are: Autism in 2012.* London: The National Autistic Society.

Bandura, A. (2006) 'Guide for constructing self-efficacy scales', in Pajares, F. & Urdan, T.C. (eds) *Self-efficacy beliefs of adolescents.* Greenwich, CT: Information Age.

Bargiela, S., Steward, R., & Mandy, W. (2016) 'The experiences of late-diagnosed women with autism spectrum conditions: An investigation of the autism female phenotype', *Journal of Autism and Developmental Disorders,* 46: 3281–3294.

Baron-Cohen, S. (2000) 'Theory of mind and autism: A review', *International Review of Research in Mental Retardation*. Academic Press: 169–184.

Baron-Cohen, S., Leslie, A.M., & Frith, U. (1985) 'Does the autistic child have a theory of mind?' *Cognition*, 21 (1): 37–46.

Baron-Cohen, S., Allen, J., & Gillberg, C. (1992). 'Can autism be detected at 18 months? The needle, the haystack, and the CHAT', *The British Journal of Psychiatry*, 161 (6): 839–843.

Beresford, B.A., Moran, N.E. Sloper, T., Cusworth, L.S., Mitchell, W.A., Spiers, G.F., Weston, K.H., & Beecham, J. (2013) *Transition to adult services and adulthood for young people with autistic spectrum conditions*. York: Social Policy Research Unit. (SPRU Working Paper; Vol. DH 2525).

Bergold, J. & Thomas, S. (2012) 'Participatory research methods: A methodological approach in motion', *Forum Qualitative Social Research*, 13 (1).

Bettelheim, B. (1967) *The empty fortress: Infantile autism and the birth of the self*. New York: The Free Press.

Biesta, G. (2007) 'Why "what works" won't work: Evidence-based practice and the democratic deficit in educational research.''', *Educational Theory*, 57 (1): 1–22.

Biesta, G. (2013) *The beautiful risk of education*. Boulder, CO: Paradigm Publishers.

Biesta, G., Allan, J., & Edwards, R. (2014) *Making a difference in theory: The theory question in education and the education question in theory*. Abingdon: Routledge.

Boaz, A., Fitzpatrick, S., & Shaw, B. (2009) 'Assessing the impact of research on policy: A literature review', *Science and Public Policy*, 36 (4): 255–270.

Bolton, S., McDonald, D., Curtis, E., Kelly, S., & Gallagher, L. (2014) 'Autism in a recently arrived immigrant population', *European Journal of Pediatrics*, 173 (3): 337–343.

Bond, C., Symes, W., Hebron, J., Humphrey, N., & Morewood, G. (2016) *Educating persons with autistic spectrum disorder: A systematic literature review*. Trim: National Council for Special Education.

Bondy, A. & Frost, L. (1998) *A picture's worth: PECS and other visual communication strategies in autism*. Bethesda, MD: Woodbine House.

Boucher, J. (2009) *The autistic spectrum: Characteristics, causes and practical issues*. London: Sage.

Bowler, D. (2007) *Autism spectrum disorders: Psychological theory and research*. London: John Wiley.

Breakey, C. (2006) *The autism spectrum and further education: A guide to good practice*. London: Jessica Kingsley Publishers.

Brede, J., Remington, A., Kenny, L., Warren, K., & Pellicano, E. (2017) 'Excluded from school: Autistic students' experiences of school exclusion and subsequent re-integration into school', *Autism & Developmental Language Impairments*, 2. doi:10.1177/2396941517737511

Brett, D., Warnell, F., McConachie, H., & Parr, J.R. (2016) 'Factors affecting age at ASD diagnosis in UK: No evidence that diagnosis age has decreased between 2004 and 2014', *Journal of Autism and Developmental Disorders*, 46 (6), 1974–1984.

Bronfenbrenner, U. (1979) *The ecology of human development*. Cambridge, MA: Harvard University Press.

Bronfenbrenner, U. (ed.). (2005) *Making human beings human: Bioecological perspectives on human development*. Thousand Oaks, CA: Sage.

Brown-Lavoie, S.M., Viecili, M.A., & Weiss, J.A. (2014) 'Sexual knowledge and victimization in adults with autism spectrum disorders', *Journal of Autism and Developmental Disorders*, 44 (9): 2185–2196.

Burns, M.K. & Ysseldyke, J. (2009) 'Reported prevalence of evidence-based instructional practices in special education', *Journal of Special Education*, 43 (1): 3–11.

Cachia, R.L., Anderson, A., & Moore, D.W. (2016) 'Mindfulness, stress and well-being in parents of children with autism spectrum disorder: A systematic review', *Journal of Child and Family Studies*, 25 (1): 1–14.

Campano, G., Ghiso, M.P. & Welch, B.J. (2015) 'Ethical and professional norms in community-based research', *Harvard Educational Review*, 85 (1): 29–49.

Casanova, E.L. & Casanova, M.F. (2018) *Defining autism: A guide to brain, biology and behavior*. London: Jessica Kingsley Publishers.

Chang, Y.C. & Locke, J. (2016) 'A systematic review of peer-mediated interventions for children with autism spectrum disorder', *Research in Autism Spectrum Disorders*, 27: 1–10.

Charman, T., Pellicano, L., Peacey, L., Peacey, N., Forward, K., & Dockrell, J. (2011) *What is good practice in autism education?* London: Autism Education Trust.

Cimera, R.E. & Cowan, R.J. (2009) 'The costs of services and employment outcomes achieved by adults with autism in the US', *Autism*, 13 (3): 285–302.

Clough, P. & Corbett, J. (2000) *Theories of inclusive education: A student's guide*. London: Sage.

Cooke, J. (2018) *We need an education*. London: Ambitious about Autism. Available at: www.ambitiousaboutautism.org.uk/why-is-this-campaign-important.

Cooper, K., Smith, L.G., & Russell, A.J. (2018) 'Gender identity in autism: Sex differences in social affiliation with gender groups', *Journal of Autism and Developmental Disorders*, 48 (12): 3995–4006.

Corker, M. & Shakespeare, T. (2002) *Disability/postmodernity: Embodying disability theory*. London: Continuum.

Corona, L.L., Fox, S.A., Christodulu, K.V., & Worlock, J.A. (2016) 'Providing education on sexuality and relationships to adolescents with autism spectrum disorder and their parents', *Sexuality and Disability*, 34 (2): 199–214.

Crane, L., Chester, J.W., Goddard, L., Henry, L.A., & Hill, E. (2016) 'Experiences of autism diagnosis: A survey of over 1000 parents in the United Kingdom', *Autism*, 20 (2): 153–162.

Cullen, M., Cullen, S., Lindsay, G., & Arweck, E. (2013) *Evaluation of Autism Education Trust training hubs programme, 2011–13: Final report.* Coventry: Centre for Educational Development, Appraisal and Research (CEDAR), University of Warwick.

Cullen, S.M. (2016) *Evaluation of the Autism Education Trust programme, 2015–2016.* Coventry: Centre for Educational Development, Appraisal and Research (CEDAR), University of Warwick.

Davenport, M., Mazurek, M., Brown, A., & McCollom, E. (2018) 'A systematic review of cultural considerations and adaptation of social skills interventions for individuals with autism spectrum disorder', *Research in Autism Spectrum Disorders*, 52: 23–33.

Davis, P. & Florian, L. (2004) *Teaching strategies and approaches for pupils with special educational needs: A scoping study.* Research Report 516. London: DfES.

Dawson, M. & Mottron, L. (2011) 'Do autistics have cognitive strengths? Should ASC be defined as disorders?' in Bolte, S. & Hallmayer, J. (eds) *Autism spectrum conditions.* Gottingen, Germany: Hogrefe.

Dawson, M., Soulières, I., Ann Gernsbacher, M., & Mottron, L. (2007) 'The level and nature of autistic intelligence', *Psychological Science*, 18 (8): 657–662.

De Clercq, H. (2012) 'The right of people with autism to live independent and full lives to the limit of their potential', in Matthews, P. & Matthews, T. (eds) *Charter of rights for people with autism: Reflections and personal experience.* Dublin: Original Writing.

De Clercq, H. (2019) 'Analysis of what makes a successful professional in autism', in Jordan, R., Hume, K., & Roberts, J. (eds) *The SAGE handbook of autism and education.* London: Sage.

Dean, M., Kasari, C., Shih, W., Frankel, F., Whitney, R., Landa, R., ... & Harwood, R. (2014) 'The peer relationships of girls with ASD at school: Comparison to boys and girls with and without ASD', *Journal of Child Psychology and Psychiatry*, 55 (11): 1218–1225.

Dekker, M. (2019) in Fletcher-Watson, S. & Happé, F. (2019) *Autism: A new introduction to psychological theory and current debate.* London: Routledge.

Department for Education (DfE) (2011) *Teachers' Standards: Guidance for school leaders, school Staff and governing bodies.* DFE-00066-2011. London: DfE.

Department for Education (DfE) (2014) *Think Autism: Fulfilling and rewarding lives, the strategy for adults with autism in England: An update.* London: DfE.

Department for Education (DfE) (2016a) *A framework of core content for Initial Teacher Training (ITT).* London: DfE.

Department for Education (DfE) (2016b) *DfE strategy 2015–2020: World-class education and care.* DFE-00087-2016. London: DfE.

Department for Education (DfE) (2018) *Children in need of help and protection: Data and analysis.* Available at: www.gov.uk/government/publications/children-in-need-of-help-and-protection-data-and-analysis

Department for Education and Department of Health (DfE/DoH) (2014). *SEND Code of Practice: For 0 to 25 years.* Available at: www.gov.uk/government/publications/send-code-of-practice-0-to-25

Department for Education and Skills (DES) (1978) *The Warnock report.* London: HMSO.

Department of Children Schools and Families (DCSF) (2008) *Early Years Foundation Stage.* Available at: http://nationalstrategies.standards.dcsf.gov.uk/earlyyears

Department of Education (2004) Individuals with Disabilities Education Act. Washington, DC.

Department of Health and Department for Education (DoH/DfE) (2017) *Transforming children and young people's mental health provision: A green paper.* Available at: www.gov.uk/government/consultations/transforming-children-and-young-peoples-mental-health-provision-a-green-paper

Dillon, G.V., Underwood, J.D., & Freemantle, L.J. (2016) Autism and the UK secondary school experience', *Focus on Autism and Other Developmental Disabilities*, 31 (3): 221–230.

Dingfelder, H.E. & Mandell, D.S. (2011) 'Bridging the research-to-practice gap in autism intervention: An application of diffusion of innovation theory', *Journal of Autism and Developmental Disorders*, 41 (5): 597–609.

Douglas, G. & McLinden, M. (2005) 'Visual impairment', in Lewis, A. & Norwich, B. (eds) *Special teaching for special children? Pedagogies for inclusion.* London: Open University Press.

Duvall S.W., Huang-Storms, L., Presmanes Hill, A., Myers, J., & Fombonne, E. (2019) 'No sex differences in cognitive ability in young children with autism spectrum disorder', *Journal of Autism and Developmental Disorders.* doi:10.1007/s10803-019-03933-1. [Epub ahead of print]

Dworzynski, K., Ronald, A., Bolton, P., & Happé, F. (2012) 'How different are girls and boys above and below the diagnostic threshold for autism spectrum disorders?' *Journal of the American Academy of Child & Adolescent Psychiatry*, 51 (8): 788–797.

Dykens, E.M., Fisher, M.H., Taylor, J.L., Lambert, W., & Miodrag, N. (2014) 'Reducing distress in mothers of children with autism and other disabilities: A randomized trial', *Pediatrics*, 134 (2).

Ecker, C. (2017) 'The neuroanatomy of autism spectrum disorder: An overview of structural neuroimaging findings and their translatability to the clinical setting', *Autism*, 21 (1): 18–28.

Edelson, S.M. (2019) 'Large-scale studies in autism: What do they show? *Autism Research Review International*, 33 (2).

Elsabbagh, M., Divan, G., Koh, Y.-J., ... & Fombonne, E. (2012) 'Global prevalence of autism and other pervasive developmental disorders', *Autism Research*, 5 (3): 160–179.

Engel, G.L (1977) 'The need for a new medical model: A challenge for biomedicine', *Science*, 196: 129–136.

Engelhardt, C.R., Mazurek, M.O., & Sohl, K. (2013) 'Media use and sleep among boys with autism spectrum disorder, ADHD, or typical development', *Pediatrics*, 132 (6): 1081–1089.

Engeström, Y. (1987) *Learning by expanding: An activity-theoretical approach to developmental research*. Helsinki: Orienta-Konultit Oy.

Equality Act (2010). Available at: www.legislation.gov.uk/ukpga/2010/15/contents

Evans-Williams, C. (2019), 'Community contribution: Dr Claire Evans-Williams, autistic person, advocate and consultant clinical psychologist', in Fletcher-Watson, S. & Happé, F. (eds) *Autism: A new introduction to psychological theory and current debate*. London: Routledge.

Farrell, S., Fidler, R., Christie, P., & Lyn-Cook, L. (2017) *AET Progression Framework*. London: Autism Education Trust.

Finkelstein, V. & French, S. (1993). 'Towards a psychology of disability', in Swain, J., Finkelstein, V., French, S., & Oliver, M. (eds) *Disabling barriers— Enabling environments*. London: Sage; Open University Press.

Fischbach, L.R., Harris, M.J., Ballan, M.S., Fischbach, G.D., & Link, B.G. (2016) 'Is there concordance in attitudes and beliefs between parents and scientists about autism spectrum disorder?', *Autism*, 20 (3): 353–363.

Fletcher-Watson, S. & Happé, F. (2019) *Autism: A new introduction to psychological theory and current debate*. London: Routledge.

Florian, L. (2007) 'Reimagining special education', in Florian, L. (ed.) *The SAGE handbook of special education*. London: Sage.

Florian, L. & Black-Hawkins, K. (2011) 'Exploring inclusive pedagogy', *British Educational Research Journal*, 37 (5): 813–828.

Fox, F., Aabe, N., Turner, K., Redwood, S., & Rai, D. (2017) 'It was like walking without knowing where I was going: A qualitative study of autism in a UK Somali migrant community', *Journal of Autism And Developmental Disorders*, 47 (2): 305–315.

Freire, P. (1972) *Pedagogy of the oppressed*. Harmondsworth: Penguin.

Frith, U. (1989) *Autism: Explaining the enigma*. Oxford: Blackwell.

Frith, U. (2012) 'Why we need cognitive explanations of autism', *Journal of Experimental Psychology*, 65 (11): 2073–2092.

Gallagher, D., Connor, D.J., & Ferri, B.A. (2011) 'Broadening our horizons: Towards a plurality of methodologies in learning disability research', *Learning Disability Quarterly*, 34: 107–121.

George, R. & Stokes, M.A. (2018) 'Gender identity and sexual orientation in autism spectrum disorder', *Autism*, 22 (8): 970–982.

Gerland, G. (2000) *Finding out about Asperger syndrome, high functioning autism and PDD*. London: Jessica Kingsley Publishers.

Giallo, R., Wood, C.E., Jellett, R., & Porter, R. (2013) 'Fatigue, wellbeing and parental self-efficacy in mothers of children with an autism spectrum disorder', *Autism*, 17 (4): 465–480.

Gill, K., Quilter-Pinner, H., & Swift, D. (2017) *Making the difference: Breaking the link between school exclusion and social exclusion*. London: Institute for Public Policy Research.

Gillberg, C. (2019) 'Autism and comorbidities: Autism plus – Implications for diagnosis, prognosis and interventions', in Jordan, R., Roberts, J.M. & Hume, K. (eds) *The SAGE Handbook of Autism and Education*. London: Sage.

Gillberg, C. & Fernell, E. (2014) 'Autism plus versus autism pure', *Journal of Autism and Developmental Disorders*, 44 (12): 3274–3276. doi:10.1007/s10803-014-2163-1

Gillespie-Lynch, K., Brooks, P.J., Someki, F., Obeid, R., Shane-Simpson, C., Kapp, S.K., Daou, N., & Shane Smith, D. (2015) 'Changing college students' conceptions of autism: An online training to increase knowledge and decrease stigma. *Journal of Autism and Developmental Disorders*, 45: 2553–2566. doi:10.1007/s10803-015-2422-9

Gillespie-Lynch, K., Kapp, S.K., Brooks, P.J., Pickens, J., & Schwartzman, B. (2017) 'Whose expertise is it? Evidence for autistic adults as critical autism experts', *Frontiers in Psycholology*, 28 March. doi:10.3389/fpsyg.2017.00438

Glazer, J.L. & Peurach, D. (2015) 'Occupational control in education: The logic and leverage of epistemic communities', *Harvard Educational Review*, 85 (2):172–202.

Goldacre, B. (2013) *Building evidence into education*. London: Bad Science. Available at: https://dera.ioe.ac.uk/17530/

Goodall, C. (2018) '"I felt closed in and like I couldn't breathe": A qualitative study exploring the mainstream educational experiences of autistic young people', *Autism and Developmental Language Impairments*, 3.

Goodchild, C. (2009) *A painful gift: Journey of a soul with autism*. London: Darton, Longman and Todd Ltd.

Goodley, D. (2013) 'Dis/entangling critical disability studies', *Disability and Society*, 28: 631–644.

Göransson, K. & Nilholm, C. (2014) 'Conceptual diversities and empirical shortcomings – a critical analysis of research on inclusive education', *European Journal of Special Needs Education*, 29 (3): 265–280, doi:10.1080/08856257.2014.933545

Gotham, K., Brunwasser, S.M., & Lord, C. (2015) 'Depressive and anxiety symptom trajectories from school age through young adulthood in samples with autism spectrum disorder and developmental delay', *Journal of the American Academy of Child & Adolescent Psychiatry*, 54 (5): 369–376.

Grandin, T. (1995) *Thinking in pictures and other reports from my life with autism*. New York: Bloomsbury.

Grandin, T. (2014) *The autistic brain: Exploring the strengths of a different kind of mind*. London: Rider.

Grandin, T. & Scariano, M. (1986). *Emergence: Labelled autistic*. Novato, CA: Arena.

Gray, C. (1994) *The social story book*. Arlington, VA: Future Horizons.

Greenwood, C.R. & Abbott, M. (2001) 'The research to practice gap in special education', *Teacher Education and Special Education*, 24 (4): 276–289.

Grinker, S.R.R. (1964) 'A struggle for eclecticism', *American Journal of Psychiatry*, 121: 451–457.

Grynszpan, O., Weiss, P.L., Perez-Diaz, F., & Gal, E. (2014). Innovative technology-based interventions for autism spectrum disorders: A meta-analysis, *Autism*, 18 (4), 346–361.

Guldberg, K. (2010) 'Educating children on the autism spectrum: Preconditions for inclusion and notions of "best autism practice" in the Early Years', *British Journal of Special Education*, 37 (4): 168–174.

Guldberg, K. (2016) 'Enhancing the impact of research and knowledge co-production in Higher Education through communities of practice', in MacDonald, J. & Cater-Steel, A. (eds) *Communities of Practice: Facilitating social learning in higher education*. Singapore: Springer.

Guldberg, K. (2017) 'Evidence-based practice in autism educational research: Can we bridge the research and practice gap?' *Oxford Review of Education*, 43 (2): 149–161.

Guldberg, K., Parsons, S., MacLeod, A., Jones, G., Prunty, A., & Balfe, T. (2011) 'Implications for practice from "International review of the evidence on best practice in educational provision for children on the autism spectrum"', *European Journal of Special Needs Education*, 26: 64–70.

Guldberg, K., Parsons, S., Porayska-Pomsta, K., & Keay-Bright, W. (2017a) 'Challenging the knowledge transfer orthodoxy: Knowledge co-construction in technology enhanced learning for children with autism', *British Educational Research Journal*, 43 (2): 394–413.

Guldberg, K., Achtypi, A., Angelidi, E., Baker, L., Bradley, R., Colombo, M., ... & Zanfroni, E. (2017b) *Transform autism education: Final report.* Birmingham: University of Birmingham.

Guldberg, K., Bradley, R., Wittemeyer, K., Briscombe, J., Phillips, C., & Jones, G. (2019a) *Good autism practice report.* London: Autism Education Trust.

Guldberg, K., Achtypi, A., D'Alonzo, L., Laskaridou, K., Milton, D., Molteni, P., & Wood, R. (2019b) 'Using the value-creation framework to capture knowledge co-creation and pathways to impact in a transnational community of practice in autism education', *International Journal of Research and Methods in Education.* doi:10.1080/1743727X.2019.1706466

Hacking, I. (2009) 'Autistic autobiography', *Philosophical Transactions of the Royal Society: Biological Sciences*, 364 (1522): 1467–1473.

Håkanson, L. (2007) 'Creating knowledge: The power and logic of articulation', *Industrial and Corporate Change*, 16 (1): 51–58.

Hallinger, P. & Heck, R. (1997) 'Exploring the principal's contribution to school effectiveness', *School Effectiveness and School Improvement*, 8 (4): 1–35.

Hammersley, M. (2005) 'Is the evidence-based practice movement doing more good than harm? Reflections on Iain Chalmers' case for research-based policy making and practice', *Evidence & Policy: A Journal of Research, Debate and Practice*, 1: 85–100.

Hammersley, M. (2006) 'What can the literature on communities of practice tell us about educational research? Reflections on some recent proposals', *International Journal of Research & Method in Education*, 28 (1): 5–21.

Hanney, S., Buxton, M., Green, C., Coulson, D.J.R., & Raftery, J.L. (2007) 'An assessment of the impact of the NHS Health Technology Assessment programme', *Health Technology Assessment*, 11 (53):1–180.

Harkavy, I. & Hartley, M. (2009) 'University-school-community partnerships for youth development and democratic renewal', *New Directions for Student Leadership*, 122: 7–18. https://doi.org/10.1002/yd.303

Hattie, J. (2008) *Visible learning: A synthesis of over 800 meta-analyses related to achievement.* New York: Routledge.

Heasman, B. & Gillespie, A. (2019) 'Neurodivergent intersubjectivity: Distinctive features of how autistic people create shared understanding', *Autism*, 23 (4): 910–921. https://doi.org/10.1177/1362361318785172

Heaton, P., & Wallace, G.L. (2004) 'Annotation: The savant syndrome', *Journal of Child Psychology and Psychiatry*, 45 (5): 899–911.

Henault, I. (2005) *Asperger's syndrome and sexuality: From adolescence through adulthood.* London: Jessica Kingsley.

Hendrickx, S. (2008) *Love, sex and long-term relationships*. London: Jessica Kingsley.

Hesmondhalgh, M. (2006) *Autism, access and inclusion on the front line: Confessions of an autism anorak*. London: Jessica Kingsley.

Higashida, N. (2013) *The reason I jump*. London: Hodder & Stoughton.

Hiller, R.M., Young, R.L., & Weber, N. (2014) 'Sex differences in autism spectrum disorder based on DSM-5 criteria: Evidence from clinician and teacher reporting', *Journal of Abnormal Child Psychology*, 42 (8): 1381–1393.

Hirvikoski, T., Mittendorfer-Rutz, E., Boman, M., Larsson, H., Lichtenstein, P., & Bolte, S. (2016) 'Premature mortality in autism spectrum disorder', *The British Journal of Psychiatry*, 208 (3): 232–238.

Hobson, P. (1990) 'Concerning knowledge of mental states', *British Journal of Medical Psychology*, 63 (3): 199–213. https://doi.org/10.1111/j.2044-8341.1990.tb01613.x

Hodkinson, P., Biesta, G., & James, D. (2008) 'Understanding learning culturally: Overcoming the dualism between social and individual views of learning', *Vocations and Learning*, 1 (1): 27–47. https://doi.org/10.1007/s12186-007-9001-y

Hollenweger, J. (2014) *Definition and classification of disability*. New York: UNICEF. Available at: www.inclusive-education.org/sites/default/files/uploads/booklets/IE_Webinar_Booklet_2.pdf

Horner, R.H., Carr, E.G., Halle, J., McGee, G., Odom, S., & Wolery, M. (2005) 'The use of single-subject research to identify evidence-based practice in special education', *Exceptional Children*, 71: 165–179.

Houlahan, K. (2019) 'Development of the All About Me tool to capture the views of autistic pupils', *Good Autism Practice*, 20 (1): 13–26.

Houston, N., Ross, H., Robinson, J., & Malcolm, H. (2010) 'Inside research, inside ourselves: Teacher educators take stock of their research practice', *Educational Action Research*, 18 (4): 555–569.

Howlin, P. (2010) 'Evaluating psychological treatments for children with autism-spectrum disorders', *Advances in Psychiatric Treatment*, 16: 133–140.

Howlin, P. (2013) 'Social disadvantage and exclusion: Adults with autism lag far behind in employment prospects', *Journal of the American Academy of Child and Adolescent Psychiatry*, 52 (9): 897–899.

Howlin, P., & Moss, P. (2012). 'Adults with autism spectrum disorders', *The Canadian Journal of Psychiatry*, 57 (5): 275–283.

Howlin, P., Goode, S., Hutton, J., & Rutter, M. (2004). 'Adult outcome for children with autism', *Journal of Child Psychology and Psychiatry*, 45 (2): 212–229.

Howlin, P., Magiati, I., & Charman, T. (2009) 'Systematic review of early intensive behavioral interventions for children with autism', *American Journal on Intellectual and Developmental Disabilities*, 114 (1): 23–41. https://doi.org/10.1352/2009.114:23–41

Hughes, B. (2000) 'Medicine and the aesthetic invalidation of disabled people', *Disability & Society*, 15 (4): 555–568.

Hughes, C. & Russell, J. (1993) 'Autistic children's difficulty with mental disengagement from an object: Its implications for theories of autism', Developmental Psychology, 29 (3): 498–510.

Humphrey, N. & Hebron, J. (2015) 'Bullying of children and adolescents with autism spectrum conditions: A "state of the field" review', *International Journal of Inclusive Education*, 19 (8): 845–862.

Humphrey, N. & Lewis, S. (2008) '"Make me normal": The views and experiences of pupils on the autistic spectrum in mainstream secondary schools', *Autism*, 12 (1): 23–46.

Humphrey, N. & Symes, W. (2013) 'Inclusive education for pupils with autistic spectrum disorders in secondary mainstream schools: Teacher attitudes, experience and knowledge', *International Journal of Inclusive Education*, 17 (1): 32–46.

Hussein, A.M., Pellicano, E., & Crane, L. (2018) 'Understanding and awareness of autism among Somali parents living in the United Kingdom', *Autism*, 23 (6): 1408–1418.

Jackson, L. (2002) *Freaks, geeks and Asperger syndrome: A user guide to adolescence.* London: Jessica Kingsley.

Jarrold, C., Boucher, J., & Russell, J. (1997) 'Language profiles in children with autism: Theoretical and methodological implications', *Autism*, 1 (1): 57–76.

Jarzabek, E. (2014) *Listening to adults on the Autism spectrum: An analysis of the phenomena of autonomy and self-determination.* Dissertation presented to the faculty of the Department of Professional Psychology, Chestnut Hill College, Philadelphia.

Johnson, M.H. (2017) 'Autism as an adaptive common variant pathway for human brain development', *Developmental Cognitive Neuroscience*, 25: 5–11. https://doi.org/10.1016/j.dcn.2017.02.004

Jones, G. (2019) 'Professional development for those working in education with students on the autism spectrum', in Jordan, R., Hume, K., & Roberts, J. (eds) *The SAGE handbook of autism and education.* London: Sage.

Jones, G., English, A., Guldberg, K., Jordan, R., Richardson, P., & Waltz, M. (2008) *Educational provision for children and young people with autism spectrum disorders living in England: A review of current practice, issues and challenges.* London: Autism Education Trust.

Jones, R.S.P., Huws, J., & Beck, G. (2013) '"I'm not the only person out there": Insider and outsider understandings of autism', *International Journal of Developmental Disabilities*, 59 (2): 134–144.

Jordan, R. (1999) *Autistic spectrum disorders: An introductory handbook for practitioners*. London: David Fulton.

Jordan, R. (2005) 'Autistic spectrum disorders', in Lewis, A. & Norwich, B. (eds) *Special teaching for special children? Pedagogy for special educational needs*. Milton Keynes: Open University Press.

Jordan, R., Jones, G. & Murray, D. (1999) *Meeting the needs of children with autistic spectrum disorders*. London: David Fulton.

Jordan, R., Roberts, J.M., & Hume, K. (2019) (eds) *The SAGE handbook of autism and education*. London: Sage.

Justice (2019) *Challenging school exclusions report*. London: Justice.

Kanner, L. (1943) 'Autistic disturbances of affective contact', *Nervous Child*, 2 (3): 217–250.

Kapp, S.K., Gillespie-Lynch, K., Sherman, L.E., & Hutman, T. (2013) 'Deficit, difference, or both? Autism and neurodiversity', *Developmental Psychology*, 49: 59–71. doi:10.1037/a0028353

Kasari, C. & Smith, T. (2013) 'Interventions in schools for children with autism spectrum disorder: Methods and recommendations', *Autism*, 17: 254–267.

Kasari, C., Freeman, S., & Paparella, T. (2006) 'Joint attention and symbolic play in young children with autism: A randomized controlled intervention study', *Journal of Child Psychology and Psychiatry*, 47: 611–620.

Kazdin, A.E. (2008) 'Evidence-based treatment and practice, new opportunities to bridge clinical research and practice, enhance the knowledge base and improve patient care', *American Psychologist*, 63: 146–159.

Kendrick, K., Jutengren, G., & Stattin, H. (2012) 'The protective role of supportive friends against bullying perpetration and victimization', *Journal of Adolescence*, 35 (4): 1069–1080.

Kenny, L., Hattersley, C., Molins, B., Buckley, C., Povey, C., & Pellicano, L. (2015) 'Which terms should be used to describe autism? Perspectives from the UK autism community', *Autism*, 20 (4): 442–462.

Kerns, C.M., Newschaffer, C.J., & Berkowitz, S.J. (2015) 'Traumatic childhood events and autism spectrum disorder', *Journal of Autism and Developmental Disorders*, 45 (11): 3475–3486.

King, C., & Murphy, G.H. (2014) 'A systematic review of people with autism spectrum disorder and the criminal justice system', *Journal of Autism and Developmental Disorders*, 44 (11): 2717–2733.

Kinnear, S.H., Link, B.G., Ballan, M.S., & Fischbach, R.L. (2016) 'Understanding the experience of stigma for parents of children with autism spectrum disorder and the role stigma plays in families' lives', *Journal of Autism and Developmental Disorders*, 46 (3): 942–953.

Kloosterman, P.H., Kelley, E.A., Craig, W.M., Parker, J.D., & Javier, C. (2013) 'Types and experiences of bullying in adolescents with an autism spectrum disorder', *Research in Autism Spectrum Disorders*, 7 (7): 824–832.

Kolb, D.A. (1984) *Experiential learning*. Englewood Cliffs, NJ: Prentice Hall.

Kowalski, R.M., & Fedina, C. (2011) 'Cyber bullying in ADHD and Asperger syndrome populations', *Research in Autism Spectrum Disorders*, 5 (3), 1201–1208.

Kreiser, N.L. & White, S.W. (2014) 'ASD in females: Are we overstating the gender difference in diagnosis?', *Clinical Child and Family Psychology Review*, 17 (1): 67–84.

Lather, P. (2004) 'Scientific research in education: A critical perspective', *British Educational Research Journal*, 30 (6): 759–772.

Lave, J. & Wenger, E. (1991) *Situated learning: Legitimate peripheral participation*. New York: Cambridge University Press.

Lawson, W. (2005) *Sex, sexuality and the autism spectrum*. London: Jessica Kingsley.

Lawson, W. (2008) *Concepts of normality: The autistic and typical spectrum*. London: Jessica Kingsley Publishers.

Lawson, W. (2010) *The passionate mind: How people with autism learn*. London: Jessica Kingsley Publishers.

Lecavalier, L., Snow, V.A., & Norris, M. (2011) 'Autism spectrum disorders and intellectual disability', in Matson, J.L. & Sturmey, P. (eds) *International handbook of autism and pervasive developmental disorders*. New York: Springer.

Leekam, S.R., Nieto, C., Libby, S.J., Wing, L., & Gould, J. (2007) 'Describing the sensory abnormalities of children and adults with autism', *Journal of Autism and Developmental Disorders*, 37 (5): 894–910.

Lehti, V., Hinkka-Yli-Salomäki, S., Cheslack-Postava, K., Gissler, M., Brown, A.S., & Sourander, A. (2013) 'The risk of childhood autism among second-generation migrants in Finland: A case–control study', *BMC Pediatrics*, 13 (1): 171.

Lemmi, V., Knapp, M., & Ragan, I. (2017) *The autism dividend: Reaping the rewards of better investment*. National Autism Project. Available at: http://nationalautismproject.org.uk/the-report

Lever, A.G. & Geurts, H.M. (2016) 'Psychiatric co-occurring symptoms and disorders in young, middle-aged, and older adults with autism spectrum disorder', *Journal of Autism and Developmental Disorders*, 46 (6): 1916–1930.

Lewis, A. & Norwich, B. (2005) *Special teaching for special children? Pedagogies for inclusion*. London: Open University Press.

Lim, N., O'Reilly, M.F., Sigafoos, J., & Lancioni, G.E. (2018) 'Understanding the linguistic needs of diverse individuals with autism spectrum disorder: Some comments on the research literature and suggestions for clinicians', *Journal of Autism and Developmental Disorders*, 48 (8): 2890–2895.

Lindsay, S., Proulx, M., Thomson, N., & Scott, H. (2013) 'Educators' challenges of including children with autism spectrum disorder in mainstream classrooms', *International Journal of Disability, Development and Education*, 60 (4): 347–362.

Locke, J., Olsen, A., Wideman, R., Downey, M.M., Kretzman, M., Kasari, C., & Mandell, D.S. (2014) 'A tangled web: The challenges of implementing an evidence-based social engagement intervention for children with autism in urban public school settings', *Behavior Therapy*, 46: 54–67.

Long, J., Panese, J., Ferguson, J., Hamill, M.A., & Miller, J. (2017) 'Enabling voice and participation in autism services: Using practitioner research to develop inclusive practice', *Good Autism Practice Journal*, 18 (2): 6–14.

Loomes, R., Hull, L., & Mandy, W.P.L. (2017) 'What is the male-to-female ratio in autism spectrum disorder? A systematic review and meta-analysis', *Journal of the American Academy of Child & Adolescent Psychiatry*, 56 (6): 466–474.

Lorenz, T. & Heinitz, K. (2014) 'Aspergers – different, not less: Occupational strengths and job interests of individuals with Asperger's syndrome', *PLoS ONE*, 9 (6): e100358.

Lovaas, O.I. (1987) 'Behavioral treatment and normal educational and intellectual functioning in autistic children', *Journal of Consultative and Clinical Psychology*, 55: 3–9.

Lundy, L. (2007) 'Voice' is not enough: Conceptualising Article 12 of the United Nations Convention on the Rights of the Child', *British Educational Research Journal*, 33 (6): 927–942.

MacBeath, J. (2012) 'Learning and teaching: Are they by any chance related?' in McLaughlin, C. (ed.) *Teachers learning: Professional development and education*. Cambridge: Cambridge University Press.

MacDonald, G. (2002) 'Transformative unlearning: Safety, discernment and communities of learning', *Nursing Inquiry*, 9 (3): 170–178.

MacKenzie, H. (2019) 'Thinking and learning', in Jordan, R., Hume, K., & Roberts, J. (2019) *The SAGE handbook of autism and education*. London: Sage.

MacLeod, A., Allan, J., Lewis, A., & Robertson, C. (2018) 'Here I come again': The cost of success for higher education students diagnosed with autism', *International Journal of Inclusive Education*, 22 (6): 683–697.

Magiati, I., Tay, X.W., & Howlin, P. (2012) 'Early comprehensive behaviorally based interventions for children with autism spectrum disorders: A summary of findings from recent reviews and meta-analyses', *Neuropsychiatry*, 2 (6): 543–570.

Magnuson, K.M. & Constantino, J.N. (2011) 'Characterization of depression in children with autism spectrum disorders', *Journal of Developmental and Behavioral Paediatrics*, 32 (4): 332–340.

Maiano, C., Normand, C.L., Salvas, M.C., Moullec, G., & Aimé, A. (2016) 'Prevalence of school bullying among youth with autism spectrum disorders: A systematic review and meta-analysis', *Autism Research*, 9 (6): 601–615.

Malow, B.A., Byars, K., Johnson, K., Weiss, S., Bernal, P., Goldman, S.E., ... & Glaze, D.G. (2012) 'A practice pathway for the identification, evaluation, and management of insomnia in children and adolescents with autism spectrum disorders', *Pediatrics – English Edition*, 130 (2): 106–124.

Mandy, W., Chilvers, R., Chowdhury, U., Salter, G., Seigal, A., & Skuse, D. (2012) 'Sex differences in autism spectrum disorder: Evidence from a large sample of children and adolescents', *Journal of Autism and Developmental Disorders*, 42 (7): 1304–1313.

Maskey, M., Warnell, F., Parr, J.R., Le Couteur, A., & McConachie, H. (2013) 'Emotional and behavioural problems in children with autism spectrum disorder', *Journal of Autism and Developmental Disorders*, 43 (4): 851–859.

Matson, J.L. & Goldin, R.L. (2013) 'Comorbidity and autism: Trends, topics and future directions', *Research in Autism Spectrum Disorders*, 7 (10): 1228–1233.

Matson, J.L., Kozlowski, A.M., Worley, J.A., Shoemaker, M.E., Sipes, M., & Horovitz, M. (2011) 'What is the evidence for environmental causes of challenging behaviors in persons with intellectual disabilities and autism spectrum disorders?', *Research in Developmental Disabilities*, 32(2): 693–698.

Maulik, P.K., Mascarenhas, M.N., Mathers, C.D., Dua, T., & Saxena, S. (2011) 'Prevalence of intellectual disability: A meta-analysis of population-based studies', *Research in Developmental Disabilities*, 32 (2): 419–436.

Mazurek, M.O., Shattuck, P.T., Wagner, M., & Cooper, B.P. (2012) 'Prevalence and correlates of screen-based media use among youths with autism spectrum disorders', *Journal of Autism and Developmental Disorders*, 42 (8):1757–1767.

Mazurek, M.O., Vasa, R.A., Kalb, L.G., Kanne, S.M., Rosenberg, D., Keefer, A., ... & Lowery, L.A. (2013) 'Anxiety, sensory over-responsivity, and gastrointestinal problems in children with autism spectrum disorders', *Journal of Abnormal Child Psychology*, 41 (1): 165–176.

McAllister, K. & Maguire, B. (2012) 'A design model: The Autism Spectrum Disorder Classroom Design Kit', *British Journal of Special Education*, 39 (4): 201–208.

McClintock, C. (2003) 'The scholar-practitioner model', in DeStefano, A., Rudestam, K.E., Rudestam, R. & Silverman, J. (2003) *Encyclopedia of distributed learning*. London: Sage.

McConachie, H., Parr, J.R., Glod, M., Hanratty, J., Livingstone, N., Oono, I.P., … & Garland, D. (2015) 'Systematic review of tools to measure outcomes for young children with autism spectrum disorder', *Health Technology Assessment*, 19 (41): 1–506.

McDonnell, A., McCreadie, M., Mills, R., Deveau, R., Anker, R., & Hayden, J. (2015) 'The role of physiological arousal in the management of challenging behaviours in individuals with autistic spectrum disorders', *Research in Developmental Disabilities*, 36: 311–322.

McElhanon, B.O., McCracken, C., Karpen, S., & Sharp, W.G. (2014) 'Gastrointestinal symptoms in autism spectrum disorder: A meta-analysis', *Pediatrics*, 133 (5): 872–883.

McLinden, M., Douglas, G., Hewett, R., Cobb, R. & Ravenscroft, J. (2016) 'Access to learning and learning to access: The role of the specialist teacher of children and young people with vision impairments in facilitating curriculum access', *British Journal of Visual Impairment*, May: 1–19. doi:10.1177/0264619616643180

Medical Research Council (MRC) (2001) *MRC review of autism research: Epidemiology and causes.* London: MRC.

Meessen, B. & Bertone, M.P. (2012). *Assessing performance of communities of practice in health policy: A conceptual framework.* Antwerp: Department of Public Health, Institute of Tropical Medicine.

Mengoni, S., Irvine, K., Thakur, D., Barton, G., Dautenhahn, K., Guldberg, K., Robins, B., Wellsted, D. & Sharma, S. (2017). 'Feasibility study of a randomised controlled trial to investigate the effectiveness of using a humanoid robot to improve the social skills of children with autism spectrum disorder (Kaspar RCT): a study protocol', *BMJ Open*, 7 (6): 1–10.

Mercer, N. & Littleton, K. (2007). *Dialogue and the development of children's thinking: A sociocultural approach.* London: Routledge.

Mesibov, G. & Shea, V. (2010) 'The TEACCH programme in the era of evidence-based practice', *Journal of Autism and Developmental Disorders*, 40: 570–579.

Mesibov, G. & Shea, V. (2011) 'Evidence-based practices and autism', *Autism*, 15: 114–133.

Mikita, N., Simonoff, E., Pine, D.S., Goodman, R. Artiges, E., Banashewski, T., Bokde, A.L., Bromberg, U., Buchel, C., Cattrell, A., Conrod, P.J., Desrivieres, S., Floor, H., … & Stringaris, A. (2016) 'Disentangling the autism-anxiety overlap: fMRI of reward-processing in a community-based longitudinal study', *Translational Psychiatry*, 6 (6): e845. doi:10.1038/tp.2016.107

Milton, D. (2012a) *So, what exactly is autism?* in Autism Education Trust Standards. London: Autism Education Trust.

Milton, D. (2012b) 'On the ontological status of autism: The "double empathy problem"', *Disability & Society*, 27 (6): 883–887.

Milton, D. (2014a) 'Autistic expertise: A critical reflection on the production of knowledge in autism studies', *Autism*, 18 (7): 794–802.

Milton, D. (2014b) 'So what exactly are autism interventions intervening with?' *Good Autism Practice*, 15 (2): 6–14.

Milton, D. & Bracher, M. (2013) 'Autistics speak but are they heard?' *Journal of the BSA Medical Society Group*, 7 (2): 61–69.

Milton, D. & McDonnell, A. (2014) 'Going with the flow: Reconsidering "repetitive behavior" through the concept of "flow states"', in Hurley, E. & Jones, G. (eds) *Promoting wellbeing and happiness*. Birmingham: British Institute of Learning Disabilities.

Ministries of Health and Education (2016) *New Zealand autism spectrum disorder guideline*. Wellington: Ministry of Health.

Moloney, P. (2010) 'How can a chord be weird if it expresses your soul? Some critical reflections on the diagnosis of Aspergers syndrome', *Disability & Society*, 25 (2): 135–148. doi:10.1080/09687590903534254

Morewood, G. (2019) 'Understanding emotional regulation in the context of whole school inclusive systems', *IncluVision*, Jan–April: 6–9.

Morgan, L., Hooker, J.L., Sparapani, N., Rinehardt, V., Schatschneider, C., & Wetherby, A. (2018) 'Cluster randomized trial of the classroom SCERTS intervention for students with autism spectrum disorder', *Journal of Consulting and Clinical Psychology*, 86 (7): 631–644.

Morgan, M.F., Moni, K.B., & Cuskelly, M. (2015) 'The development of research skills in young adults with intellectual disability in participatory research', *International Journal of Disability, Development and Education*, 62 (4): 438–457. doi:10.1080/1034912X.2015.1028905

Moriña, A. (2017). 'Inclusive education in higher education: Challenges and opportunities', *European Journal of Special Needs Education*, 32 (1): 3–17.

Mottron, L., Dawson, M., Soulieres, I., Hubert, B., & Burack, J. (2006) 'Enhanced perceptual functioning in autism: An update, and eight principles of autistic perception', *Journal of Autism and Developmental Disorders*, 36 (1): 27–43.

Murray, D. (1992) 'Attention tunnelling and autism', in *Living with autism: The individual, the family, and the professional*. Originally presented at the Durham Conference, UK. Proceedings obtainable from Autism Research Unit, School of Health Sciences, University of Sunderland, Sunderland SR2 7EE, UK.

Murray, D., Lesser, M., & Lawson, W. (2005) 'Attention, monotropism and the diagnostic criteria for autism', *Autism*, 9 (2): 139–156. doi:10.1177/1362361305051398

Myers, B.J., Mackintosh, V.H., & Goin-Kochel, R.P. (2009) '"My greatest joy and my greatest heart ache': Parents' own words on how having a child in the autism spectrum has affected their lives and their families' lives", *Research in Autism Spectrum Disorders*, 3 (3): 670–684.

Nader, A.M., Courchesne, V., Dawson, M., & Soulières, I. (2016) 'Does WISC-IV underestimate the intelligence of autistic children?', *Journal of Autism and Developmental Disorders*, 46 (5): 1582–1589.

Nastasi, B., Varjas, K., Schensul, S.L., Tudor Silva, K., Schensul, J.J., & Ratnayake, P. (2000) 'The Participatory Intervention Model: A framework for conceptualizing and promoting intervention acceptability', *School Psychology Quarterly*, 15 (2): 207–232.

National Autism Center (NAC) (2009) *National Standards Report. The National Standards Project – addressing the need for evidence-based practice guidelines for autism spectrum disorders*. Randolph, MA: National Autism Center.

National Children's Bureau (NCB) Briefing. (2017) *Mental health provision in schools and colleges*. Available at: www.ncb.org.uk/sites/default/files/uploads/Supporting%20Mental%20Health%20in%20Schools%20and%20Colleges.pdf

National Council for Special Education (NCSE) (2015) *Supporting autism with autism spectrum disorder in schools*. NCSE Policy Advice Paper No.5. Dublin: NCSE.

Ne'eman, A. (2010) 'The future (and the past) of autism advocacy, or why the ASA's magazine, *The advocate*, wouldn't publish this piece', *Disability Studies Quarterly*, 30 (1).

NICE (2013) *Social and emotional wellbeing for children and young people*. London: NICE.

NICE Clinical Guidelines (2011) 'Autism spectrum disorder in under 19s: Recognition, referral and diagnosis', in *Clinical Guideline 142*. London: NICE.

NICE Clinical Guidelines (2013) 'Autism spectrum disorder in under 19s: Support and management', in *Clinical Guideline 170*. London: NICE.

Nicolaidis C, Raymaker D, McDonald K, Dern, S., & Ashkenazy, E. (2011) 'Collaboration strategies in nontraditional community-based participatory research partnerships: Lessons from an academic–community partnership with autistic self-advocates', *Progress in Community Health Partnerships*, 5 (2): 143–150.

Nind, M. (2006) 'Conducting systematic review in education: A reflexive narrative', *London Review of Education*, 4 (2): 183–195.

Nind, M. (2014) *What is inclusive research?* London: Bloomsbury Academic.

Noens, I. & van Berckelaer-Onnes, I. (2004) 'Making sense in a fragmentary world: Communication in people with autism and learning disability', *Autism*, 8 (2): 197–218. doi:10.1177/1362361304042723

Norwich, B. (2002) 'Education, inclusion and individual differences: Recognising and resolving dilemmas', *British Journal of Educational Studies*, 50 (4): 482–502.

Norwich, B. (2013) *Addressing tensions and dilemmas in inclusive education: Living with uncertainty.* London: Routledge.

Norwich, B. & Lewis, A. (2007) 'How specialized is teaching children with disabilities and difficulties?' *Journal of Curriculum Studies*, 39 (2): 127–150.

O'Brien, A. (2018) *AET Post-16 Autism Standards.* London: Autism Education Trust.

O'Dell, L., Bertilsdotter Rosqvist, H., Ortega, F., Bronlow, C., & Orsini, M. (2016) 'Critical autism studies: Exploring epistemic dialogues and intersections, challenging dominant understandings of autism', *Disability & Society*, 31 (2): 166–179.

Odom, S.L., Brantlinger, E., Gersten, R., Horner, R.H., Thompson, B., & Harris, K.R. (2005) 'Research in special education: Scientific methods and evidence-based practices', *Exceptional Children*, 71: 137–148.

Odom, S.L., Collet-Klingenberg, L., Rogers, S.J., & Hatton, D.D. (2010) 'Evidence-based practices in interventions for children and youth with autism spectrum disorders', *Preventing School Failure: Alternative Education for Children and Youth*, 54 (4): 275–282. doi:10.1080/10459881003785506

OECD (2010) *PISA 2009 at a glance.* Paris: OECD Publishing. http://dx.doi.org/10.1787/9789264095298-en

Ofsted (2019) *The education inspection framework May 2019.* No. 190015. Manchester: Ofsted.

Oliver, M. (1996) *Understanding disability: From theory to practice.* Basingstoke, Hampshire: Macmillan.

Orsini, M. & Davidson, J. (2013) 'Introduction: Critical autism studies: Notes on an emerging field', in Davidson, J. & Orsini, M. (eds) *Worlds of autism: Across the spectrum of neurological difference.* Minneapolis, MN: University of Minnesota Press.

Osborne, L.A., McHugh, L., Saunders, J., & Reed, P. (2008) 'Parenting stress reduces the effectiveness of early teaching interventions for autistic spectrum disorders', *Journal of Autism and Developmental Disorders*, 38 (6): 1092–1103.

Ozonoff, S., Rogers, S., & Hendren, R.L. (2003) *Autism spectrum disorders: A research review for practitioners.* New York: American Psychiatric Publishing.

Parker, E. (2017) 'An actor-network theory reading of change for children in public care', *British Educational Research Journal*, 43 (1): 151–167.

Parsons, S. & Cobb, S. (2014) 'Reflections on the role of the 'users': Challenges in a multidisciplinary context of learner-centred design for children on the autism spectrum', *International Journal of Research and Method in Education*, 37 (4): 421–441.

Parsons, S. & Kasari, C. (2013) 'Editorial: Schools at the centre of educational research in autism: Possibilities, practices and promises', *Autism*, 17: 251–253.

Parsons, S., Guldberg, K., MacLeod, A., Jones, G., Prunty, A., & Balfe, T. (2011) 'International review of the evidence on best practice in educational provision for children on the autism spectrum', *European Journal of Special Needs Education*, 26 (1): 47–63.

Peeters, T. & Jordan, R. (1999) 'What makes a "good" practitioner in the field of autism?' *Good Autism Practice*, April 1999: 85–89.

Pellicano, E., Dinsmore, A., & Charman, T. (2014) 'What should autism research focus upon? Community views and priorities from the United Kingdom', *Autism*, 18 (7): 756–770.

Perepa, P. (2015). 'Impact of cultural perceptions on diagnosis of autism'. Available at: http://nectar.northampton.ac.uk/9162/2/Perepa20159162.pdf

Peters, R. & Brooks, R. (2016) 'Parental perspectives on the transition to secondary school for students with Asperger syndrome and high-functioning autism: A pilot survey study', *British Journal of Special Education*, 43 (1): 75–91. https://doi.org/10.1111/1467-8578.12125

Peters, S.J. (2010) *Democracy and higher education: Traditions and stories of civic engagement*. East Lansing, MI: Michigan State University Press.

Petrina, N., Carter, M., & Stephenson, J. (2014) 'The nature of friendship in children with autism spectrum disorders: A systematic review', *Research in Autism Spectrum Disorders*, 8 (2): 111–126.

Phillips, B.N. (1993) 'Challenging the stultifying bonds of tradition: Some philosophical, conceptual and methodological issues in applying the scientist-practitioner model', *School Counselling Quarterly*, 8: 27–37.

Pilling, S., Baron-Cohen, S., Megnin-Viggars, O., Lee, R., & Taylor, C. (2012) 'Recognition, referral, diagnosis, and management of adults with autism: Summary of NICE guidance', *British Medical Journal*, 344, e4082.

Poplin, M. (2011) 'Valuing a plurality of research methodologies in the field of LD', *Learning Disability Quarterly*, 34 (Issue I of II): 150–152.

Potter, C. & Whittaker, P. (2001) *Enabling communication in children with autism*. London: Jessica Kingsley.

Prizant, B., with Fields-Meyer, T. (2015) *Uniquely human: A different way of seeing autism*. New York: The Associated Press.

Prizant, B., Wetherby, A., Rubin, E., Laurent, A., & Rydell, P. (2006) *The SCERTS Model: A comprehensive educational approach for children with autism spectrum disorders. Volume 1: Assessment*. Baltimore, MD: Paul Brookes Publishing Co.

Putnam, C. & Chong, L. (2008) 'Software and technologies designed for people with autism: What do users want?' in *Proceedings of the 10th international ACM SIGACCESS conference on computers and accessibility* (pp. 3–10). ACM.

Ravet, J. (2011) 'Inclusive/exclusive? Contradictory perspectives on autism and inclusion: The case for an integrative position', *International Journal of Inclusive Education*, 15 (6): 667–682.

Ravet, J. (2013) 'Delving deeper into the black box: Formative assessment, inclusion and learners on the autism spectrum', *International Journal of Inclusive Education*, 17 (9): 948–964.

Ravet, J. (2015) *Supporting change in autism services: Bridging the gap between theory and practice*. London: Routledge.

Reed, P., Osborne, L.A., & Corness, M. (2007) 'The real-world effectiveness of early teaching interventions for children with autism spectrum disorder', *Exceptional Children*, 73 (4): 417–433.

Reichow, B. (2012) 'Overview of meta-analyses on early intensive behavioral intervention for young children with autism spectrum disorders', *Journal of Autism and Developmental Disorders*, 42: 512–520.

Reichow, B., Volkmar, F.R., & Chiccetti, D.V. (2008) 'Development of the evaluative method for evaluating and determining evidence-based practices in autism', *Journal of Autism and Developmental Disorders*, 38 (7): 1311–1319.

Reid, K. & Valle, J.W. (2004) 'The discursive practice of learning disability: Implications for instruction and parent–school relations', *Journal of Learning Disabilities*, 37 (6): 466–481. https://doi.org/10.1177/00222194040370060101

Remington, B., Hastings, R.P., Kovshoff, H., Espinosa, F., Jahr, E., & Brown, T. (2007) 'Early intensive behavioral intervention: Outcomes for children with autism and their parents after two years', *American Journal on Mental Retardation*, 112 (6): 418–438.

Richler, J., Huerta, M., Bishop, S.L., & Lord, C. (2010) 'Developmental trajectories of restricted and repetitive behaviors and interests in children with autism spectrum disorders', *Development and Psychopathology*, 22 (1): 55–69.

Riddick, B. (2008) 'Parents' perspectives on receiving, searching for and evaluating information relating to autistic spectrum disorders: Sorting the wheat from the chaff', *Good Autism Practice Journal*, 9 (1): 58–66.

Rose, J. (2009) *Identifying and teaching children and young people with dyslexia and literacy difficulties*. London: DCSF.

Roth, I. (2010) *The autism spectrum in the 21st century: Exploring psychology, biology and practice*. London: Jessica Kingsley.

Rowley, E., Chandler, S., Baird, G., Simonoff, E., Pickles, A., Loucas, T., & Charman, T. (2012) 'The experience of friendship, victimization and bullying in children with an autism spectrum disorder: Associations with child characteristics and school placement', *Research in Autism Spectrum Disorders*, 6 (3): 1126–1134.

Royal College of Pathology website. (2019) Available at: www.rcpath.org

Russell, T.L. (2001) *The no significant difference phenomenon.* Raleigh, NC: North Carolina State University.

Rynes, S.L., Bartunek, J.M., & Daft, R.L. (2001) 'Across the great divide: Knowledge creation and transfer between practitioners and academics', *The Academy of Management Journal,* 44: 340–355.

Saggers, B. (2015) 'Student perceptions: Improving the educational experiences of high school students on the autism spectrum,' *Improving Schools,* 18 (1): 35–45.

Sahlberg, P. (2010) 'Rethinking accountability in a knowledge society', *Journal of Educational Change,* 11: 45–61.

Sainsbury, C. (2000) *The martian in the playground: Understanding the school-child with Asperger's syndrome.* Bristol: Lucky Duck Publishing.

Salomone, E., Charman, T., McConachie, H., & Warreyn, P. (2015) 'Prevalence and correlates of use of complementary and alternative medicine in children with autism spectrum disorder in Europe', *European Journal of Pediatrics,* 174 (10): 1277–1285.

Schon, D.A. (1987) *Educating the reflective practitioner.* San Francisco, CA: Jossey-Bass.

Schroeder, J.H., Cappadocia, M.C., Bebko, J.M., Pepler, D.J., & Weiss, J.A. (2014) 'Shedding light on a pervasive problem: A review of research on bullying experiences among children with autism spectrum disorders', *Journal of Autism and Developmental Disorders,* 44 (7): 1520–1534.

Scottish Intercollegiate Guidelines Network (SIGN) (2016). *Assessment, diagnosis and interventions for autism spectrum disorders.* Edinburgh: SIGN. (SIGN publication no. 145). Available at: www.sign.ac.uk

Scottish Government (2011) 'Scottish Strategy for Autism'. Available at: www.gov.scot/Publications/2011/11/01120340/0

Shah, H. & Chung, K. (2009) 'Archie Cochrane and his vision for evidence-based medicine', *Plastic and Reconstructive Surgery,* 124 (3): 982–988. doi:10.1097/PRS.0b013e3181b03928

Shakespeare, T. & Watson, N. (2001) 'The social model of disability: An outdated ideology?', in Barnartt, S. & Altman, B. (eds) *Exploring theories and expanding methodologies: Where we are and where we need to go.* Bingley: Emerald Group Publishing Limited.

Shields, J. (2001) 'The NAS Early Bird programme: Partnership with parents in early intervention', *Autism,* 5: 49–56.

Shore, S.M. (2003) *Beyond the wall: Personal experiences with autism and Asperger syndrome.* Shawnee Mission, KS: Autism Asperger Publishing Company.

Silberman, S. (2016) *Neurotribes: The legacy of autism and how to think smarter about people who think differently.* Crows Nest, Sydney: Allan & Unwin.

Simonoff, E., Pickles, A., Charman, T., Chandler, S., Loucas, T., & Baird, G. (2008) 'Psychiatric disorders in children with autism spectrum disorders: Prevalence, comorbidity, and associated factors in a population-derived sample', *Journal of the American Academy of Child & Adolescent Psychiatry*, 47 (8): 921–929.

Simpson, P. (2017) 'Transforming educational provision for children and young people with autism using the Autism Education Trust materials and training programme', *Good Autism Practice Journal*, 18 (1): 13–19.

Simpson, P., Vining, Y., Cropley, R., & Horton, D. (2015) *A guide to the use of the AET programme materials by local authorities, support services and schools.* London: Autism Education Trust.

Sinclair, J. (1993) 'Don't mourn for us', Autism Network International Newsletter, *Our Voice*, 1 (3). Available at: www.autreat.com/dont_mourn.html

Sinclair, J. (2010) 'Being autistic together', *Disability Studies Quarterly*, 30 (1).

Singal, N., Ware, H., & Bhutani, S.K. (2017) *Inclusive quality education for children with disabilities.* Doha: World Innovation Summit for Education.

Skokauskas, N. & Gallagher, L. (2012) 'Mental health aspects of autistic spectrum disorders in children', *Journal of Intellectual Disability Research*, 56 (3): 248–257.

Slee, R. (2010) *The irregular school: Exclusion, schooling and inclusive education.* London: Routledge.

Soke, G.N., Rosenberg, S.A., Rosenberg, C.R., Vasa, R.A., Lee, L.C., & DiGuiseppi, C. (2018) 'Self-injurious behaviors in children with autism spectrum disorders enrolled in the Study to Explore Early Development', *Autism*, 22 (5): 625–635. doi:10.1177/1362361316689330

Sorensen, P. (2004) 'Managers' learnings in action: The scholar-practitioner, organization development and action research', in Coghlan, D., Dromgoole, T., Joynt, P., & Sorensen, P. (eds) *Managers learning in action: Management learning, research and education.* London: Routledge.

Souders, M.C., Zavodny, S., Eriksen, W., Sinko, R., Connell, J., Kerns, C., … & Pinto-Martin, J. (2017) 'Sleep in children with autism spectrum disorder', *Current Psychiatry Reports*, 19 (6), 34.

Soulieres, I., Zeffiro, T.A., Girard, M.L., & Mottron, L. (2011) 'Enhanced mental image mapping in autism', *Neuropsychologia*, 49 (5): 848–857.

Sproston, K., Sedgewick, F., & Crane, L. (2017) 'Autistic girls and school exclusion: Perspectives of students and their parents', *Autism & Developmental Language Impairments*, 2.

Sreckovic, M.A., Brunsting, N.C., & Able, H. (2014) 'Victimization of students with autism spectrum disorder: A review of prevalence and risk factors', *Research in Autism Spectrum Disorders*, 8 (9): 1155–1172.

Stahmer, A.C. (2007) 'The basic structure of community early intervention programs for children with autism: Provider descriptions', *Journal of Autism and Developmental Disorders*, 37: 1344–1355.

Stahmer, A.C., Reed, S., Lee, E., Reisinger, E.M., Connell, J.E., & Mandell, D.S. (2015) 'Training teachers to use evidence-based practices for autism: Examining procedural implementation fidelity', *Psychology in the Schools*, 52: 181–195.

Stevenson, L.J. & Gernsbacher, M.A. (2013) 'Abstract spatial reasoning as an autistic strength', *PLoS ONE*, 8 (3).

Tager-Flusberg, H., Edelson, L., & Luyster, R. (2011) 'Language and communication in autism spectrum disorders', in Amaral, D., Dawson, G., & Geschwind, D. (eds) *Autism spectrum disorders*. Oxford: Oxford University Press.

Tanwar, M., Lloyd, B., & Julies, P. (2017) 'Challenging behaviour and learning disabilities: Prevention and interventions for children with learning disabilities whose behaviour challenges: NICE guideline 2015', *Archives of Disease in Childhood-Education and Practice*, 102 (1): 24–27.

Terzi, L. (2014) 'Reframing inclusive education: Educational equality as capability equality', *Cambridge Journal of Education*, 44 (4): 479–493.Thomas, G. & Pring, R. (eds) (2004) *Evidence-based practice in education*. Maidenhead: Open University Press.

Thomas, G. (2012) 'Changing our landscape of inquiry for a new science of education', *Harvard Educational Review*, 82 (1): 26–51.

Thomas, G. & Loxley, A. (2007) *Deconstructing special education and constructing inclusion*. Maidenhead: Open University Press.

Thullen, M. & Bonsall, A. (2017) 'Co-parenting quality, parenting stress, and feeding challenges in families with a child diagnosed with Autism Spectrum Disorder', *Journal of Autism and Developmental Disorders*, 47 (3): 878–886.

Timpson, E. (2019) *Timpson review of school exclusion*. London: Department for Education.

Trent, S.C., Artiles, A.J., & Englert, C.S. (1998) 'From deficit thinking to social constructivism: A review of theory, research, and practice in special education', *Review of Research in Education*, 23: 277–307.

Trevarthen, C. (1979) 'Communication and cooperation in early infancy: A description of primary intersubjectivity', in Bullowa, M. (ed) *Before speech: The beginning of human communication*. Cambridge: Cambridge University Press.

Tuchman, R., Hirtz, D., & Mamounas, L.A. (2013) 'NINDS epilepsy and autism spectrum disorders workshop report', *Neurology*, 81 (18): 1630–1636.

UN (1989) *Convention on the rights of the child*. Geneva: Office of the High Commissioner of Human Rights.

UN General Assembly (2015) Transforming our world: The 2030 Agenda for Sustainable Development, A/RES/70/1. Available at: www.refworld.org/docid/57b6e3e44.html

UNESCO (1994) *The Salamanca statement and framework for action on special needs education*. Paris: UNESCO.

US Department of Education, Office of the Deputy Secretary (2004) *No Child Left Behind: A toolkit for teachers*. Washington, DC: Author.

US Department of Education Institute of Education Sciences National Center for Education Evaluation and Regional Assistance (2003) *Educational practices supported by rigorous evidence: A user friendly guide*. Washington, DC: US Institute of Education Sciences.

Van Schalkwyk, G.I., Klingensmith, K., & Volkmar, F.R. (2015) 'Gender identity and autism spectrum disorders', *The Yale Journal of Biology And Medicine*, 88 (1): 81–83.

Vanclay, F. (2003) 'International principles for social impact assessment', *Impact Assessment and Project Appraisal*, 21 (1): 5–12, doi:10.3152/147154603781766491

Vaughn, S. & Fuchs, L.S. (2003) 'Redefining learning-disabilities and inadequate response to instruction: The promise and potential problems', *Learning Disabilities Research and Practice*, 18: 137–146. http://dx.doi.org/10.1111/1540–5826.00070

Vygotsky, L. (1978) *Mind in society*. Cambridge, MA: Harvard University Press.

Wallace, S., Coleman, M., & Bailey, A. (2008) 'Face and object processing in autism spectrum disorders', *Autism Research*, 1 (1): 43–51.

Wallace, S., Parr, J., & Hardy, A. (2013). *One in a hundred: Putting families at the heart of autism research*. London: Autistica.

Walmsley, J. (2004) 'Inclusive learning disability research: The (nondisabled) researcher's role', *British Journal of Learning Disabilities*, 32 (2): 65–71.

Walmsley, J. (2010) 'Research and emancipation: Prospects and problems', in Grant, G., Ramcharan, P., Flynn, M., & Richardson, M. (eds) *Learning disability: A lifecycle approach* (2nd ed.) Maidenhead: Open University Press.

Ward, M. (2005) 'A historical perspective of self-determination in special education: Accomplishments and challenges', *Research & Practice for Persons with Severe Disabilities*, 30 (3): 108–112.

Warren, M.R., Oh Park, S., & Tieken, M.C. (2016) 'The formation of community engaged scholars: A collaborative approach to doctoral training in educational research', *Harvard Educational Review*, 86 (2): 233–260.

Watkins, L., O'Reilly, M., Kuhn, M., Gevarter, C., Lancioni, G.E., Sigafoos, J., & Lang, R. (2015) 'A review of peer-mediated social interaction interventions for students with autism in inclusive settings', *Journal of Autism and Developmental Disorders*, 45 (4): 1070–1083.

Wedell, K. (1993) 'Special needs education: The next 25 years', in *Briefings for the National Commission for Education*. London: Heinemann.

Wei, X., Jennifer, W.Y., Shattuck, P., McCracken, M., & Blackorby, J. (2013) 'Science, technology, engineering, and mathematics (STEM) participation among college students with an autism spectrum disorder', *Journal of Autism and Developmental Disorders*, 43 (7): 1539–1546.

Weisz, J. & Jensen, P. (1999) 'Efficacy and effectiveness of child and adolescent psychotherapy and pharmacotherapy', *Mental Health Services Research*, 1: 125–157.

Wenger, E. (1998) *Communities of practice: Learning, meaning, and identity.* Cambridge: Cambridge University Press.

Wenger, E., Trayner, B., & de Laat, M. (2011) *Promoting and assessing value creation in communities and networks: A conceptual framework.* Heerlen, the Netherlands: Ruud de Moor Centrum, Open University of the Netherlands.

Wenger-Trayner, E. & Wenger-Trayner, B. (in press) *Learning to make a difference.* Cambridge: Cambridge University Press.

Williams, D. (1996a) *An inside-out approach.* London: Jessica Kingsley.

Williams, D. (1996b) *Like colour to the blind.* London: Jessica Kingsley.

Williams, E.I., Gleeson, K., & Jones, B.E. (2019) 'How pupils on the autism spectrum make sense of themselves in the context of their experiences in a mainstream school setting: A qualitative metasynthesis', *Autism*, 23 (1): 8–28.

Winburn, E., Charlton, J., McConachie, H., McColl, E., Parr, J., O'Hare, A., ... & Adams, S. (2014) 'Parents' and child health professionals' attitudes towards dietary interventions for children with autism spectrum disorders', *Journal of Autism and Developmental Disorders*, 44 (4): 747–757.

Wing, L. (1996) *The autistic spectrum.* London: Constable.

Wittemeyer, K., Charman, T., Cusack, J., Guldberg, K., Hastings, R., Howlin, P., Macnab, N., Parsons, S., Pellicano, L., & Slonims, V. (2011) *Educational provision and outcomes for people on the autism spectrum.* London: Autism Education Trust.

Wong, C., Odom, S.L., Hume, K., Cox, A.W., Fettig, A., Kucharczyk, S., Brock, M.E., Plavnik, J.B., Fleury, V.P., & Schultz, T.R. (2014) *Evidence-based practices for children, youth, and young adults with Autism Spectrum Disorder.* Chapel Hill, NC: The University of North Carolina.

World Health Organization (WHO) (2018) *International statistical classification of diseases and related health problems* (11th revision). Geneva: WHO.

Yoder, P.J. & Stone, W.L. (2006) 'Randomized comparison of two communication interventions for preschoolers with autism spectrum disorders', *Journal of Consulting and Clinical Psychology*, 74: 426–435.

Youdell, D. & Lindley, M. (2019) *Biosocial education: The social and biological entanglements of learning.* London: Routledge.

Zablotsky, B., Boswell, K., & Smith, C. (2012) 'An evaluation of school involvement and satisfaction of parents of children with autism spectrum disorders', *American Journal on Intellectual and Developmental Disabilities*, 117 (4): 316–330.

Zaidman-Zait, A., Mirenda, P., Duku, E., Vaillancourt, T., Smith, I.M., Szatmari, P., … & Zwaigenbaum, L. (2017) 'Impact of personal and social resources on parenting stress in mothers of children with autism spectrum disorder', *Autism*, 21 (2): 155–166.

Index

Note: Figures are in *italics*. The acronym AET stands for Autism Education Trust, CYP for children and young people, and GAP for good autism practice.

ABA (Applied Behaviour Analysis) 56–57

abilities 5, 10, 35, 45, 64, 73, 173; cognitive 85; individual 53, 135; masking disabilities 28; pre-verbal 28; savant 45; in typical development 25; uneven profiles of 144

acceptance: of autism 6, 8, 17, 58, 68, 71, 73, 74, 80; of differences 156; of rights of people with disabilities 115; and scholar-practitioners 188

access to learning 4, 134, 164

ACER (Autism Centre for Education and Research) 170, 175

action research 105

active listening 58

adapting the curriculum, teaching and learning 133, *142*, 142, 163–167

Addressing Inequalities principle, from *The Autism Dividend* 80

ADHD (Attention Deficit Hyperactivity Disorder) 38–39

AET Competency Framework 157, 170–171, 174

AET National Standards 148, 157, 158, 170, 171, 172, 174

AET professional development programme 169–181, *171*

AET Progression Framework 162–163

AET Schools Programme 156

AET training programme *171*

age of diagnosis 36–37

agency 61, 116, 119, 192; of autistic people 57, 58, 80, 101, 133–134, 150, 162; and double empathy 52; of policymakers and researchers 101; of teachers 4, 191

'All about me' tool, to support person-centred planning 145

All Party Parliamentary Group on Autism (APPGA) 129, 154

Ambitious about Autism 83, 170

American Psychological Association (APA) 102, 187

anti-bullying 155, 160

anxiety 16, 20, 21, 58, 64, 136, 177; and biological and medical evidence 33, 38, 39, 40, 42, 46; and GAP in education 144, 151, 152, 158, 161, 164, 165–166

APA (American Psychological Association) 102, 187

APPGA (All Party Parliamentary Group on Autism) 129, 154

Applied Behaviour Analysis (ABA)
56–57
Asperger syndrome 25, 26, 31, 39
assessment: diagnostic 35–36, 38, 79,
95, 152–153; educational 108, 121,
143–144, 160–161, 162, 177–178;
multidisciplinary 43, 118
assistive tools 6
attention 28, 32, 38, 45, 164; joint 29,
54, 57, 59, 99, 137
Attention Deficit Hyperactivity
Disorder (ADHD) 38–39
attention span 51
attitudes, to autism 18, 117, 157, 159,
177; social science contributions to
77, 79–81, 84, 86
attitudinal barriers, to inclusion and
acceptance 6, 117
Australia, guidelines for autism
education in 132
autism: definitions of 15–16; holistic
understanding of 15–22, *19*,
191; as impairment 6, 16–17, 45,
172–173; as neurodevelopmental
condition 15, 24, 25, 111, 124; as
transactional condition 5–6, 172; as
way of being 5–6, 8, 173, 179
Autism and Education in England
154
autism awareness 158, 160
Autism Centre for Education and
Research (ACER) 170, 175
autism developmental pathway 24,
143
Autism Dividend, The 80
Autism Education Trust *see* AET
autism friendliness
autism lens 180
"autism plus" 38
autism spectrum 8–9, 25
autism terminology 9, 10, 29–30, 31
autistic focus 26, 30, 32, 45, 49, 50
autistic knowledge base 62–74
autistic narratives 9–10, 63, 65–67,
69, 72, 73–74
autistic perspectives 62–74
autistic rights 63, 68, 70, 74
autistic self-narratives 63

"autistic symptoms" 37
autistic voice 63, 67, 74, 149
autonomy 54, 80, 96, 102, 162, 180

Baron-Cohen, Simon: 48, 71–72
barriers: attitudinal 6, 117; to
belonging 115; diagnoses as 73;
environmental 18; to inclusion 17,
84; to learning 11, 117, 121, 122,
127, 134, 155, 161; to participation
17, 115, 127, 158; physical 158;
social 11, 17; societal 75–91, *82*;
systemic 18
Beadle, Dean 35
behavioural criteria, for
understanding autism 15, 19, 62
behavioural factors 119
behavioural norms 67
behavioural psychology 56–57
behaviourism 56, 57, 131
behaviours that challenge 20, 39, 40,
42–43, 60, 88
beliefs 11, 48, 86, 88, 115, 117, 157
belonging 69, 71, 114, 115, 120, 191
Bettelheim, Bruno 23
bias, research 99–100
biology 23–46, 47, 119, 124; *see also*
bio-psycho-social-insider model, of
disability
bio-psycho-social-insider model, of
disability x, *xi*, 15–22, *19*
bio-psycho-social model, of disability
19, 21
Blackburn, Roz 28
body language 29, 54
Boulder Model 187
brains and brain-imaging studies
24–25, 51, 67–68, 71–72
Breakey, Christine 66
Bronfenbrenner, Urie 75, 76, 105–106
bullying 42, 83, 89–90, 129, 155–156,
160; cyber 90, 160, 167

causal relations 100, 189
Central Coherence 48–49, 50, 60
cerebral cortex 24
challenges, faced by autistic people
6, 16, 131, 136, 177, 184; and

bio-psycho-social model 19; and GAP in education 141, 143–147, 162, 165–166; and neurodiversity movement 69, 70, 71; and social differences 29; societal 75–91, *82*
challenging behaviours 20, 39, 40, 42–43, 60, 88
change 3, 5, 6; in classrooms 97, 101, 111, 133–134, 164, 169–181, *171*, 178; persons with autism 45–46, 73, 164; resistance to 26, 30, 50, 164; social 184, 188; in routine 7, 50
Children and Families Act (2014) 126–127
choice, for autistic people 58, 59, 73, 96, 102, 133–134, 150, 180
Choice and Control principle, from *The Autism Dividend* 80
citizen science 186–187
classrooms 99, 100–101, 109, 120, 190
Cochrane, Archie 92
Code of Practice, SEND (2014) 126, 127–128, 147, 150–151, 155, 161
cognition 39, 47, 48, 51, 85, 119
collaboration 43–44, 60, 132, 137, 170, 174, 179; in AET programme 174–175; with parents and carers 141, *142*, 150–153; research 181, 183–184
common needs and pedagogy 122–123
communication: behaviour as 42–43; expressive 27, 28, 29, 54, 137, 143–144; non-verbal 1, 2, 27, 29, 54, 95; receptive 27
communities of learning 123
communities of practice 190–191
community-engaged scholarship and research 183–187
co-morbidities 71; biology/medical contributions to 23, 37–39, 42, 43, 44, 46; social science contributions to 86–87, 90
Competency Framework, AET 157, 170–171, 174
complexity, of autism and autistic people 20, 49, 87

Comprehensive Treatment Models (CTMs) 55, 94
contextual, case-based research 185, 186
Continuous Professional Development (CPD) 5, 111, 130, 153–156, 157, 169–181, *171*
control: difficulties with 31, 32, 48, 137; giving the autistic child 6, 59, 148; controlled research 40, 96, 98, 99–100, 105, 185–186, 187
conversation 28–29, 85
co-occurring medical conditions *see* co-morbidities, medical
coping strategies 57, 58, 137
core deficit models, of autism 48
CPD (continuous professional development) 5, 111, 130, 153–156, 157, 169–181, *171*
criticism, autistic experience of 42
CTMs (Comprehensive Treatment Models) 55, 94
culture 18, 81, 86, 88, 121, 189; *see also* social factors
curing autism 8, 16, 17, 45–46, 67, 68, 70–71, 190
curriculum 6, 64, 118, 121–122, 130–131, 134; adapting the 43, 133, 135–138, 142, 158, *162*, 163–167, 174, 178; ecological 141; and foundational skills 138; inclusive 120–121; and special interests 4; therapeutic 135, 136
cyber bullying 90, 160, 167

data triangulation 108
Dawson, Michelle 8
decision-making, involvement of CYP in 59, 72–73, 108, 147, 148, 150
Dekker, Martin 69
deliberative pedagogy 187
Department for Education (UK) 126, 128–129, 132, 163, 170
Department of Education (US) 99, 103, 104
depression 38, 39, 42, 86–87, 136, 152

developmental approaches, to
teaching 131
developmental differences 24–25,
111, 141
developmental difficulties 25, 26–29,
136
developmental disabilities 8, 39, 81,
118
developmental histories 36
developmental pathway, of autism
24, 143
developmental psychology, and
psychosocial interventions
53–55
diagnosis 26, 35–37, 38–39, 45–46,
85, 88, 151, 152
diagnostic and statistical manuals
16–17, 25, 29–30, 32, 37, 38, 62
diagnostic assessment 35–36, 38, 79,
95, 152–153
diagnostic criteria 15, 24–26, 27, 31,
35, 44–45, 66–67, 71
diagnostic process 35–37, 45–46
diagnostic tools 36
diet 20, 37, 40–41, 43, 88, 160
different way of being, autism as 5, 8,
60, 142–143, 173, 179
dimensions of pedagogy 122–124
Disability Act (1995) 116–117
disability discrimination 157
disability rights 8, 17
discovery mode, of developmental
science 105–106
discrete trial training 56
discrimination 17, 77, 80, 127, 157
distinctive group differences, of
autistic CYP 123, 133–135
distinctive group needs, of autistic
CYP 114, 123, 136; see also GAP, in
education
distinctive pedagogy, for autism 123,
124, 139, 170
distress 2, 6, 20, 30, 31, 34, 66
double empathy problem 7, 52–53
DSM (Diagnostic and Statistical
Manual) 16, 25, 38
dynamic relationships 6, 173
dysregulation 31, 57–58

Early Intensive Behaviour(al)
Intervention (EIBI) 55, 56, 96
Early Years Autism Project (EYAP)
107–109
Early Years Foundation Stage, in
England 140
EBP (evidence-based practices) 92,
97, 101–104, 132, 174, 191
EBT (evidence-based treatment)
92
eclectic approaches, to intervention
57, 124–125
ecological curriculum 141
ecological systems theory 75–76
Education, Health and Care Plans
(EHCPs) 127, 154
Education Inspection Framework,
Ofsted 129, 130
education systems 18, 77, 78, 86, 121,
129, 156
educational assessment 108, 121,
143–144, 160–161, 162, 177–178
educational equity 183–184
educational needs, of autistic
children 86, 164; see also Special
Educational Needs
effective interventions, core
components of 59–60
effectiveness studies 98
efficacy studies 98
EHCPs (Education, Health and Care
Plans) 127, 154
EIBI (Early Intensive Behaviour(al)
Intervention) 55, 56, 96
emancipatory research 183
Emergence: Labeled Autistic 65
emotional connectivity 52
emotional dysregulation 57–58, 137
emotional engagement 52
emotional health 147–148, 151, 167
emotional identification 29
emotional regulation 31, 57–58, 59,
137, 166; see also SCERTS
emotional wellbeing 88, 164, 166
empathy 7, 52–53, 79
empowerment 6, 69, 107, 129, 134,
186
enabling environments 60, 140, 141

enabling voices of autistic CYP 141, *142*, 147–150

engagement, of autistic CYP 34, 41, 52, 60, 72, 118, 121; and GAP in education 144–145, 149, 150, 158, 164; social science contributions to 85, 88

Engel, George L. 19

enthusiasms 32, 33

environmental accommodations 159

environmental barriers 18; *see also* barriers, to learning

environmental changes 6, 137

environmental factors 19, 20–21, 42, 119

environments: fostering social inclusion *142*, 142, 158–160; physical 20, 22, 30, 60, 84, 138; social 6, 42, 43, 131, 167

epilepsy 25, 39, 71, 72, 86–87

epistemological integrity, of autism research 74

Equality Act (2010) 116–117, 157

equality of opportunity 43, 127

equity 78, 81, 116–117, 119, 183–184

ethics 133, 143, 186, 187

ethos 8, 76, 107, 111, 120, 141, 156, 157; fostering social inclusion *142*, 142, 158–160

Evans-Williams, Claire 49

everyday functioning 96

evidence, hierarchies of 103

evidence-based interventions 80

evidence-based practices (EBP) 92, 97, 101–104, 132, 174, 191

evidence-based research 104

evidence-based treatment (EBT) 92

evidence-informed practice 101–104, 191

exclusion, social 18, 42, 77, 81, 85, 89

exclusion diet 40

exclusions, school 81, 83–84, 114, 129, 153, 154, 157, 158

Executive Functioning 48, 50, 138, 164

exercise 41, 159, 160

exosystem 76

expertise 4, 5, 44, 62–63, 184; and evidence-informed practice 101, 102, 103, 109–110; and inclusive practice 115, 124, 125, 130

explanatory power, of theory 48, 49

expressive communication 27, 28, 29, 54, 137, 143–144

EYAP (Early Years Autism Project) 107–109

facial expressions 21, 28, 29, 54

falsifiability, of theory 48

family 11, 60, 75–76, 87–90, 124, 138, 139; and GAP in education 145, 152, 153, 161

feelings, of others 29, 48, 52

flapping 58, 63

focus, autistic 26, 30, 32, 45, 49, 50

focused interventions 55, 94, 103

food intolerances 40

foundational skills, for learning 138

four-part teaching cycle 155

Freaks, Geeks and Asperger Syndrome 65

friendships 29, 89–90, 134, 158

Frith, Uta 48, 49

GAP, in education 1–11, 140–168, *142*

gastrointestinal conditions 19, 38, 40, 46

gender 81, 83, 84–85, 86, 87

general systems theory 19

generalisation 49, 57, 89, 109, 138, 143

genetics 15, 21, 23, 24, 41, 42, 71–72

Gerland, Gunilla 8

Gillespie, Alex 53

good autism practice, in education 1–11, 140–168, *142*

good teaching 105, 109

Goodchild, Christopher 66

Grandin, Temple 65

Greece, AET case study in 178–180

Grinker, Roy 19

group differences, of autistic CYP 122, 123, 133–135, 140

group needs, of autistic CYP
114, 123, 136; see also GAP, in
education

Hacking, Ian 8, 63–64
health 20–21, 23, 37, 43, 44, 46
hearing 7, 20, 34, 122
Heasman, Brett 53
Higashida, Naoki 65
high-functioning autism 25, 44, 70
Hobson, Peter 51, 52
holistic understanding, of autism
15–22, 19, 191
humanism 6, 19, 57
hyper-arousal, cognitive 39
hyper/hyposensitivities, sensory 25,
30, 33, 159

IBS (Irritable Bowel Syndrome) 38
ICD (International Classification of
Diseases) 16, 25
ICT (Information and Communication
Technology) 166–167
ID (Intellectual Disability) 37, 39, 41,
42, 183
IDEA (Individuals with Disabilities
Education Act) 17, 93
identity 8, 67, 68, 69, 72, 85, 87, 188
identity construction 173, 190
identity first language 8
IEP (Individual Education Plan) 145
imitation 29, 53–54
impairment, autism as 6, 16–17, 45,
172–173; and pedagogy 122, 130,
134; and social disability 18
implementation science 103
impulsivity 38–39
inattention 38–39
inclusive education 17, 77, 78,
113–125, 126–139, 156
inclusive principles 126, 140–168, 142
inclusive research 182–183
individual abilities 53, 135
Individual Education Plan (IEP) 145
Individuals with Disabilities
Education Act (IDEA) 17, 93
Information and Communication
Technology (ICT) 166–167

information processing 50, 135,
137–138
Initial Teacher Training (ITT) 128
insider perspectives, on autism xi,
10, 15–22, 19, 62–74
Institute for Public Policy Research
(IPPR) 84
integrative inclusionist model, of
inclusion for autistic CYP 114
Intellectual Disability (ID) 37, 39, 41,
42, 183
intensive interventions 17, 55, 56, 60,
94, 96, 118
intentionality 51–52
interactive expertise 101
interests, of autistic CYP 4, 25, 26,
30, 135, 137–138; and GAP 141,
143–147; and gender 85; and
monotropism 32; and teaching 72;
see also special interests
International Classification of
Diseases (ICD) 16, 25
international implications, of AET
programme 178–180
inter-professionalism 43–44
intersectionality 86–87
inter-subjectivity theories 51–53, 57
intervention research 59, 93, 95, 98,
101
interventions: core components of
effective 59–60; focused 55, 94,
103; (non)intensive 17, 55, 56, 59,
60, 94, 96, 118; therapeutic 44,
54–55, 94, 134, 135, 136
IPPR (Institute for Public Policy
Research) 84
Ireland, guidelines for autism
education in 132
Irritable Bowel Syndrome (IBS) 38
isolation, social 29, 84, 88, 89, 149,
153
Italy: AET case study in 178–180;
inclusive education in 115, 120
ITT (Initial Teacher Training) 128

Jackson, Luke 63, 65
joint attention 29, 54, 57, 59, 99, 137
Jordan, Rita 49, 52??

Kanner, Leo 26
knowledge: co-creation of 106, 181; *know-how* and *know-that* of x, xi–xii; transfer of 97, 103, 104, 105
knowledge bases *xi*, 9, 21, 22, 191; autistic 62–74, 184; and evidence-informed practice 101, 102–103, 104, 106

labelling, with a diagnosis 35, 114
language 24, 27, 28–29, 49, 63–64, 65, 72, 86; to describe autism 5, 8–9, 173; autistic 101; body 28, 29, 54; identity first 8; literal understanding of 29, 50; person first 8
language delay 26, 27, 28, 37, 54
language skills 28, 29, 54, 57
Lawson, Wenn 32, 34, 67
leadership 126, 128, 129–130, 171, 176, 177; and GAP in education 141, *142*, 156–158, 160
learning: from autistic perspectives 62–74; as expanding involvement with a system 173; structured 164–165
learning and development 76, 135; in GAP framework 140, 141, 161
learning differences 121
learning difficulties 1, 27, 70, 176
learning disabilities 4, 25, 86, 183
learning environments 11, 60, 90, 121, 177; and GAP in education 143, 158–159, 164, 165, 166
learning partnerships 176
learning styles 57, 120, 146
learning to access 134, 135, 138
Liam case study 2–3, 4, 6–7, 20–21
Life-long Perspective principle, from *The Autism Dividend* 80
limited diet 40
linguistic diversity 81, 86, 121
literal understanding, of language 29, 50
lived experiences, of autism 60, 63, 102, 106, 184
loneliness 89
low-arousal approach, for autism education 7, 137

macrosystem 76–79
mainstream schools 2, 4, 43, 148, 154; and inclusive practice 114, 115–116, 120, 127–128, 130; social science contributions to 78, 84, 89, 90
management 128, 130, 141, *142*, 156–158, 160
marginalised identities 87
Martian in the Playground 64–65
masking 28, 85
measuring progress, of autistic CYP *142*, 142, 160–163
medical assessment 35–36, 38, 79, 95, 152–153
medical comorbidities 23, 37–39, 42, 43, 44, 46, 71, 86–87, 90
medical domain, contributions from the 23–46
medical model, of disability 9, 10, 20, 179; focus on deficits/impairments 16–17, 18, 45, 57, 67; and needs-based perspective on autism 114; and neurodiversity 71
Medical Research Council (MRC) 60
mental health 2, 21, 37, 41–42, 43, 136; and GAP in education 149, 155, 160, 165, 166; social science contributions to 83, 84, 88, 89, 90
mesosystem 75–76
methodologies 93, 98–99, 101, 104–107, 187, 189
methods, teaching 103, 118, 121, 156, 164, 178
microsystem 75–76, 87–90
Milton, Damian 7, 8, 34, 52, 62–63, 72, 145, 146–147
minority populations 86
models of disability 10, 16–21, *19*; *see also* bio-psycho-social(-insider) model, of disability; medical model, of disability; social model, of disability
monotropism 32
moral values 77–78
motivation 52, 53, 58, 90, 100, 121, 144, 164
MRC (Medical Research Council) 60

multi-agency working 88–89, 107
multidisciplinary practice 36, 43, 60, 107–108, 118
mutual adaptation 5–6, 172–173
myths, around autism 79–80

narratives, autistic 9–10, 63, 65–67, 69, 72, 73–74
National Council for Special Education (NCSE) 95, 132
National Council on Severe Autism 70
National Institute of Health and Care Excellence (NICE) 36, 59–60
National Professional Development Centre (NPDC) 59, 103, 138
National Standards, AET 148, 157, 158, 170, 171, 172, 174
NCLB (No Child Left Behind Act) 93, 103–104
NCSE (National Council for Special Education) 95, 132
needs-based perspective, on inclusion 114
neurodevelopmental condition, autism as 15, 24–25, 111, 124
neurodiversity 67–72
neurotypicality 42, 53, 67
New Zealand, guidelines for autism education in 132
NICE (National Institute of Health and Care Excellence) 36, 59–60
No Child Left Behind Act (NCLB) 93, 103–104
non-intensive interventions 59
non-social media 167
non-verbal communication 1, 2, 27, 29, 54, 95
normalisation 66–67, 68, 73
Norway, inclusive education in 115, 120
NPDC (National Professional Development Centre) 59, 103, 138

obsessions 32, 33
ODD (Oppositional Defiant Disorder) 38

Ofsted (Office for Standards in Education, Children's Services and Skills) 126, 129, 130
ongoing professional development 169–181, *171*
Oppositional Defiant Disorder (ODD) 38

parents 86, 87–89, 90; collaboration with 141, 144, 150–153
participation, of autistic CYP 8, 72–73; and anxiety 144; barriers to 17, 115, 127, 158; community 133, 134, 162, 163, 173, 180, 190, 192; in decision-making 147, 150; and GAP 143; and inclusion 77, 78, 119, 120; and leadership 156; in learning 134, 159; and sensory processing difficulties 150; and stress 144
participation, of people with intellectual disabilities in research 182–183
participatory research 105, 106, 183
pathology 16–17, 29–30, 68
pedagogy: for autism 123, 124, 139, 170; common 122; deliberative 187; dimensions of 122–124; inclusive 113–125, 126–139; SEND 126–129
peers 54, 83, 84, 89–90, 149, 155, 159
perception, sensory 7, 15, 16, 33, 52, 53–54, 60, 64
performance management 130, 157
person first language 8
Personalised Actions principle, from *The Autism Dividend* 80
person-centred planning 145, 146
physical environment 20, 22, 30, 60, 84, 138
play 28, 50, 54, 55, 57, 137, 161
policy shifts 76–79
polytropism 32
positive and effective relationships theme, of GAP framework 140–141
positive behaviour 56, 132
positive flow 145

Post-16 settings 117, 129, 130, 171, 175; and GAP in education 152, 158, 163, 167
practical knowledge 133, 185
practice: evidence-based 92, 97, 101–104, 132, 174, 191; evidence-informed 101–104, 191
practice-based evidence 182
practice-based knowledge and policy *xi*
practitioner relationships 32, 133
practitioner-based research 107–109
prevalence: of autism 41, 81; of co-occurring mental health conditions 42; of epilepsy 39; of intellectual disability 41
pre-verbal abilities 28
primarily generative research designs 105
primary intervention, under Response to Intervention model 118
Prizant, Barry 5, 31, 32, 57–58
processing the world, a different way of 29–33
professional development 5, 111, 130, 153–156, 157; AET programme of 169–181, *171*
Progression Framework, AET 162–163
psychological factors 18, 19, 20, 21, 41
psychological functioning 16, 49, 51, 60
psychological interventions 134
psychology, contributions from 47–61
psychosocial interventions 53–55, 57–59
public awareness and understanding 78, 79–81
pupil voice 148

qualitative methodologies 84, 105, 149
quality of life 4, 38, 46, 68–69, 81, 83, 152, 161, 186
quantitative methodologies 96, 105

Randomised Controlled Trials (RCTs) 99
rationale, for teaching 130–131
Ravet, Jackie 43–44, 99, 114, 123, 124
RCTs (Randomised Controlled Trials) 99
Reason I Jump, The 65
reasonable adjustments 43, 116–117, 129, 176–177, 178; and GAP in education 157, 158, 161, 164
receptive communication 27
reflective practice 10; *see also* scholarly practitioner, the
refrigerator mother theory 23
regression 37
reinforcement 42, 55, 56
relationships 29, 50, 58, 61, 96, 139, 149, 150; classroom 109, 190; parental 88; peer 83, 84, 89–90, 149, 155, 159; positive and effective 140–141; practitioner 32, 133; romantic 29; and sex 166; social 51, 137
research *xi*, 95, 96–97, 99–100, 187
research-practice gap 97–101, 103
Response to Intervention (RTI) 117, 118, 119
restricted and repetitive behaviours 30–31, 32, 33
rights, of disabled individuals 8, 17
rights-based perspective, on inclusion 114
rigidity, of thought and behaviour 30–31, 32, 33
romantic relationships 29
RTI (Response to Intervention) 117, 118, 119

Sainsbury, Claire 64–65
Salamanca World Conference on Special Needs Education 76–77
sameness, insistence on 30
savantism 45, 79
scholarly practitioner, the 182–192
school exclusions 81, 83–84, 114, 129, 153, 154, 157, 158
school experiences 72, 85, 87–90, 153
Schools Programme, AET 156

scientist-practitioner model 187
Scottish Intercollegiate Guidelines
Network (SIGN) 36, 44
Scottish Strategy for Autism 44
screening 35–36, 79
secondary intervention, under
Response to Intervention model
118
self-esteem 8, 16, 42, 72, 85, 136–137
self-narratives, autistic 63
SEN (Special Educational Needs) 78,
83, 115, 127
SEND (Special Educational Needs
and Disabilities) 81, 113, 120,
126–128, 183; and GAP in
education 147, 150–151, 155,
161
sensitivity: sensory 2, 7, 20, 33–34,
40, 138; to social signals 29, 136
sensorimotor behaviours 30
sensory audits 159
sensory environments 4, 43, 83, 137,
144, 164
sensory functioning 53
sensory hyper/hyposensitivities 25,
30, 33, 159
sensory integration 33
sensory perception 7, 15, 16, 33, 52,
53–54, 60, 64
sensory processing 33–35, 37, 57–58,
60, 64, 135; and GAP in education
144, 150, 158, 159, 162, 166
sensory seeking 33
sensory sensitivities 2, 25, 30, 33–34,
40, 138, 159
sex education 166
sexuality 50, 87
Shore, Steven 25
siblings 89, 152, 153
SIGN (Scottish Intercollegiate
Guidelines Network) 36, 44
silent clapping 34
Sinclair, Jim 52, 64
Singer, Judy 67–68
sleep disturbance 20, 37, 38, 39, 40,
41, 42; and educational planning
144; and family life 88; and playing
of video games 167

social and emotional learning 29,
89–90, 136, 144, 162, 166, 172
social approaches 29
social barriers, to participation and
inclusion 17
social change 184, 188
social cognitive approach, to
intervention 58
social communication 15, 25, 26–29,
36, 53–54, 59, 137, 162; see also
SCERTS
social differences 29
social environments 6, 42, 43, 131,
167
social exclusion 18, 42, 77, 81, 85, 89
social expectations 30
social factors 16, 19, 20, 21, 41 +
chapter 6
social inclusion 77, 114, 142, 147,
158–160, 164
social independence 29
social information, noticing and
responding to 29
social isolation 29, 84, 88, 89, 149,
153
social learning theory 190
social media 70, 76, 167
social model, of disability 9, 10, 17,
18, 114; see also bio-psycho-social
model
social motivation 52
social orienting hypotheses 52
social relationships 51, 137
social sciences, contributions from
75–91, *82*
social signals, sensitivity to 29, 136
social understanding 52, 54, 59, 134,
135, 136; and GAP in education
159, 161, 162, 164
social withdrawal 42
socialisation 37, 136
societal barriers 72
socio-environmental factors 20
sociology 10
socio-political factors 18
special education 17, 79, 115, 131
Special Educational Needs (SEN) 78,
83, 115, 127

Special Educational Needs and Disabilities (SEND) 81, 113, 120, 126–128, 183; and GAP in education 147, 150–151, 155, 161
special gifts 79
special interests 4, 26, 32, 33, 85
specialist pedagogy 120
Specialisterne 69
specificity 49
staff development 154–155, 157; see also professional development
statistics *82*, 96
stereotypes 25, 30, 36, 66, 79, 80, 85
stigma 18, 35, 42, 72, 73, 79, 80, 86, 88
Strategy 2015–2020 – World-class Education and Care 128
strengths, of autistic CYP 5, 121, 123, 127, 190; current evidence for 18, 25, 44–45, 67, 68, 69, 97; and GAP in education 141, 143–147, 150, 155, 156, 160–161; and professional development 171, 173–174, 176, 177, 178
stress 2, 144, 147, 177, 180; and mental health 42; parental 88, 151–152, 153; and school exclusion 158; and sensory sensitivities 33–34; triggers for 165–166
structural language skills 28
structured learning and teaching 158–159, 164–165, 176, 180
success, for CYP on the autism spectrum 163–167
sudden noises 7, 20
suicide 136
support structures 80, 113, 159
Sustainable Development Goals, United Nations 77
systemic barriers 18

TAE (Transform Autism Education) project 178, 179, 181
targeted support, for autistic CYP *142*, 142, 160–163
task analysis 55
Teachers' Standards 126, 128
teaching methods 103, 118, 121, 156, 164, 178

terminology, autism 9, 10, 29–30, 31
tertiary intervention, under Response to Intervention model 118
theory *xi*, 11, 49; cognitive 48; double empathy 7, 52–53; ecological systems 75–76; falsifiability of 48; general systems 19; inter-subjectivity 51–53, 57; refrigerator mother 23; and scholar-practitioner 187–188, 189; social learning 190; see also Central Coherence; Executive Functioning; monotropism; Theory of Mind
Theory of Mind 7, 48, 49, 50
therapeutic curriculum 135, 136
therapeutic interventions 44, 54–55, 94, 134
therapy 55, 59, 61, 132, 134, 163
Think Autism strategy 79
Thinking in Pictures: My Life with Autism 65
thinking processes 16
three-step process, of Applied Behaviour Analysis 56
Timpson Review of School Exclusion 83–84
touch sensitivity 7, 34
training programme, AET *171*
transactional approach, to understanding autism 5, 6, 51, 52, 53, 57, 172
Transform Autism Education (TAE) project 178, 179, 181
Transforming Children and Young People's Mental Health Provision 165–166
transitions 20, 30–31, 50, 80, 83, 88–89, 138, 150; and GAP in education 150, 151, 164
triad of impairments 26
triangulation, data 108
triggers 20, 42, 43, 165
typical development 25

UDL (Universal Design for Learning) 120–121, 135, 177
UNCRC (United Nations Convention on the Rights of the Child) 77, 147

understanding strengths, interests and challenges 141, 143–147, *162*
understanding the individual theme, of GAP framework 140
UNESCO (United Nations Educational, Scientific and Cultural Organization) 77
uneven ability profiles 144
Uniquely Human 5, 57
United Nations 77, 147
Universal Design for Learning (UDL) 120–121, 135, 177
universality 49
unstructured periods 50

values 8, 11, 76, 99, 110, 157; AET programme 176, 178, 180; and inclusive practice 111, 114, 119, 120, 123, 124, 134; moral 77–78; scholar-practitioner 187, 188
variables, research 95, 96–97, 99–100, 187
visual impairments 122, 130, 134

visual sensitivity 34
visual supports 138, 165
visual thinking 65
voice: autistic 63, 67, 74, 149; pupil 148

Warnock report 115
wave model 118–119
We Need an Education 83
wellbeing: 4, 116, 136, 142, 165; current evidence for 37, 44, 69, 74; emotional 88, 164, 166; and GAP in education 144, 147–148, 161, 163–167; parental 88
whole-school approaches 137, 156, 171, 176, 177
Williams, Donna 62
Wing, Lorna 26
workforce development, to support autistic CYP 141, *142*, 153–156
Working Together with Your Child's School 152
worldviews 9, 21